Cruise through History

ITINERARY 14

AUSTRALIA, NEW ZEALAND AND THE PACIFIC ISLANDS

SHERRY HUTT

Copyright © 2020 by Sherry Hutt

All rights reserved. No part of this book may be reproduced or transmitted in any form or by any means, electronic or mechanical, including photocopying, recording, or by any information storage and retrieval system without the written permission of the author, except where permitted by law.

Bound: ISBN: 978-1-942153-21-4

Epub: ISBN: 978-1-942153-20-7

TABLE OF CONTENTS

Preface 5
Acknowledgements 9
Introduction – Stories of the Southern Seas 11
Map of Itinerary XIV- Australia, New Zealand
and the Pacific Islands 14
Timeline 15
At Sea - Search for a Great Southern Continent 17

Australia

    Sydney - More than a Harbor 31
    Sydney - Characters of Kings Cross 49
    Marvelous Melbourne 61
    Hobart, Tasmania: Port Arthur and the Transportation Era 75
    Adelaide – Hahndorf: A Little Bit of Germany in
    South Australia 91
    Wild West of Australia in Fremantle 107
    Aboriginal Heart of Australia 123
    Broome of Pearls and Poets 133
    Darwin of the Air 149
    Independent Queenslanders of Brisbane 163

New Zealand

    New Zealand History, Part I: Maori Strong and Resilient 177
    New Zealand History, Part II: Travels with Captain Cook
    in New Zealand 193

New Zealand History, Part III: Waitangi: A Treaty in Translation 207

New Zealand History, Part IV: Wairu: From War to New, New Zealand 219

Wine and Coffee in Auckland..231

Art Deco Napier..245

Wellington Girl – Kathryn Mansfield...259

Christchurch Rising 273

Dunedin: A Little Bit of Scotland in New Zealand 287

FRENCH POLYNESIA

Island Gods 303

The French in French Polynesia..321

Paul Gauguin in Tahiti 341

The Real Captain Bligh 365

Bora Bora – Operation Bobcat and the Beautiful Isle 381

EASTER ISLAND

Katherine Routledge Legacy of Easter Island 393

Walking Moai of Easter Island...409

PITCAIRN ISLAND

Bounty Mutineers Escape to Pitcairn Island 429

INDEX 439

PREFACE

Cruise through History is a collection of short stories grouped by the sequence of many popular cruise itineraries, rather than by country, or period of history. As the stories move from port to port, they randomly move through time. The stories are all true. They introduce the traveler to the history and culture of a port through the story of a long-ago, or not so long-ago, resident, whose exploits left a castle, a palace, or a lovely site that can be explored on a cruise ship shore excursion.

The host character for each port stop is chosen for their inspiring actions and the visible culture left behind. Some names will be familiar, presented in these volumes with depth to their personality. Other characters will become new friends, too long unrecognized. Either way, stories offer a new twist to the school-age history of place, drawn together to put travels in a fascinating context for the short-term visitor.

No apology is made for the choice of subjects. They have been chosen in an arbitrary manner on the whim of the author, accumulated from past travels, for your enjoyment. The desire is that the reader will share the fun. No attempt is made to be politically correct, or give a chamber of commerce gloss to stories evident in remnants of the past. Knowledge of history can teach us a great deal about ourselves, and the human condition, but only if it is honest and fairly told. No doubt it is the quest for "real" that draws adults to travel as often and for as long as they are able.

The desire to seek knowledge, about distant places and times, fuels international tourism. Many travelers who found history in school to be dull, later in life seek to fill gaps in their knowledge, with personal experience. Travel is the opportunity for events of one's life to give rich meaning to the human condition and to enjoy stories of fact for which fiction is no rival.

Praise is due to the many historians and other scholars who have delved deeply into source data, to ponder minute details of history for pedagogical pursuits. Such information is mined here, with attribution, for the lively details, to heighten the traveler's enjoyment of the past. History is a public good. The more it is enjoyed, the more it will be valued.

Apology is due to those who hoped to foster disciplined scholarship in the author. This is reading for an out-of-the classroom experience. Footnotes are inserted to give due credit to scholars, who have provided valuable information, and to remind the reader that these stories are true. The presence of source notes is not to feign an academic appearance. Editorial sidebars and fun bits are in the footnotes.

When there are gaps in the facts, or mysteries remain, they are not supplemented by fiction. Rather, an effort is made to look at the known as a guide to the unknown. The reader can draw their own conclusions, daydream through the gaps, and enjoy the reason that so much popular fiction and movies are drawn from historical facts.

These stories are offered to give historical context to the sites often visited as cruise destinations. In these stories, meet the characters who walked the same streets in the past, that visitors walk today. Go beyond the castle ruins to envision the people who built them and lived there.

The itineraries in this series have stories at each port that seek to inspire cruise travelers to rise out of their deck chairs and investigate a destination with honesty and irreverence, or the potential traveler to rise from the sofa and embark on a Cruise through History. There is no stigma of a school assignment. Earn an "E" for enjoyment.

Itineraries in the Cruise through History series available and forthcoming:

1. **London to Rome - 2014**
2. **Rome to Venice – 2014**
3. **Ports of the Eastern Mediterranean - 2019**
4. **Ports of the Black Sea - 2019**

5. Ports of Arabia to the Atlantic, across the Southern Mediterranean – coming 2021

6. Ports of the Atlantic Coast of North America, with Cuba and Bermuda – coming 2021

7. Ports of the Pacific Coast of North America, with Hawaii – coming 2021

8. **Mexico, Central America, and the Caribbean Islands – 2015**

9. **Ports of South America –2017**

10. **Ports of the British Isles - 2020**

11. **Ports of the Baltic Sea – 2018**

12. **Ports of the North Sea - 2020**

13. Ports of Africa, India and Southeast Asia – coming 2021

14. **Australia, New Zealand and the Pacific Islands – 2020**

15. Ports of the Far East, including Indonesia – coming 2021

Cruise through History – Shakespeare as Travel Writer – coming 2021

Find all the story books at **cruisethroughhistory.com**.

Author & Husband on Bora Bora

ACKNOWLEDGEMENTS

Writing travel stories began as therapy from the world of Washington, D.C. Thanks are due to the Summer Citizens program at Utah State University, Logan, and to the several cruise lines, book clubs and community associations that have given me opportunities to share stories with their guests and students.

Much appreciated are those who helped to produce the series, including: Digby and Rose, publisher, art director, and publicist; Lisa Lynn Aispuro and Robert Palmer research assistance. Diana Verkamp, created the CTH logo and additional photos are by Chris and David Greinke. Thanks go to Elizabeth Herrgott at Feast Studios for CTH video stories.

These stories would not be possible without the treasure trove of material in libraries and used bookshops. I am indebted to the Battery Park Book Exchange, Asheville NC, the Lanier Library, Tryon, NC, and the Library of Congress. In this increasingly paperless world, bookstores and libraries provide solace and an opportunity to revive our humanity.

Much appreciation is due to those who apply their skill to preservation and protection of heritage resources in the United States and around the world. The greatest thanks go to my husband, Guy Rouse, who has lugged my camera equipment all over the world for over thirty years. So many good times, so many photos, have all become the fabric of memory and the inspiration for stories.

All photos and art are property of Cruise through History, unless otherwise noted, and all rights are reserved. No use may be made of the photos, art and text, the construction of history in stories, without prior permission of the author.

INTRODUCTION
Stories of the Southern Seas

In this itinerary of stories, cruise the Southern Seas to the Great Southern Continent. In the great migration from Southeast Asia and Melanesia, ancient people came to islands of Polynesia and Easter Island, until they reached the southern boundary of attractive climate in New Zealand. Earlier, people came from New Guinea, south into Australia. Centuries later, the vast Southern Seas, places of myth and mystery to Europeans, were sought by adventurous sea captains. In the nineteenth century, Europeans came to Australia, by force of British law, while France colonized Polynesia. In recent history, Polynesia, Australia and New Zealand are seen as some of the most attractive places on earth to live. Locals are protective of their cherished environments.

In this collection of stories are tales of explorers, who mapped Australia, New Zealand and Polynesia, and of the indigenous peoples they encountered. Follow Able Tasman in Australia and Tasmania and James Cook as he stops along a route in New Zealand. Infamous Captain William Bligh has his own story in this collection. Contrary to Hollywood movies, Bligh is viewed differently in the realities of history. He came to Polynesia to collect breadfruit, a fool's errand for slave-owning Englishmen, and a mission made infamous in the Mutiny on the Bounty. Bligh lived through the mutiny, on the force of will and excellent skills as a mariner, to become part of the history of Australia in New South Wales.

First residents of the Southern Seas feature prominently in this itinerary. In each port, indigenous people are part of the ongoing story, integral to history and future of each place. Endearing is the Aboriginal Heart of Australia, told in Songlines, the literal dots of cultural understanding. In New Zealand, the Maori are Strong and Resilient, through times of the Treaty of Waitangi and its ambiguous translation. In New Zealand, the Treaty began a war, rather than came at its conclusion. The story here, is the evolution of Maori and European co-existence from the incident at Wairu, that led from War to a New, New Zealand of today.

In Polynesia, experience the Island Gods, never fully vanquished when the French colonized French Polynesia. The story of the French in French Polynesia is an ode to the lack of virtue in colonizing cultures. Paul Gauguin discovered French pretentiousness, so far from home, when he sought primitive people in Tahiti, through whom he channeled his passion in art. The story of Bora Bora is a short story from party animals, the Arioi warriors of ancient history, to Operation Bobcat in World War II and the festive atmosphere that is everlasting at Bloody Mary's.

On Easter Island, learn the secrets of Walking Moai and the Rapa Nui people for whom the stone giants protected their *mana*. Then sail on the *Mana*, the purpose-built schooner of Katherine Routledge, who spent more than a year on Easter Island, prior to World War I, documenting genealogies of the remnants of Rapa Nui people. Routledge began a personal adventure in science, which brought world-wide attention to the importance of preservation of Rapa Nui culture, through the emerging field of ethnography, and enhanced regard for women in science.

As in all itineraries in Cruise through History, stories in ports of call are offered to enhance the lure and fun of shore visits. In Australia, begin in Sydney, by going deep into the streetscape, where Sydney is More than a Harbor. Then venture into the notorious King's Cross section of Sydney, where Characters of King's Cross include two women gang mavens, artists, the muse for Priscilla Queen of the Desert, and the unsolved mystery of the disappearance of the woman whose crusade to preserve the neighborhood may have ended in her death.

Travel around the coast of Australia to Marvelous Melbourne, built by new wealth of the gold rush and sustained today by an environment largely devoted to the arts. In Hobart, Tasmania, visit Port Arthur for the story of the Transportation Era in Australia. Not all emigres from Europe were transportees. In Adelaide, Hahndorf is A Little Bit of Germany in South Australia. Enjoy a walk in the old world, within the new, and end the day with strudel in a German style café.

The Wild West of Australia lives on in Fremantle, home of the World Heritage Site Transportation Era prison and a streetscape of territorial pubs, cafés and coffee bars. Broome, an outpost of pearl divers, is the ideal location for mystery stories Of Pearls and Poets. History of Darwin was made by flyers of double winged and single engine aircraft, until it became famous as a port in the airplane race of the century. End the Australia tour with Independent Queenslanders of Brisbane. Brisbane, begun as a Transportation Era prison site, grew into a most desirable, multicultural city, along the Brisbane River, which provides a frame today to entertainment, arts and recreation, in view of historic buildings of the heart of the city.

In New Zealand, the opening story of ports is Wine and Coffee in Auckland. Wander the streets of Auckland from its beginnings at the port, up the street in time to the town hall, now an orchestra venue. The historic city is vibrant with coffee bars, as it adds new layers of its story, preserved with the old. Napier and Christchurch, New Zealand were devastated by earthquakes. In Napier the story is regrowth as an Art Deco gem in the southern hemisphere. Christchurch is Rising amidst recent leveling of its Gothic Revival core, with a spirit of regeneration that is inspiring.

Turn to New Zealand literature in Wellington and Dunedin. In Wellington Girl meet Katherine Mansfield, outrageous in life and inspiring writers forever after. Although she lived in Europe and England, her stories are set in emotions of Wellington, told with honesty and clarity, which makes her a favorite daughter of the city today. Dunedin is a Little Bit of Scotland in New Zealand. Founded by Scots, hallmark of the city is a statue of Robert Burns on the city center, at the beginning of a writers' walk, inspiration to modern writers of literary prizes. In Dunedin visit a Scottish castle and wander streets of Scottish architecture, as if home were not far away.

This volume of Cruise through History ends with the story of Mutineers on the Bounty Escape to Pitcairn Island. To complete the story of Captain Bligh, which began in Polynesia and Australia, learn the fate of the mutineers after they parted company with Bligh. Life on Pitcairn is a strange tale for the modern world. It ends with a mystery, that asks the question, did Fletcher Christian end his days, on an island in the middle of the South Pacific, or in Portsmouth, England, home of the Royal Navy, which traversed the seas hunting for him? All the stories are for you to enjoy.

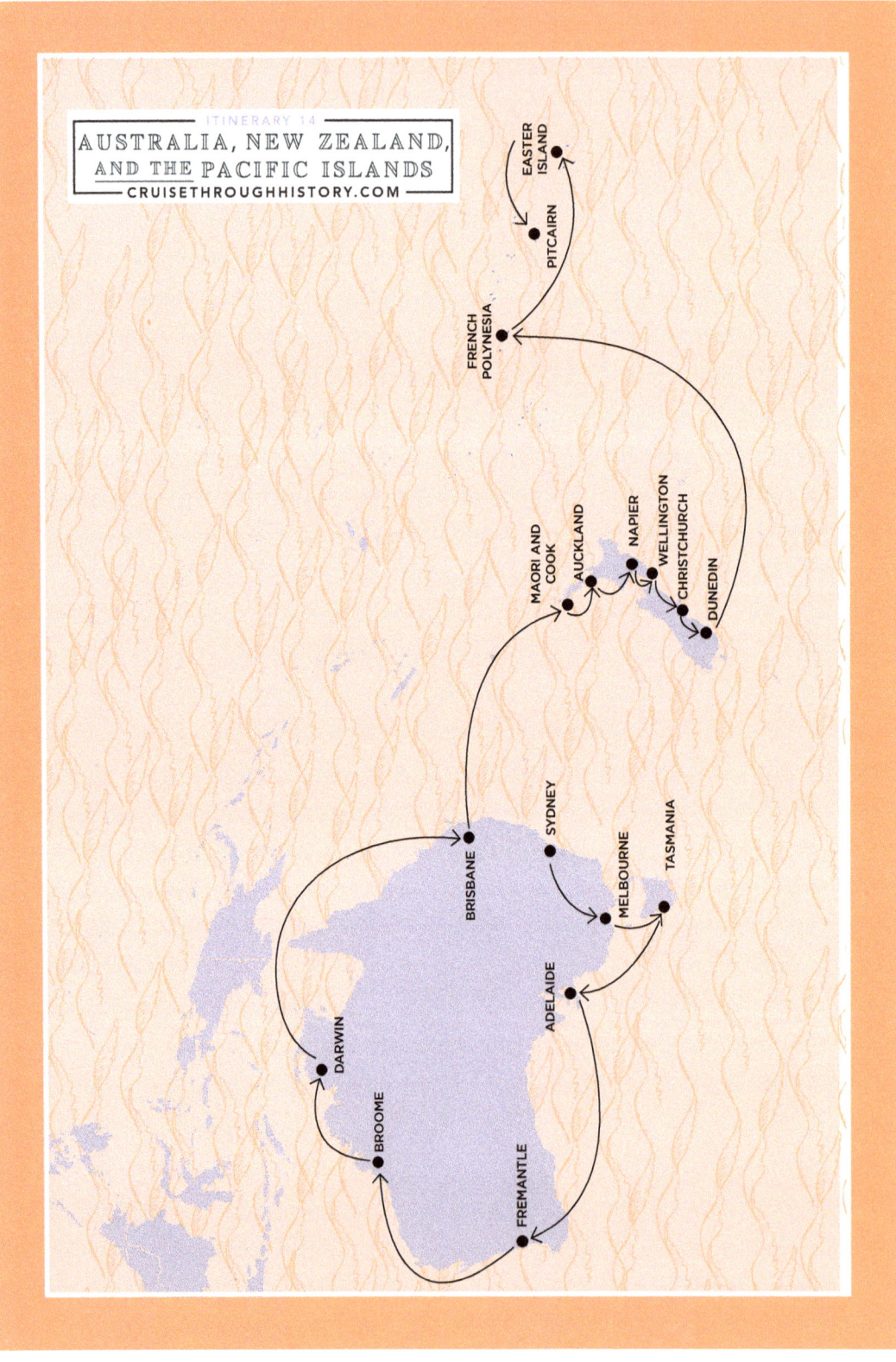

Cruise Through History
Itinerary XIV

Timeline | cruisethroughhistory.com

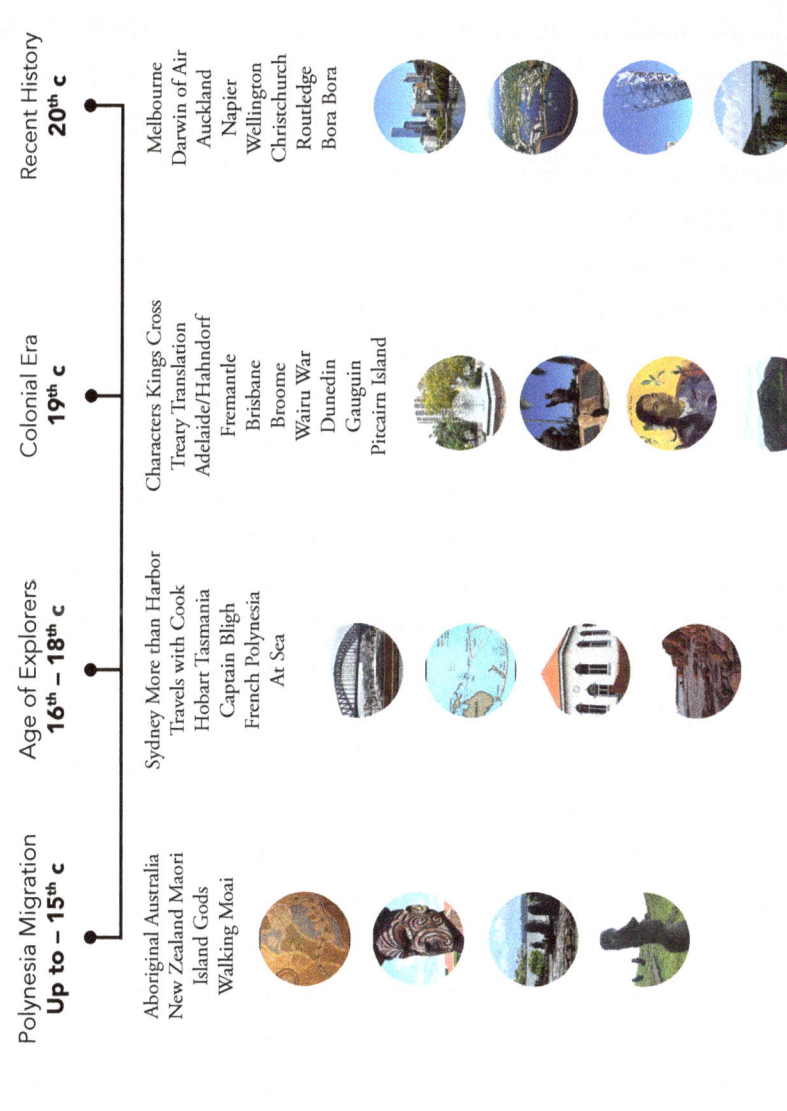

| Polynesia Migration | Age of Explorers | Colonial Era | Recent History |
| Up to – 15th c | 16th – 18th c | 19th c | 20th c |

Polynesia Migration (Up to – 15th c)
- Aboriginal Australia
- New Zealand Maori
- Island Gods
- Walking Moai

Age of Explorers (16th – 18th c)
- Sydney More than Harbor
- Travels with Cook
- Hobart Tasmania
- Captain Bligh
- French Polynesia
- At Sea

Colonial Era (19th c)
- Characters Kings Cross
- Treaty Translation
- Adelaide/Hahndorf
- Fremantle
- Brisbane
- Broome
- Wairu War
- Dunedin
- Gauguin
- Pitcairn Island

Recent History (20th c)
- Melbourne
- Darwin of Air
- Auckland
- Napier
- Wellington
- Christchurch
- Routledge
- Bora Bora

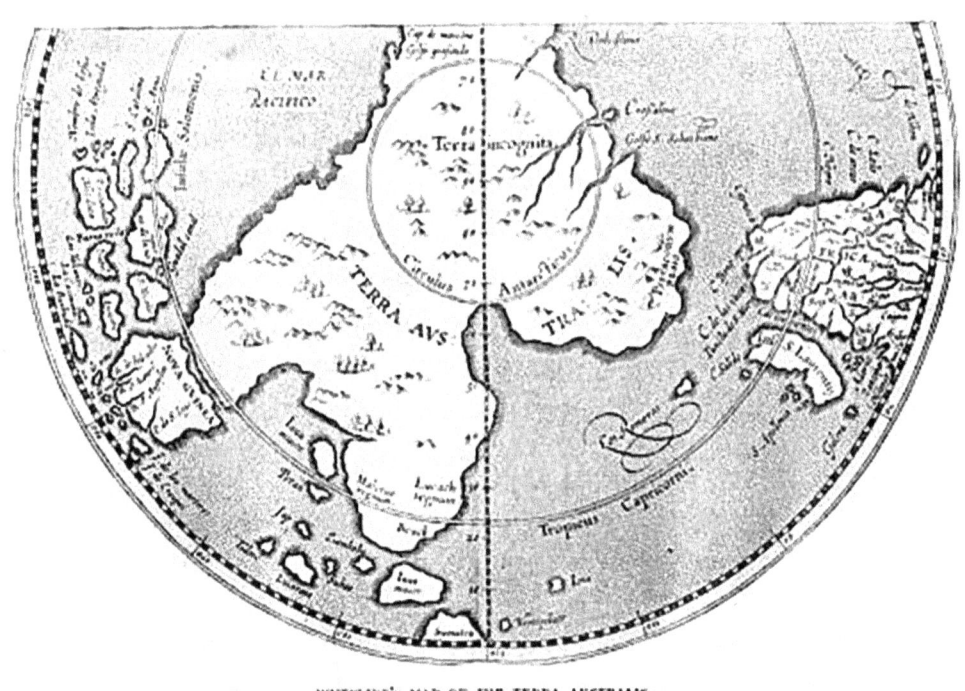

Terra Australis 1597 credit Gutenberg Australia

AT SEA
SEARCH FOR A GREAT SOUTHERN CONTINENT

Second century maps of Greeks and Romans, such as Ptolemy in 150 CE, included a Great Southern Continent no one had ever seen. It seemed logical to the ancients that such a land mass must exist. Marco Polo, more than a millennium later, promised there was a continent of gold below Java. Of course, he wrote from jail, through an interpreter, of a land he had never seen.

Early masters of the seas of the Far East were Dutch. The seventeenth century Dutch East India Company (DEIC) was a world leader in corporate, shareholder endeavors. Their purpose in exploration was for stockholder profit, not scientific research, religious missionary outpost sites, or colonization. Dutch captains saw no profit lurking in arid northern Australia. They lingered no further south than Java, where plantations filled their ships with profitable commodities.

James Cook sailed to New Zealand in search of the Great Southern Continent for England in the latter half of the eighteenth century. His secret sailing instructions told him there must be such a place between Cape Horn and New Holland in the southern Pacific Ocean. When he sailed around New Zealand, he proved that it was an island and not the tip of the sought-after new continent. Years later, when Cook sailed from Botany Bay, now Sydney Harbor, up the east coast of Australia, he considered himself a failure for not turning east from New Zealand to search the open sea.

Cook was a keen observer and a diligent note taker. He was not an anthropologist. Along the coast of Australia, he observed hunter-gatherer people, of a lifestyle basic beyond his prior experience. He observed no Maori style forts, farms, or settlements. In Cook's European sensibility, this was *Terra Nullius*, the land of no one. When he claimed the east coast of Australia for the crown of England, he had no idea of the vast real estate beyond, or that it would take two hundred years to sort out land claims, due to his mistaken assumptions.

This is the short story of discovery and conquest of a continent. Australia was not *terra nullius*. Those who agonize over Cook's mistake, might consider the consequences for Aboriginal land rights resolved today, if Cook had attempted, or asserted a treaty which extinguished Aboriginal land rights. In this look at history as we find it, the story ends with land rights defined by court decree. Against a history of disease, violence and anger, all Australians can find solace in the law.

Dutch Masters of the Eastern Oceans

Portuguese are due credit for being the first among Europeans in an Age of Discovery to reach Australia. In 1516, a Portuguese fort was built on Timor. Finding no gold, or trading ports, they sailed away.

Spanish explorer Luis Vaes de Torres arrived in a strait between New Guinea and the upward reaching peninsula of north eastern Australia, now known as York Peninsula, in 1606. He captured twenty hostages, which he considered candidates to become interpreters and guides to the interior. He sailed to Manila with his human cargo, leaving behind his name. Torres Strait Islanders have no fond memories of their namesake.

Also, in 1606, Dutchman Willem Jansz sailed to the Spice Islands, looking for New Guinea. He veered south in error and landed on Cape York, at the top of the Australian York peninsula. He was greeted by spear throwing locals. The Dutch were undeterred.

With a solid base of operations in Java, the DEIC sent several more ships south to the north coast of Australia, which was recorded on maps as Arnhem Land. Between Arnhem Land and York Peninsula is the Gulf of Carpentaria. Dutch navigators mapped the area between Java, known then as Dutch Batavia, and the western side of the York Peninsula in the gulf, up through the 1640s.

The Dutch became familiar with Aboriginal Australians they regarded as most wretched creatures. When the DEIC enslaved locals in Java to work sugar plantations, the Dutch saw no potential either in farmland, or potential slaves in the northern territory. Another Dutchman, Maarten van Delft, made contact in 1705, with Tiwi people on the tiny island north of Darwin today.

Though people were friendly, unless and until Dutchmen tried to take non-volunteer interpreter trainees, the Dutch saw no economic potential in the Southern Continent.

A century later, Mathew Flinders had contact with Aboriginals in the same area, and saw their life little changed. Yolngu people of Arnhem Land adopted some gardening practices of their northern neighbors, the Macassans, who came to their land to collect sea cucumber. Macassans collected great amounts of the sea urchins, to trade in China. Since Yolngu did not regard the catch as food, they had no issue with the roaming, short-term visitors, who left them alone.

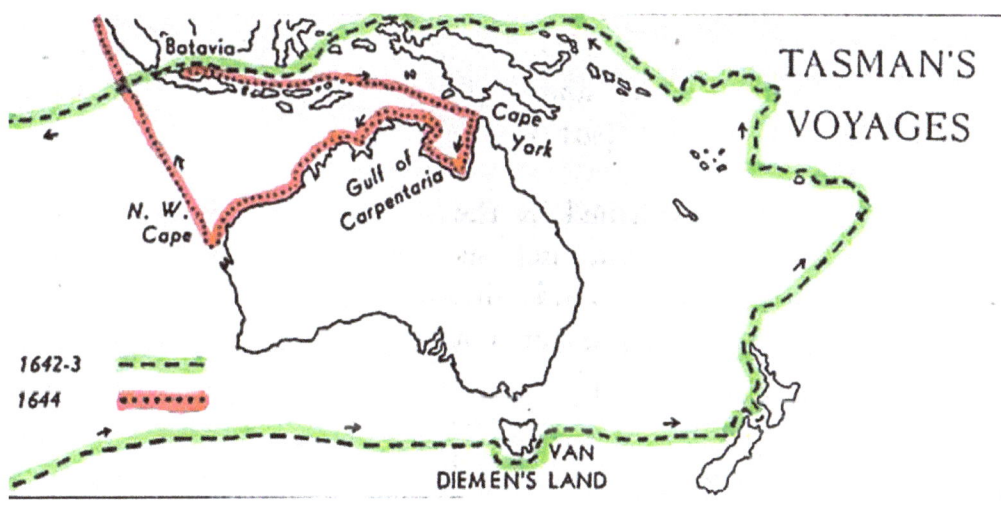

Tasman Map (credit Gutenberg Australia)

The great Dutch explorer of the era in Australia was Abel Tasman[1], who sailed for the DEIC in 1642 and 1644. In his 1642 voyage to the Spice Islands, Tasman went from the Cape of Good Hope to Mauritius, known as a preferred stop in the Indian Ocean. Instead of heading northeast, Tasman sailed due east and discovered the island south of the Australian continent, which he named Van Dieman's Land. Several centuries later, in an attempt to remove the stain of involvement in the Transportation Era, the island name was changed to Tasmania, in honor of the Dutchman.

---

[1] Abel Tasman was born in 1603 in Holland and died in Java, then known as Batavia in 1659.

From Van Dieman's Land, Tasman continued east to New Zealand. He sailed up the west side of the North Island and then northeast to Tonga. There Tasman turned northwest to New Guinea and the Spice Islands, known as Moluccas. Tasman made a further voyage in 1644, where he mapped Australia, from the east side of the York Peninsula, along the northern coast, to the point he turned south. The west coast of Australia was previously known to Dutch sailors, notably as a place they were blown in unfavorable winds. Tasman had an idea of the enormity of the southern continent. He found nothing to recommend it.

The Dutch were great keepers of secrets about their travels. Tasman's journal was not published until 1898. Tasman spent his final years as a manager of operations for the DEIC in Java.

Britain Claims the Continent

Dampier Peninsula, Australia (photo credit Creative Commons.org)

The first British landing in Australia of note was the pirate William Dampier. Journals of his travels are fabulous tales of adventure. Some of which are true. In a circumnavigation of the globe in search of treasure in 1688, Dampier spent time along the west coast of Australia, repairing his ship. His records of Aboriginals, flora, and fauna sparked the interest of King William III. Dampier's 1697 book, *A New Voyage Round the World* was a best seller in his time.

In 1699, Dampier had a royal commission to explore the west coast of Australia. Before he could reach the Australian coast, his ship was in such a perilous condition, that he beached on the shore. The great adventurer ended up rescued by a merchant ship and returned to England in 1701. His next book, *A Voyage to New Holland* in 1703, gave him the aura of a shipwreck survivor.

Plants Found in New Holland by William Dampier (credit Gutenberg Australia)

Dampier was removed from the Royal Navy for cruelty to crew. His circumnavigation adventurers were as a pirate. In his later voyage in the South Pacific, to capture treasure of Manila Galleons headed to Acapulco, Dampier gained notoriety as the captain who left Alexander Selkirk marooned on Juan Fernandez Islands. Selkirk complained about seaworthiness of the ship. Selkirk was right. The ship sank. Selkirk was rescued by another English adventurer, Woods Rogers, which is another story.[2]

---

[2] Selkirk claimed to be the inspiration for Robinson Crusoe, written by Daniel Defoe in 1719.

Captain James Cook came to the South Pacific to observe the transit of Venus, a marker in measuring earth's distance from the sun. Then he went looking for the Great Southern Continent. He proved that New Zealand was an island, not the tip of a continent. Turning west, Cook discovered Botany Bay, so called for the collection of plants accomplished by his botanists.

James Cook (credit Gutenberg Australia)

In the rubric of Cook's day, when making contacts with advanced cultures, trade treaties were in order. If the location held hostile inhabitants, it was avoided unless strategic. If of value in commerce, Britain landed the military. If the land appeared uninhabited, it was considered *terra nullius*, the land of no one. Cook knew of New Holland, the land beyond the southern sea. If the east coast of an uncharted land mass was not New Holland, then it was claimable for England.

Cook claimed the east coast of Australia as New South Wales. He recorded seeing few people with spears and no farms, homes, or canoes. He saw no one with whom he could make a treaty. No chieftain asserted himself. Cook saw the land in what he reported as a *pure state of nature*.[3]

Conquest of Land in an Age of *Terra Nullius*

In the late nineteenth century, England was desperate to find a new location for exile of convicts. The American colonies were in revolt, curbing the availability of New England as a venue. Prison ships in the Thames were overloaded denizens of disease. Worse yet, the ships put incarceration within view of Londoners. When Cook submitted his report, it was timely and useful information.

---

[3] Flood, at 25.

In 1788, English settlers came to the Sydney Basin. The first to arrive were opportunist officers of the New South Wales Company, determined to control land and commerce. Poor farmers, with barely the means to pay for passage, looked to Australia as a place to become prosperous land owners, without the stigma of social class that limited social and economic mobility in England. In this new place, possibilities were limitless, or so new arrivals thought.

Aboriginal Australians looked at new arrivals with interest. As long as they were few in number, Aboriginals retreated from the coast. As long as no chief asserted land ownership, where land could be bargained for in sale, as in New Zealand, settlers established farms and ranches.

As the number of settlers increased, and farms became more numerous, new arrivals were in competition for Aboriginal food supply. Europeans were efficient at shooting game and trapping fish. Farms displaced areas of traditional seed collection. Aboriginal people were amiable in dealing with newcomers until their survival was threatened. They saw the survival line crossed before Europeans realized the impact of their actions.

Many Australians consider January 26, 1788, Australia National Day. For Aboriginal Australians, the day is a mark of pain. In that year, not only did British arrive to settle and establish farms, French military ships arrived. French confrontation with Aboriginals was hostile and left natives apprehensive when dealing with foreigners.[4] Then, British convict ships arrived. Convicts stole from Aboriginals. There was an incident in which convicts were speared and Aboriginals died.

In 1789, another small pox epidemic spread through Australia. Whether brought by Europeans or Macassans, the result was death of half the population of Eora people. Eora are a reference to the population of Aboriginal peoples of eastern Australia. Depletion numbers were catastrophic. Deaths from disease exacerbated the decline in Aboriginal births, the result of years of Aboriginal women contracting venereal disease from random sailors of various nations.

---

[4] Aboriginals thought the French were strange creatures. The French sailors had no beards so Aboriginals thought they were women until a Frenchman bared his bottom. Aboriginals were wary of men who traveled with sheep instead of women.

When Aboriginals stole food from settlers, the response was armed settlers hunting and shooting peaceful camps of Aboriginal women and children. Aboriginal warriors retaliated by driving settler sheep or cattle over a cliff. Freed British convicts were given open land to settle further into the interior. Aboriginals responded by burning farms. Clearly the land was not *terra nullius*.

From *Terra Nullius* to Aboriginal Australian Land Rights

1814 Thomson Map of Australia, New Zealand and New Guinea

As the nineteenth century began, Europeans looked at natives with a paternalistic view. Missionaries came to Australia to distribute food, education and Christianity to Aboriginals. Governor Lachlan Macquarie in Sydney began a school for Aboriginal children. Mixed raced children, though not abandoned by Aboriginal family groups, were collected by British agents and brought to boarding schools. The children were taught to become British citizens in what is termed the Stolen Generation. Some children prospered and others did not.

While hostilities escalated in the first decades of the nineteenth century, Britain continued to encourage settlers to occupy *empty* territory. In Melbourne, a Native Police Force was begun, in which Aboriginals with tracking skills were given horses and guns. They tracked groups of Aboriginals retaliating the conquest of their land by burning settler farms. Violence increased.

The number of Aboriginal deaths due to violence during this period is subject to debate today. Looking across sources, there is some agreement that twice as many Aboriginals died due to violence than did settlers. The number of deaths from disease was likely four times the number.

Britain considered setting aside land reserved for Aboriginals. Unable to find Aboriginal leaders to negotiate a treaty, picture signs were created and posted as warnings for consequences of raids. The British failed to understand Aboriginal social organization, even after decades of interaction.

The British failed to appreciate that consolidating disparate Aboriginal peoples onto a single land area required one group to trespass on gathering lands of another. Aboriginals did not want to be forced into war with other Aboriginals. They appreciated scarcity of food sources and consequences for encroachment on territory of others. If settlers realized prior land use by Aboriginals, they ignored indications of prior ownership, not recognized by their government.

The century from 1820 to 1920, was a period of settler expansion, Aboriginal response and devastating Aboriginal population decline due to disease. To visualize the extent of settler impact on the land, draw a line from Adelaide northeast to Brisbane on a map. The area from the line to the coast, once land of Aboriginal peoples, was controlled by settlers. The area above the line includes desert, hardly able to support a healthy population of hunter-gatherers. Draw an arc coast to coast above Perth to Broome, to visualize settlement of Europeans on the western habitable coast. Arid red desert lies between coasts. This land was left to Aboriginal occupants.

Add to the mix, increased technology of guns to the six-shot revolver. Settlers had the most recent technology in guns. Aboriginals, rapidly becoming dependent upon European food, also mastered European weapons. Some Aboriginals had older guns and little ammunition.

Aboriginal Protection Societies proliferated from the 1840s, supported by church groups given land by the government. Societies fed and educated Aboriginals in locations remote to cities. Missionaries gave from the heart, based on a European vision of humanity. Charles Darwin visited Australia in 1836, and proclaimed Aboriginals to be a doomed race. Social Darwinism, the idea of stronger races prevail, was popular in Europe until the later twentieth century.

In the 1930s, government response to crisis in Australia was a policy of assimilation. Through education, Aboriginal people could adopt British knowledge. The assumption was that British knowledge would enable Aboriginals to become more accepting of British lifeways. British lifeways included strata of social class, in which people of color were at the lowest rung.

The 1960s was a decade of social movements and demonstrations across the globe on issues of human rights. In Australia, the government policy shifted to ending assimilation and preserving culture. The question faced by the Australian government was how to preserve Aboriginal culture in remote areas, where there were few social services, and most acute despair.

When the government required equal pay and provision for housing for families of ranch hands, few ranchers could afford to retain Aboriginal workers. Unemployment among Aboriginals increased. Substance abuse increased. Dependency upon government support increased. People who functioned as hunter-gatherers for thousands of years, became government dependents within a century. Most poitent, government decided for Aboriginals what was in their best interests. Government evolved from conqueror, to paternal assistance, to caretaker of Aboriginals.

Aboriginal Land Rights March in Melbourne 1968 (Photo credit News Ltd/Newspix)

The 1970s began an era of land rights determination. Gurindji people claimed aboriginal title to traditional lands from among Crown Land. There were no treaties to extinguish their claim. The Gurindji were awarded ten square miles of cattle station land in 1975. By 1991, the land was deserted. The experiment seemed a failure. Failure in fact was considered progress in concept.

The 1981 Pitjantjatjara Land Rights Act acknowledged a corporate clan body of Aboriginal people, given forty square miles of land in South Australia. The corporation has control of rents and income from land, although it shares mining royalties with the government. The Act established a means to recognize an Aboriginal group, resolve land rights, and manage income and benefits to members, without requiring an identified tribal leader, a concept foreign to Aboriginal culture.

In 1992, the High Court of Australia considered the case of Eddie Mabo's claim for land rights determination. The Mabo Case is historic. The court overturned the 1788 determination of Britain, that Australia was *terra nullius*. Cook's Mistake became Cook's Redemption. Due to Cook's failure to acknowledge land ownership, there are no treaties to bar present-day claims to native title.

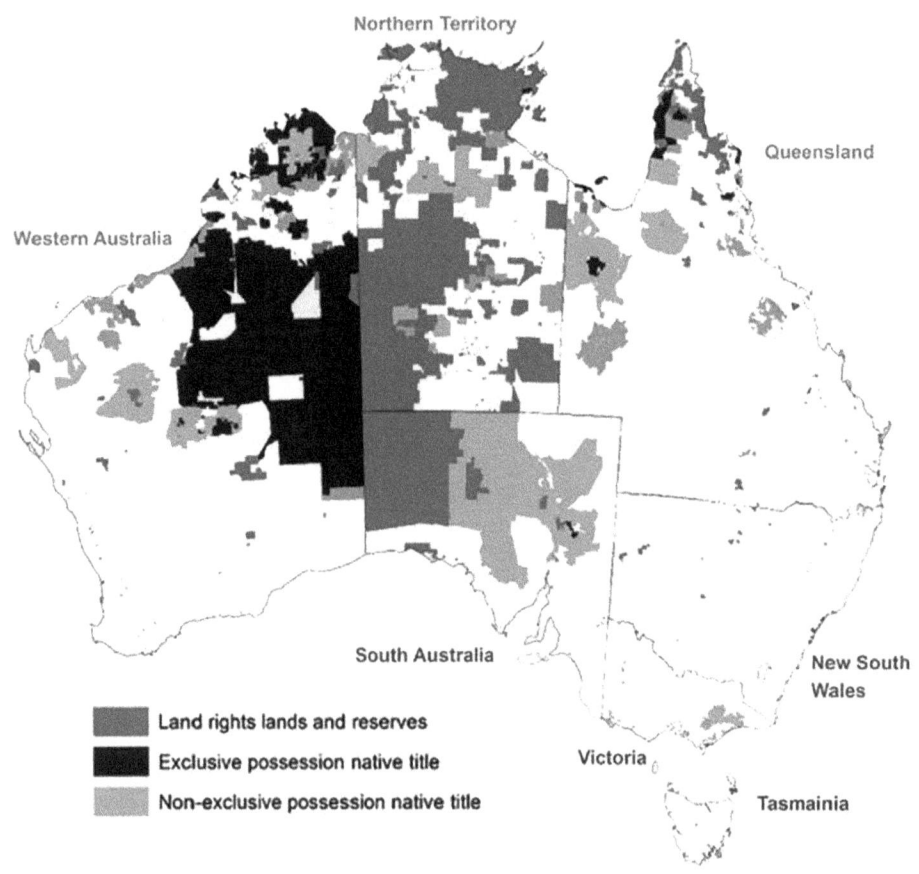

Aboriginal Land Rights (credit Wiki commons)

Native Title is defined in Australian law as indigenous inhabitants' interests in land, whether communal, group, or individual, under traditional law and custom of the group. In *Wik Peoples v. Queensland*, in 1996, the court clarified the Mabo case to hold that Native Title is not extinguished by government granted leases to land. Court law was made into parliamentary law in the 1998 Native Title Amendment Act, which establishes a process to adjudicate land claims. The Indigenous Land Fund was established to provide for purchase of land and cover administrative costs.

Two hundred years of land management under an assumption of *terra nullius* could not be resolved in two decades. The process is a beginning. Deeply held prejudices do not melt with the passage of law. In 2008, Prime Minister of Australia, Kevin Rudd gave a formal apology for centuries of government policy toward Aboriginals. That too, is part of the process of healing.

Sixty-five thousand years ago, humans migrated into Australia looking for space upon which to thrive. In the interim, the world has become highly populated. Living in close space, amicably, was resolved by Aboriginal Australians for thousands of years prior to European *discovery*. Living together amicably today is still a quest.

Governor Lachlan Macquarie

AUSTRALIA
Sydney – More than a Harbor

Entrance to Sydney Harbor

The sail-in experience of the Sydney Harbor is the reason Australia cruise itineraries book to capacity as soon as they are offered. A cruise provides the best introduction to Sydney. Few harbors of the world offer such drama as a sail into sight of the Sydney Opera House on the point, with the high-rise buildings pushed back, and the green of the Royal Botanic Gardens framing the view. Cruise ships move under the bridge, within earshot of growls emanating from Taronga Zoo, on the opposite shore, and come to dock where the first settlers arrived. On shore is Captain William Bligh in bronze, one of the first governors of New South Wales, there to greet everyone.

Once on the Sydney dock, what next? Some visitors head to Bondi Beach, or one of the many lovely beaches along the shore outside the harbor to the south of the city. Some visitors are whisked onto big buses for a quick ride around, before returning to the harbor area to wander around the Sydney Opera House, for a close-up view at icon architecture in a perfect setting.

There is more to Sydney than the harbor. It may not be obvious at a first look. Beyond the harbor and the preserved area of The Rocks, that is the early immigrant section, with the warehouses and small flats for new arrivals, there is a palisade of incredibly tall and imposing commercial buildings, the product of economic success of recent decades. The Sydney most visitors would enjoy seeing is spread across both sides of the sprawling Royal Botanic Gardens, and several harbors from the Overseas Passenger Terminal in the center, to the east at Cowper Wharf, and to the west at the newly redeveloping Ultimo area, of former heavy industry around Darling Harbor.[5]

To comfortably venture beyond the harbor, it is helpful to understand the history of the city. Sydney grew by fiat, in clumps.[6] It was founded as a depot to support Transportation Era prison camps. Early governor Lachlan Macquarie, who thought he might create a city in the first decades of the nineteenth century, was admonished for his efforts and recalled to London. He was followed by Governor Ralph Darling, who paved streets and royally cashed in on housing subdivisions, although he was adamant that Sydney should not have a theatre.[7]

There is greater depth to history in Sydney than can be encapsulated in a short story.[8] Development, from supply depot, to a city of international stature, not often seen in a non-capital city, is told in six segments, through its buildings, representative of layers of city history. The story begins, where Sydney began, at The Rocks, then moves to efforts of Governor Macquarie to create a city. Next comes Sydney's literal Golden Age, funded by gold mining, and built of

---

[5] When complete, Ultimo will be the upcoming hotspot destination. The Aquatic Center is open and the WildLife Sydney Zoo is scheduled for opening in 2019.
[6] The capital of Australia is Canberra, a master-planned capital, begun in 1908. As a compromise to Sydney and Melbourne, the larger competitive siblings, the capital was placed mid-way between them, inland from either harbor. In Australia, the capital of government does not compete with commerce.
[7] A harbor and city neighborhood, among other places, are named for Darling.
[8] Historic walks of Sydney to learn city history in depth can be found online at: cityofSydney.nsw.au

golden Sydney sandstone. In the twentieth century, Sydney was impressed by architectural phases of the world as it went through Art Deco, in the industrial age, to modernism's steel and glass, to finally settle on icon architecture, which requires this story to return to the harbor and the Opera House.

Sydney is still a young city, compared with cities of Europe. It is still under construction. For the cruise visitor, enthralled by the harbor, this story begs to create a deeper view of the port city.

The Rocks

The Rocks

Sydney began as a consequence of the Transportation Era. It was not a prison site. Captain James Cook extolled the possibilities of Botany Bay in 1770. Islands of the bay, outside the immediate Sydney Harbor, became the venue for notorious prisons of the Transportation Era. Those prisons have a separate story in this Itinerary.

Monument to Settlers at Sydney Rocks

Prisoner transportees were deposited in the area that would become Sydney in the late eighteenth century. These men and women were deemed non-dangerous. They were punished by the journey, then left to fend for themselves as farmers, in virgin turf, more forest and rock than farmland. The name *The Rocks* comes from available material, mixed with mud, used to build the first homes. So far from anything familiar, with Aboriginal occupants of the land not pleased to see intruders, the first settlers were like people deposited on another planet. This was home.

Little is left of the first arrivals in Sydney. Their homes melted around them in the rain. One of the earliest buildings preserved today is the John Cadman Cottage, first built in 1816. A modest structure now, amidst surrounding buildings, when built it would have seemed a palace. Cadman must have appreciated the cottage as his home from 1827 to 1845. He began life in Sydney as a transporté in 1798. He persevered to a pardon in 1821, and a position as a harbor official, which included the benefit of this home near the pier.

Cadman Cottage

All new arrivals to Sydney came through The Rocks. Modest apartments were built, which were small and densely arranged, on back streets. The Rocks was a place of lanes leading around warehouses. There were no wide streets or boulevards. Crammed between the water and the hill, upon which the Sydney Harbor Bridge pylons are now rooted, thousands of people lived. Their only dream was to leave The Rocks for wilderness farming. These were city people imaging a life as farmers; knowing nothing, possessing no skills for farming, and being provided few tools.

In 1900, the plague broke out in Sydney. It began in The Rocks. People were dispersed to other marginal housing. Buildings were torn down. New brick warehouses and shops were built. The Rawson Institute for Seaman, close to Cadman Cottage, was built in 1909. This home for old sailors replaced the Sailors' Church built in 1859, on the same site. Commercial buildings of early twentieth century red brick, and sandstone of the Victorian era, line roads of The Rocks today.

Construction of the Sydney Harbor Bridge in 1932, required removal of early-built remnants of The Rocks. Local rocks, which were used to build a retaining wall for the approach to the bridge, form a severe backdrop to preserved early twentieth century flats. Tented markets fill the streets under the bridge today. This fun place to shop for visitors, approximates what life was like two centuries earlier, when tented markets were the mainstay of shopping in Sydney.

Harbor to Harbor View under Sydney Bridge

Territorial Era

Sydney Mint of Lachlan Macquarie

Sydney transitioned from a random settlement at The Rocks, to a formative city of stature, during the administration of Governor Lachlan Macquarie. His achievements are considerable in light of tumultuous circumstances in which he governed. He was appointed in 1809, to quell the Rum Rebellion, which had been the undoing of his predecessor, Captain William Bligh. He was recalled in 1821, under similar circumstance as faced Bligh, when powerful locals felt their controlling grip on the city was slipping.[9]

---

[9] Macquarie made enemies when he issued orders prohibiting drinking on Sunday, taxed rum, and cut the number of bars authorized to operate in Sydney. Considering that taxes were paid in rum, Macquarie ordered a double. See generally, Robert Hughes, The Fatal Shore, Knopf, New York, 1987. Still the best read on the era.

Captain Bligh was a naval officer sent to New South Wales to contend with self-empowered officers of the New South Wales Company, a company more mercantile than military. Major General Macquarie landed in Sydney with his own loyal company of army stalwarts. He quashed remnants of self-appointed tyrants in a land that required, as he saw it, military rule. He became the last of the military governors. His legacy was to create a welcome place for civilian rule.

Macquarie established a mint for the first official local currency, using Spanish coins with the center punched; transitioned cricket grounds to the signature city park, Hyde Park, in 1810; and began the first bank of New South Wales. He named the continent Australia in 1817, in honor of the choice of names given by Mathew Flinders, the first to circumnavigate the continent in 1804.

Like Bligh, Macquarie ran into problems when his actions compromised control of freemen in the province. The issue became **freemen** versus **freedmen**. Macquarie's tenure oversaw the development of a court system, transitioning from military to civilian justice. Macquarie preferred a more egalitarian form of justice, involving freedmen. Large landowners in New South Wales preferred to replicate social exclusions of the British rule of law. Large landowners prevailed.

As governor, Macquarie could grant pardons and issue travel authorization to convicts. There was a practice in New South Wales, enjoyed by large landowners, of not granting a pardon, or travel authorization at the expiration of a sentence served. Macquarie's practice of granting pardons increased the number of freedmen, at the expense of freemen's access to unpaid labor. By the time Macquarie was recalled to London, there was a population in Sydney exceeding 36,000, of which freedmen exceeded the number of freemen. Officially, Macquarie was recalled for improvident spending on public works. In truth, he was another victim of territorial politics.

The Territorial Era of Macquarie is easily seen in Sydney in Hyde Park, established in 1810, and the Royal Botanic Gardens. Many of his building projects lie in, or on, the park periphery and between Macquarie Street and Mrs. Macquarie Street. Beyond the Mint on Macquarie Street, is the colonial Parliament House, built in 1811. The building was originally intended as part of a hospital.

Hyde Park Fountain

Macquarie took pride in hiring convicts, enabling their transition to productive life in Sydney. He granted a commission to convicted forger Francis Howard Greenway, to be his architect.[10] Greenway built the next building on Macquarie Street in 1817, the Hyde Park Barracks, which provided housing to former convicts. Greenway then began stables in 1817, which became the Conservatorium of Music, nestled into the Royal Botanic Garden, dedicated by Macquarie, and positioned on Mrs. Macquarie Street. Today the gardens are the place to view the harbor bridge.[11]

Greenway was the architect for the Macquarie Lighthouse in 1818, seen on entrance to Sydney Harbor. Just prior to the dedication of the lighthouse,

---

[10] Francis Howard Greenway was born in England in 1777, transported to Botany Bay in 1812, for the crime of forgery, and died in Sydney in 1837.

[11] The statue of Prince Albert was placed at the Conservatory of Music entrance in 1866.

Macquarie presented Greenway with his pardon. Greenway went on to build St. James Church in 1819, which sits on Queen's Square across from the Mint Museum on Macquarie Street.

Transportation of British convicts to Australia ended in 1840, although prison populations were maintained for decades longer. Growth in Sydney was sustained by small numbers of free settlers seeking land. Little civic construction occurred absent the availability of convict labor.

Victorian Golden Age

Queen's Square

In 1851, a rambling prospector, Edward Hammond Hargraves discovered gold in hills outside of Sydney. The ensuing rush of thousands of hopeful prospectors ended the Transportation Era, sent thousands of new settlers to Sydney of their free will, at their own cost, and broke the hold on the city of the few large landowning aristocrats. Gold brought an egalitarian age to Sydney.

Hardy adventurers, veterans of the California gold rush, returned to Australia, or came for the first time. A significant number of prospectors came from China. Those who remained, founded Chinatown in Sydney, a visible neighborhood today. In all, it is estimated that 370,000 people came to various sites in Australia by 1860, all in search of gold. Many stayed to build cities.

The gold rush era in Australia, and the opportunity to spend new-found wealth in a home of open social opportunities, coincided with the reign of Queen Victoria in England. The Victorian Era is regarded as the period from 1838 to 1901. Queen Victoria proclaimed city status on Sydney, self-government to New South Wales, and in 1901, the Commonwealth of Australia was created.

Sydney was home to shipbuilders. Woolloomooloo was an international harbor. Darling harbor handled coastal shipments from farms around the coast, and from Tasmania. Produce came to market at Paddy Market, on Hay Street, on the city's west side, while new immigrants and sailors populated Woolloomooloo and Kings Cross on the east side. Sydney was vibrant.

Victorian era architecture displayed exuberance of the age. The architectural style was eclectic, often called revival architecture. One building could include Greek columns, Gothic windows and medieval turrets. Bold decoration became popular. In Sydney, the popular building material was golden Sydney sandstone. In a few decades of the latter nineteen century, Sydney sprouted many massive public buildings in the Victorian style, all of local Sydney sandstone.

A stunning example of Victorian architecture, and a statement of identity for the government, is seen in the State Library of New South Wales, established in 1826, and which received its home on Macquarie Street in 1845.[12] Five years later, the Australian Museum opened, with its Greek Revival style entry, looking out on Captain Cook Park. The massive St. Andrews Cathedral, the

---

[12] The statue in front of the library is that of General Sir Richard Bourke, 8th Governor of New South Wales, from 1831 to 1837. He is noted for emancipation of convicts and for dedicating the site on the Yarra River, which became Melbourne. An Irish Catholic, Bourke separated church and state, taking the Anglican church out of state funding. He proclaimed that Native Australians could only sell land to the state, which resold it to settlers.

centerpiece of Hyde Park, sitting with its side adjacent to the park, was built through the 1860s. The impressive Colonial Secretary's Office joined the library on Macquarie Street in 1875. In the 1880s, the Town Hall and Post Office opened, clearly making a statement of solid city presence.

Library New South Wales

Late in the nineteenth century, Victorian architecture transitioned to a playful mode. Building styles evolved into Art Nouveau, where embellishments included leaves and mythical ladies. There are a few commercial buildings in Sydney in Art Nouveau style.

Art Deco Sydney

Art Deco, as an architectural style, grew out of the post-World War I age of rapid industrialization in Europe. In the 1930s, the style was popularized in Australia by local architects. Art Deco is characterized by clean lines, integration of industrial building materials, such as steel and block, into the building exterior, and large forceful block letters, with stylized structural embellishments as minimal decoration. Sometimes referred to as Moderne, Art Deco is sharp edged; not to be confused with Art Nouveau, with its flowing flora and maidens with soft gowns.

Art Deco Museum of Contemporary Art on Circular Quay

The age of Art Deco in Sydney is exemplified by the Museum of Contemporary Art on Circular Quay. The building was originally designed to house the former iteration of Maritime Services, as the key piece of a total redesign of Circular Quay.[13] Building plans were drawn in 1940, then shelved during the World War II years. In 1952, the building was completed from the 1940 design.

Smaller in scale, and more daring in execution, are the Art Deco buildings of Kings Cross. The Kings Cross version of urban renewal, in the post-depression

---

[13] Circular Quay is lined with the Writers Walk, dotted with plaques honoring Australian writers. Among them is a plaque honoring Robert Hughes, author in 1987 of *The Fatal Shore*, the history of Transportation Era Australia.

years, includes colorful Art Deco buildings, such as the Empire Hotel and the Metro Theatre.

Connecting north and south Sydney is the Sydney Harbor Bridge, which opened in 1932. The bridge pillars are classic Art Deco arches. Across the harbor, on Olympic Drive in North Sydney, is the former ferry transport dock area, turned into an amusement park. In 1935, Luna Park opened to delight Sydney. The Hair Raiser entrance has swallowed attendees in her oversized mouth, in several iterations. The current Hair Raiser was installed in 1994, using a 1950 design.

Sydney Luna Park & Hair Raiser Entrance

Steel and Glass Sydney

Rapid growth of Sydney, in times of financial downturn of the 1970s, resulted in steel and glass buildings, some of which beg for replacement. The era also produced some keepers. Among them, the 1975 Sydney Tower, with a glass-bottom observation deck, ringing a restaurant, that is 879 feet above the street. It has been popular with tourists, enjoying the view since 1981.[14]

---

[14] If visitors prefer, they can climb 1,504 stairs to the observation deck.

The Sydney central business district today is a forest of imposing steel tower buildings. On the fringes are smaller in scale, colorful versions of 1970s architecture. South of Darlinghurst, in the expanding residential and business neighborhoods, that move toward Frog Hollow, are apartment buildings, that house the population in an upscale environment.[15] Sydney has matured as a city, which can absorb a growing population with style.

Visiting Sydney Today

Opera House on Bennelong Point

It is typical for any walking tour of Sydney history to begin and end at the iconic Sydney Opera House. At each stage in the history of Bennelong Point, on which the Opera House sits, it was a place of significance for inhabitants of the area. For ancient Aboriginal people, the spot was a shell midden, that

---

[15] Try Sticky Fingers for dining with the locals.

was a central place of fishing and gathering. In 1798, convict labor was used to build Fort Macquarie on the Point, critical to protection of Britain's interest in the colony. The fort, another project of Governor Macquarie, by architect Greenway, was demolished in 1901. It looked like a castle, with its round turrets and crenellated crown tower.

In 1955, an international competition was held to solicit proposed plans for an opera house.[16] The prize-winning architect was Jørn Oberg Utzon, a Dane. His plan for precast concrete shells, with a radius of 246 feet each, clad in New South Wales quarried pink granite, opened to the public in 1973. The building has two large performance venues; the concert hall and the Joan Sutherland Theater. There are smaller performance spaces in the lower-level podium of the structure. Also, on the lower level, are restaurants and gathering places along the waterfront.

Sydney Opera House

---

[16] One of the judges was Eero Saarinen, architect of the New York City Pan Am Airport Terminal, which is an icon of modern design. Saarinen is reputed to have picked the winning entry.

End Walk around Harbor

The opening of the Sydney Opera House gave an instant boost to the reputation of the city and its architect. The city of Sydney became recognizable to the world, based on its singular harbor. Utzon garnered the coveted Pritzker Architecture Prize in 2003. Typical historic preservation recognition guidelines, of a time-honored structure, of significance over fifty to one hundred years, was put aside. The Sydney Opera House was listed as a heritage asset by the National Trust of Australia in 1983, and by City of Sydney Heritage in 2000. In 2007, the site was included as a World Heritage Site by the cultural arm of the United Nations.

Today cruise guests either dock under the gaze of Captain Bligh, or take a tender to the excursion pier at the base of Sydney Harbor Bridge. The harbor walk, from the passenger docks, runs along a path through The Rocks, along the Circular Quay, past the Art Deco Contemporary Art Museum and its modern cube addition, over the Writers Walk, and up the shaded stars to the Macquarie Street Fountain, also known as the Allen C. Lewis Memorial Fountain, donated in tribute by the company that built Sydney, the Concrete Construction Group. Here, in full view, is the Sydney Opera House, with the Sydney Harbor Bridge backdrop. Voilà.

Pausing to catch a breath, in part of the Royal Botanic Garden, just south of the Sydney Opera House, puts visitors in touch with the literal foundation stone of Sydney. This is the place of the Tarpeian Way stone quarry, from which building blocks of Victorian Sydney were cut. On the open grounds today, is the sobering sculpture of artist Kimio Tsuchiya, installed in 2000, entitled *Memory Is Creation without End*. The artwork is composed of bits of demolished buildings of Sydney, returned to the site from which they began.[17]

There is more to Sydney than the harbor. Continue walking south on Macquarie Street, away from the harbor, to delve deeper into the times through which Sydney developed, from a landing point for frightened settlers, to a destination point for expectant visitors. No one should leave Sydney dissatisfied, thinking there is nothing more to the place than the harbor.

---

[17] Tarpeian Rock in Rome is the cliff over which criminals were thrown to their death in the era of Roman Emperors.

Sydney - Characters of Kings Cross

Enter Kings Cross

Deep in the city of Sydney, away from the harbor, where few visitors now go, is where locals lived, who gave the city its enduring character. Residents, sometimes raucous and dangerous, or outspoken and poetic, came to live in the Kings Cross section of town, from the early twentieth century. They were drawn to the area of small homes and streets, which were affordable. The monuments here are not to royals, parliamentarians and generals.[18] The buildings are not grand. Kings Cross is an icon of Sydney, for the people who lived in the homes and streets, where their life story became part of the fabric of the place. They are the characters of Kings Cross.

---

[18] The one war memorial is the dandelion, El Alamein Memorial Fountain dedicated to losses in battle in Egypt.

Central Sydney is divided by the Royal Botanical Gardens, with the docks of the Overseas Passenger Terminal to the north, on the west side of the Gardens. This where the city began at The Rocks. This area of first immigrants, became an area of warehouses, then businesses and stately homes. Today, the west side of the Gardens has as its anchor the iconic Sydney Opera House. Visitors pass high-rise office towers and migrate toward the early and current government buildings, through Hyde Park, to museums. The west side story is of national and city history.

To the east of the Royal Botanical Gardens, is the place the Aboriginals called *Woo moo*, which became Woolloomooloo, a residential area. Here are small docks, used by local fishermen, now known as Finger Wharf. The land stretches out to Potts Point, where its high ground was purchased by wealthy business and political leaders of New South Wales. On the low ground, the commercial area of Kings Cross grew at the place major thoroughfares crossed. The commercial area of bars and dingy clubs serviced men of the Royal Australian Navy, who were based on Garden Island, just off the mainland. By World War II, Garden Island was joined to the mainland.

Cowper Wharf Woolloomooloo

In 1923, the governor of New South Wales put his name on Darlinghurst development, on what is now Darlinghurst Street. He carefully selected residents to live in single family, large homes, with lovely gardens. Then the

Great Depression happened. Today, Darlinghurst Street flows into Victoria Street at Kings Cross. Respectable Darlinghurst gave way to the Red-Light District of Kings Cross, with its rows of small shops and affordable flats, rented by immigrants and artists.

The artist community gave Kings Cross a caché, together with affordable housing for young professionals, that led to an area revitalization in the 1940s and 1950s, after the war. By the 1970s, the area had a patina of historic charm. Kings Cross was attractive to developers, of the urban renewal mode, who came into conflict with local residents, who wanted Kings Cross to stay as it was. Eventually, the developers went elsewhere. Today, streets of Kings Cross are lit at night with a cluster of neon. Residents enjoy delightful small shops and cafés of Darlinghurst Street.

Along Darlinghurst are historic plaques, giving notoriety to personalities of local fame.[19] Carlotta, the first transgender resident and star of Les Girls, has her plaque, although her show is closed.[20] Other residents of Kings Cross noted were famous and infamous. Stories of a few at told here.

Five of the many characters of Kings Cross are included in this short story, chosen to take visitors through time, in evolution of the place. The queens of Kings Cross, in the 1920s and 1930s, were rival gang leaders, who divided their turf, becoming wealthy on prostitution and illegal liquor sales. Kate Leigh was the Queen of Surry Hills, of western Woolloomooloo, and Tilly Devine was the Queen of Darlinghurst. In the 1940s and 1950s, the artists were non-violent, yet outspoken, and just as controversial. Sir William Dobell's art spurred a major legal battle, while his neighbor Dame Mary Gilmore spoke her mind on the radio. Social activist, neighborhood preservationist and newspaper owner, Juanita Nielson disappeared in 1975, during a property dispute. These five people shared a place, over time, where they imparted a bit of themselves to the neighborhood.

---

[19] See generally the useful website: cityofsydney.nsw.gov. Last accessed September 27, 2018.
[20] Carlotta was the muse for the 1994 movie, *Priscilla, Queen of the Desert*.

Two Queens of Kings Cross

Quiet Streets of Kings Cross

In an effort to control crime and violence, in the part of Sydney off-limits to respectable people, the New South Wales assembly acted, in the first decades of the twentieth century, to prohibit street prostitution, end sales of cocaine by pharmacists, and prohibit guns in the city. Also enacted in 1916, were six o'clock closing laws, requiring bars to close in the evening and on weekends. Criminal minds considered the possibilities handed to them. They acquired razors instead of guns, and opened brothels and establishments, that sold prohibited drink on the sly.

Kate Leigh, also known as Beahan, Barry and Ryan, was born in 1881. She grew up learning to be tough in an abusive family setting. Looking demure in her jail booking photos in 1917, she acquired over one hundred convictions, arising from sales of illegal liquor and cocaine. At her high point, Kate had twenty establishments in the Kings Cross area, serving working class to high end clients. She bottled her own beer, which had a reputation for quality. Kate also had a reputation for never backing down from a fight. Her body guards carried razors.

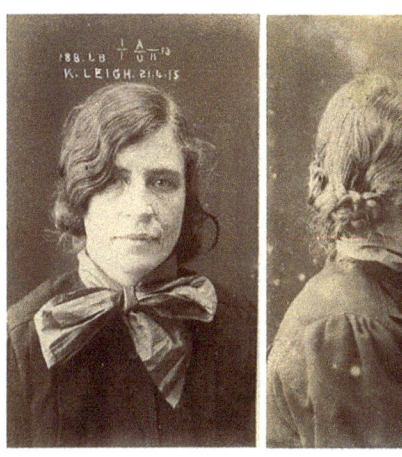 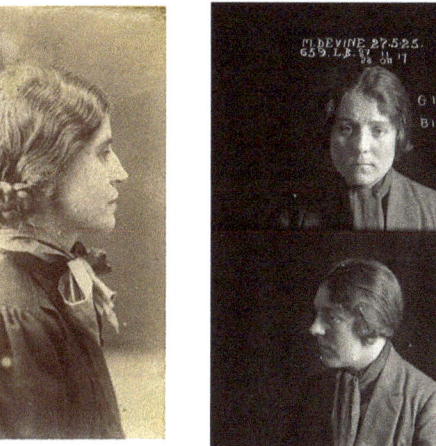

Kate Leigh & Tilly Devine Mug Shots (public domain)

Tilly Devine was born in 1900, in England. She financed herself in New South Wales as a prostitute, when she realized her husband had no ambition for work. Tilly had a passion for diamonds. She could make more money running brothels, than working in one. Since the law prohibited men from running a brothel, Tilly saw an opening for an enterprising woman.

Tilly's early booking photos depict a dowdy businesswoman. Over the years of opening new brothels, and over two hundred arrests, Tilly became a blond, wore excessive jewelry and carried her own razor, which she never hesitated to use. In Darlinghurst, police worked for Tilly.

Kate and Tilly were rivals. The sight of each other in the streets of Kings Cross, was impetus to spur a fist-fight. Local legend has Kate jumping from a street car at the sight of Tilly, to give her a punch in the nose. When Tilly remarried, Kate waited until three in the morning, after the wedding party, to send in fire trucks. Late that same night, an undertaker arrived to wake the newlyweds, informed that there had been a death in the house. The pair harassed each other's customers and trashed each other's business property.

The police stood neutral in gang fights, until war erupted. Noted as an historic event, on August 8, 1929, the Battle of Kellett Street was an all-out gang battle. Much alcohol was involved.

By 1948, Kate and Tilly met to bury the hatchet. Everyone they knew was either dead, or in prison. After World War II, there were fewer military men at the naval yard. Then in 1950, the government lifted the six o'clock closing ban, cutting into their business. The number of honest policemen became overwhelming. Fortunately, in the depressed property market of Kings Cross, where the queens helped keep prices low, the rivals diversified their portfolio and bought land.[21]

Kate became a philanthropist, endowing public charities. Revenue agents investigated Tilly's source of wealth, given her flamboyant display of diamonds. When no criminal wrongdoing was proven, government agents assessed Tilly for back income taxes. Unable to keep pace with Kate's philanthropy, Tilly held fundraisers for her favorite charity, herself.

Kate died in 1964, at the age of eighty-three. No doubt, her only regret in life of was dying prior to Tilly. When Tilly died in 1970, of cancer, at the age of seventy, her eulogy was delivered by the police commissioner. He is reputed to have said: *she was a villain, but who am I to judge?*

Defining What is Art

Sir William Dobell was born in New South Wales in 1899. Recognized in his teens as a brilliant artist, he came to a flat in Kings Cross in 1924. From his window, Dobell had a box seat to gang wars. During World War II, Dobell was a war artist, who recorded emotion, that a camera did not.

William Dobell by Max Dupain
(public domain)

---

[21] Tilly's purchase of property in Darlinghurst could not have pleased Governor Darling.

In 1943, Dobell entered a portrait he painted of fellow artist, Joseph Smith, into competition for the Archibald Prize. The coveted annual award, not only had a cash prize, it guaranteed display space in the New South Wales Gallery of Art. Over his life, Dobell won the award several times. His first award, almost ended his career as an artist.

Dobell's portraiture was more than replication of life in paint. His talent, that eventually captured attention of the Crown, leading to his knighthood, was in the early days thought of as extreme. Dobell saw a subject as a personality and painted as such. His art was new to the public eye.

When Dobell was announced as the winner of the Archibald Prize, for his portrait of Joseph Smith, two unsuccessful contestants brought a legal action, claiming the work was caricature, not art. The court was required to define what is art. The public entered the fray, arguing in social gatherings. Everyone became an art critic. The city was divided in anger, over the definition of art.

Dobell was harassed. He was spit upon when in the street. His new phone rang incessantly. He became a nervous wreck. He stopped painting. Years later, he painted only landscapes. Joseph Smith was ruined as a painter. Fame of his portrait, eclipsed his own work.

The court became an oracle of the law, when the justice ruled that the portrait was a distortion, intended to also be a likeness of the subject.[22] The decision came to an ultimate decision that the painting was a portrait. Dobell received the prize. The ruling ended the case, not the discourse.

When Dobell died in 1970, he left all his assets to a foundation, which established the Dobell Prize for painting. An award has been given each year, since 1993. His legacy as an agent of change in defining art is remembered in Kings Cross, in the galleries, and throughout Australia.

---

[22] Greek oracles were always profound, but vague, leaving pronouncements to interpretation.

Utopia in the Cross

Art Deco at Kings Cross

Dame Mary Gilmore was Dobell's neighbor in Kings Cross in 1933. She was sixty-eight and an accomplished poet, when she arrived and sat for her portrait by Dobell. Gilmore's first book of poetry was published in 1910. She received the Order of the British Empire in 1937, despite political views she held throughout her life. She was always more of a communist than socialist.

When she was a youthful idealist, at twenty-eight in 1893, influenced by a dear friend, Gilmore followed her passion to Paraguay, to live in a utopian settlement. Disillusioned by circumstances in Paraguay, although never losing her zeal for speaking to needs of those impoverished, Gilmore returned to Australia in 1902. From 1908 to 1931, she wrote the women's section of *The Australian Worker*, a labor newspaper. Gilmore's poetry immortalized what she saw in Kings Cross.

During the Great Depression, Gilmore wrote for the *Tribune*, the local communist newspaper. During the war, she penned a poem, one line of which is enshrined on the Australian ten-pound note. Gilmore wrote, *no foe shall gather our harvest*. The phrase boosted wartime morale.

Gilmore was knighted for her memoirs in prose and poetry, which preserved memory of colonial days in Australia. At her death in 1962, at ninety-seven, Gilmore was accorded a state funeral. She was a known figure in Kings Cross for her opinions and for her willingness to give thoughts wings.

Dame Mary Gilmore 1912 (public domain)

Neighborhood Preservation

Juanita Nielson was born in 1937. In the 1970s, she moved from the posh section of Potts Point, to live on Victoria Street, in Kings Cross. Her home was in a working-class area of rental properties, which were called bohemian, as a polite term for slum area, popular with artists. In this place, memories of Kate, Tilly, Dobell and Gilmore were part of a colorful mélange. Nielson thought such heritage deserved preserving.

Nielsen became publisher of a local distribution newspaper called *NOW*. The paper gave exposure to local issues, including tenants' plight. Retaining a supply of low-cost housing for low-wage workers, in the face of urban renewal and burgeoning high-rise developments, became a cause for Nielson. She appreciated the value of historic preservation, in a time when the concept was newly forming as an important civic responsibility, to retain historic character of neighborhoods.

Heritage Office Kings Cross

In Sydney of the 1970s, the effort to halt development, preceding city historic zoning, was led by organized labor in the form of a strike. A building, or an area to be protected, was stated as a Green Ban. Residents of the area of a Green Ban opposed removal of older buildings for high-rise development, or destruction of a natural area of historic significance, such as a place of Aboriginal Bushmen. Green Bans, controversial at the time, are credited today with retaining historic Sydney neighborhoods, which are attractive to high-rent commercial and residential tenants, as well as popular with visitors. Kings Cross is such a place preserved.

Juanita Nielsen used her voice through *NOW*, to help organize a resident action group to preserve homes on Victoria Street, where she lived. The property developer, who was at the time buying lots on Victoria Street, was not happy. He had millions of pounds at risk, paying thousands of pounds a day in interest, while Nielson and residents obstructed new development.

Reverting to days of Kate and Tilly, property developers employed thugs to harass tenants into leaving their homes. Windows were smashed. Utilities were pulled from flats, rendering them uninhabitable. Mass eviction notices were served. The head of the residents' action group was abducted. When he was returned home, he claimed no memory of what happened, or the identity of his abductors. Through the fray, Nielsen defended the tenants and refused to vacate her home.

On the evening of July 4, 1975, Nielsen went to the local bar, the Carousel Club, ostensibly to meet a man, who wished to buy advertising space in her paper. She was never seen again. A week later, her handbag was found by the side of a highway, outside of the city.

Juanita Nielsen (public domain)

There are many theories on the disappearance of Juanita Nielsen, and no answers. In 1977, after lengthy investigation and dredging of the harbor, three arrests were made and a trial was held. Three men were charged with conspiracy to kidnap. Edward Trigg, an employee of the Carousel Club, owned by one of the developers of Kings Cross, was found guilty and served three years in prison. Of the other two employees of the club charged, one served a short jail sentence and the other was acquitted. Today, the murder case remains an unsolved mystery.

Today, the section of Victoria Street, where Nielsen worked to preserve homes, is retained as an historic district of Sydney. Her home at 202 Victoria Street was listed on the Historic Register in 2012, for its history as housing of early twentieth century Sydney, and as residence to Nielsen. In 2014, a section of a Woolloomooloo street was named Juanita Street, in honor of Nielsen.[23]

---

[23] Ian Walker, Sydney Council to rename Woolloomooloo street in honor of Juanita Nielsen, murdered in 1975, in Daily Telegraph, August 13, 2014, dailytelegraph.com.au. Last accessed Sept. 26, 2018.

Visiting Kings Cross Today

To enjoy a bit of Sydney beyond the harbor, Opera House and museums, either take the Big Bus as is runs through Kings Cross, or take the underground train to Kings Cross station and walk Darlinghurst Street. Be warned. At night the area is as unruly a scene of drugs and high alcohol consumption, as it was in the days of Kate and Tilly, only minus razor gangs. Visitors come to the Cross at night, to take photos of neon signs, packed into one place.

During the day, small shops and cafés of Darlinghurst Street are filled with locals and visitors, enjoying the less flamboyant side of Sydney. Art Deco architecture preserved, is home to new shops, enjoying resurgence of residential use, this time home to affluent young professionals. Hills of Potts Point are pricey real estate once again. Governor Darling would like this place.

Walk Darlinghurst Street and look down at the embedded plaques, which tell the history of Kings Cross. Then look up into the galleries, of the next generation of artists, writers, bloggers and characters, who are illuminating Kings Cross with their stories.

MARVELOUS MELBOURNE

Marvelous Melbourne

Melbourne is the capital of the Australian province of Victoria, not the entire country. It is blasphemy to state that to Melbourne locals. After all, Melbourne took its turn as the national capital. Though Melbourne is the second city in Australia today, it is the first in arts and education, giving it some basis for conceit of primacy. The history of Melbourne has always involved competition with Sydney. Competition has not rendered it a copy of the elder city.

The site of Melbourne was inhabited for forty-thousand years, by at least three Aboriginal groups, prior to the first Europeans, who decided to establish a settlement. In competition between locals and newcomers for survival in the unforgiving environment, Aboriginal people suffered. The story of Aboriginal Australia has its own tale, lest it be lost among tales of settlers.

Melbourne was founded as a city of free and enterprising people, with an intentional desire to separate from less seemly history, in the forced Transportation Era of Australia. Coincidental to Melbourne's founding, gold was discovered in Australia. Melbourne was the center of a gold rush and instant prosperity. That prosperity is seen today, in a city of nineteenth century grandeur.

Not all of the history of Melbourne shines in the light of today. Where there was boom, there was bust. The age of gold was short-lived. The new English residents came in conflict with the existing Aboriginal residents. Culture shock impacted historic and new residents, living in tandem.

In less than two centuries, Melbourne grew as a perennial city of immigrants to Australia. Diversity too, is evident in the central city. Inclusion of city residents is seen in new public spaces, intended to bring people to the center city, to relax and mingle. Arts and education facilities seem to proliferate in Melbourne, as fast as the population grows.

This is a short story, of the relatively short history, of an amazing city of culture, that opens easily to visitors. It is a story of exclusion and inclusion. It is a story of leadership and finding a defining image, apart from competition with Sydney. It is a story of what makes Melbourne Marvelous.

Gold Rush City

Early in the nineteenth century, errant fishermen and adventurers, seeking land to farm, entered the bay that became Port Phillip, the eventual site of Melbourne. Concerned that the French may claim land within their sights, British governors of Tasmania tried to establish a penal colony on the bay, as was established in Tasmania. Their efforts failed.

Enterprising businessmen stepped ahead of the absentee overseer government in London, to form Port Phillip Association, with the intent of establishing their own commercial colony. John Batman came to Port Phillip in 1835. As a farmer, who became a success in Tasmania, he knew good farm land when he saw it. He put together an investment group, made up of the core of business and governmental leaders in Tasmania, in short, the new elite, of the new land.

FitzRoy Gardens Melbourne

Ignoring the fact that only a government can make a treaty with another government, Batman drafted a treaty, ostensibly with tribal leaders of the Wurundjeri, a tribe of Aboriginals, living in the area. The document formed Tasman's self-assumed rights to six hundred thousand acres of land, surrounding the bay. Batman assumed his treaty replaced necessity of purchase.

On the basis that possession is ownership, another man in Tasmania, acting with the same goals as Batman, dispensed with a treaty and moved into the bay with his camp followers. John Pascoe Fawkner brought a group of farmers to the bay. They quickly established ownership by fiat, by plowing land. Fawkner was about to bring a second group to the bay, when Batman arrived.

Since neither Fawkner, nor Batman, had actual property rights to land in Australia, they astutely decided that joinder was their best course. Crown officials arrived to tell the men what they knew. That is, only a government can establish a new colony. Acknowledging that the government had little ability to enforce law, in the face of self-help colonists, and acknowledging inability of the government to accomplish, at great cost, that which Fawkner and Batman accomplished, British officials in Tasmania affirmed the obvious and established a town at the site of their settlement.

British agents officially created that which Batman and Fawkner could not. A land survey office was opened, where British officials sold land to settlers, on surveyed plots. In short order, Melbourne was created, with a bureaucracy and a post office, by 1836, financed by land sales.

In less than three years, Melbourne grew from a minor settlement, to the most populous city in Australia. In 1839, Charles La Trobe was appointed Superintendent of the new district within New South Wales. Residents of Melbourne were not satisfied with being a second city to Sydney. They would accept nothing less than designation as the capital city, of a new province. They agitated for twelve years, while the farming and ranching industry grew. Finally, in 1851, in recognition of the substantial wool exports to Britain, Victoria Province was created out of New South Wales. Melbourne was the province capital. La Trobe was province governor.

After a century of Britain transporting people to populate Australia, at government expense, and not by their choice, the outpost in the sparsely settled province of Victoria bloomed with new residents, traveling great distances, at their own expense, and of their free will.[24] In a word, the reason for the sudden success of Melbourne was gold. Melbourne population doubled in one year.

Melbourne went from unremarkable to Marvelous, with the sparkle of gold. The gold rush started in 1851, just after the gold rush in California. Hopeful fortune-seekers, late to opportunities in California, had a fresh opportunity in Victoria. The gold rush in Australia hit a high point in 1856, drawing more opportunists, who might have otherwise headed to California, or Alaska. The torrent of miners arriving in Melbourne continued to the late 1860s. Gold mining on a smaller scale, controlled by fewer owners, continued for decades longer.

---

[24] The total permanent population was less than 80,000; 23,000 of whom lived in Melbourne.

Superintendent La Trobe

The center of Melbourne was built on the gold economy. The city looks as though it was built within a few decades, which it was. This was the era of Victorian architecture, so named for the Queen of England, who launched her own style of architecture. Large brick buildings, with decorative domes, towers with turrets and abundant decoration, are features of the eclectic Victorian style. Less staid than high, fluted columns and center-peaked roof lines of Neo-classical Roman architecture, the style adopted for Melbourne fit well into newly-wealthy, frontier tastes.

Royal Exhibition Building WHS

Imagine homes filled with oversized, elaborately carved, heavy wood furniture, upholstered in leather, or red velvet. Gas lamps lit homes, with large rooms. The newly wealthy lived as though in a large city, belying the fact that they were in the midst of an unsettled land. Victorian style homes provided an illusion of connection to England.

Britain benefited greatly from the gold economy in Australia. Miners were charged a fee to mine for gold, regardless of success. When minors objected to the license fee, Britain proposed an export duty. Miners were rebellious. They formed unions, to resist government intrusion on their wealth. Miners knew the mother country was too remote, and too lightly staffed, to enforce taxes.

It was the better part of government discretion, not to push miners too hard. Britain received enough revenue from mining licenses to boost its central economy and pay debts of disastrous wars elsewhere in the empire. Soon enough, Melbourne became a consumer city, buying exports from England. As long as it was boom time in Melbourne, England profited.

Leading the growth of Melbourne, at the time of the gold rush boom, was the first provincial lieutenant governor, Charles La Trobe.[25] It was La Trobe's interest in gardens, the arts, education and social responsibility, seen in the Melbourne Hospital, that established the personality of Melbourne from inception, as a grand city of the arts. His mark on the city can still be seen in the center city plan, which includes parks and promenades. Educational institutions are named for him, and a main street, in the central business district, is La Trobe Street.

At age fifty, experienced in civic management, from his prior appointment as an administrator of a transportation colony in New South Wales, under governor FitzRoy, La Trobe built his legacy informed by his life as an educated, world traveler. Unlike newly rich miners in Victoria, or fortune-seeking opportunists, who took advantage of government positions in New South Wales, building personal estates and enjoying income from slave labor of prison inmates, La Trobe had enjoyed an advantaged life-style from a young age. Although he profited from his land in Victoria, amassing personal worth was secondary to fashioning a civilized home far from England. By building a city to his taste, La Trobe gave the new city elite an image of who they desired to be.

The mark of La Trobe can be seen in the Parliament House, begun in 1855, a number of churches, built between 1855 and 1880, and the first railway in

---

[25] La Trobe was born in the United States and traveled with Washington Irving. He is the nephew of Benjamin Henry Latrobe, the father of American architecture, who designed the United States Capital building, among other notable commissions.

Melbourne, which opened in 1854. Educated residents required schools and scientific societies. The Royal Society of Victoria in Melbourne received its charter in 1859.

Flinders Street Rail Station

By 1880, Melbourne was second only to London in size. It was number one in the world in per-capita wealth. Gold miners who struck it rich, and those who made a fortune servicing their needs, tended to stay in the city. Melbourne added a new word to the lexicon of city planning: suburban sprawl. With access to a rail car, suburban sprawl was seen in the growing number of residential neighborhoods.

Fortunately for Melbourne, when the money was pouring in, city fathers spent the income on infrastructure, rather than increasing size of a government bureaucracy. Increasing land values, and dependence on gold, could not last. By 1891, gold miners decamped for Western Australia. The population of Melbourne stopped growing. Land speculators caught short, lost their investments. Jobs were reduced. A high number of people were unemployed, with no government, or other safety net. The city population held steady at a half million.

Twentieth Century Melbourne

Modern Melbourne

Melbourne received a boost in 1901, when it became the capital of the new Commonwealth of Australia. The honor was short lived. By 1905, Sydney, the vibrant port city, eclipsed Melbourne to become the capital. The Parliament House remains as a reminder of what once was.

Without gold, Melbourne had little to sustain an economy. The city had an unremarkable first few decades of the twentieth century. There were financial panics and depression. Two world wars provided little but employment for residents. The Marvelous city lost its shine.

In the post-World War II era, Melbourne received immigrants from Europe, then the Near East. The population of Jews in Melbourne, less than two percent of the city overall population, was the largest of any Australian city. New residents created a building boom in residences and infrastructure. Slum areas were cleared for mid-century, high-rise, state-owned apartments. The influx of new residents increased to include Asian countries, when Australia openly ended the largely informal White Australia policy, between 1949 and 1973.

When in 1956, Melbourne hosted the Summer Olympics, the city looked truly international. The games should have been an opportunity for the city to display its new century look. Instead, the games became a lesson in international politics, into which Melbourne was thrust. Egypt boycotted the games to protest the Suez Crisis. The Netherlands, Spain and Switzerland boycotted Melbourne to protest the Soviet invasion of Hungary. Communist People's Republic of China stayed home to protest the inclusion of the Republic of China.

As a high note in the games, East and West Germany participated, as a single German entry. Australians dominated gold medals in track and swimming. After a bloody competition, in which Hungary faced Russia in water polo, Hungary took home the gold.

Given all the hostility during the 1956 Olympic games, a unifying closing ceremony was needed. Instead of teams marching behind their flags, all the athletes entered the closing ceremonies as a mingled group. The practice has become an Olympics tradition.

Melbourne, with its fragile economy, over the century, was hard hit in the world-wide financial crisis of the late century. The new millennium promises to be the best for Melbourne, since the high of the gold years. Growth is rational and organic. Building projects, such as the Southlands and Docklands, have created premium real estate, in under-utilized areas. Tourism to the city is on the rise. From 2010 to 2017, Melbourne was voted the most livable city by *the Economist*.[26]

No doubt, one of the factors, which places Melbourne high on the list of choice cities in which to live, is its dedication to the arts. The new era of Melbourne is one in which public spaces, in which to linger, center around new and historic arts venues. Melbourne, no longer the first city in government in Australia, has become the first city of the arts. It is a world-wide reputation.

---

[26] For 2018, 2019 and 2020, Melbourne dropped to number 2 in world ranking.

Arts Capital of Australia

Melbourne Theatre

When it comes to the arts, Melbourne has taken on the world to display preeminence. When the internationally recognized Metropolitan Museum of Art in New York touted abstract expressionism in the 1950s, as the new art of the age, Melbourne artists formed a society to stand their ground on figurative art. Their group, the Antipodeans, was comprised of six artists from Melbourne and one from Sydney. Their exhibition, which challenged the art world, was mounted in the Victorian Artist's Society building in Melbourne. The Artist's Society was founded in 1856, in Melbourne. The building dates to 1888, founded as a place to promote Australian arts.

Viewed as reactionary, by emerging Australian Impressionists, the Antipodeans were given a showing at the British Museum. The show gave attention to the growing art world in Australia. Artists such as abstractionist Roger Kemp

(Francis Roderick Kemp),[27] stained glass artist Leonard French and sculptor Inge King, benefited from the exposure.

Continuing to exhibit its recognition as arts capital of Australia, the Melbourne skyline includes designation of a group of towering buildings, ringing the harbor, dedicated to Australian artists Sidney Nolan, Howard Arkley, Arthur Boyd and Charles Edward Conder. Residential towers incorporate themes from the artists in the architecture. Charles Conder, the only one of the four, who did not spend most of his life in Melbourne, is credited with bringing French Impressionist art to expression in Melbourne, toward the end of the nineteenth century. The artists who developed in Melbourne's artistic climate, look to Conder as one of their inspirations.

Sidney Nolan, Melbourne native, is known for his stylized paintings of Australian history.[28] Most notable are twenty-seven paintings of infamous bushranger Ned Kelly, who went to the gallows in Melbourne in 1880. Nolan's rendition of armor worn by the outlaw Kelly, is the inspiration for a modern frieze in the base of the Nolan apartment building in the Docklands development. Nolan's 1971 *Snake*, installed in the Museum of Old and New Art in Hobart, Tasmania, is an arrangement of sixteen-hundred, twenty small paintings, which, when mounted and viewed at a distance, reveal a snake across the wall.

Melbourne native, Howard Arkley[29] painted in black and white and vivid colors, applied with an airbrush. His style was commentary on suburbia in Melbourne. His final show brought him fame at the 1999 Biennale in Venice, just prior to his death at age forty-eight.

Arthur Boyd[30] enjoyed a successful career as an artist in Melbourne. Known for his Impressionistic paintings of Australian landscapes, Boyd was a proponent of figurative art in the 1950s, when international forums promoted Impressionism. Fourth generation artist, and supporter of young artists, Boyd is equally remembered for his philanthropy.

---

[27] Roger Kemp 1908- 1987(Melbourne); Leonard French 1928 – 2017, given Order of the British Empire in 1968; Inge King 1915 Berlin – 2016 Melbourne.
[28] Sidney Nolan, born 1917 Melbourne, died 1992 London.
[29] Howard Arkley, born 1951 Melbourne, died 1999 Melbourne.
[30] Arthur Boyd, born 1920, died 1999 Melbourne.

A Walk Around Marvelous Melbourne, the Art City, Today

Victoria Library

Melbourne now boasts one of the highest concentrations of private art galleries in the world, showcasing local and international artists. Installations of street art join historic monuments, to render a walk around the city an outdoor gallery. The National Gallery Victoria, NGV International and Ian Potter, is housed in two buildings, so vast is the collection. The two buildings anchor an open-air stroll along the water and bridge, taking visitors past performing arts and gallery venues, on both sides of the Yarra River.

On the far side of the downtown rectangle, are the historic Melbourne Museum and State Library Victoria. The walk from the Yarra to the Melbourne Museum, goes beyond the World Exposition Building, minus the two wings, otherwise looking as it did in 1880. Between the two clusters of museums is the Fitzroy Garden, with the recreation of the house of the father of Captain James Cook. Cook never lived in the house. Pity for him. At the time of his journey around the southern islands, the banks of the Yarra River never looked as they do today.

Home of James Cook's Father in Melbourne FitzRoy Gardens

Melbourne deserves an overnight stay, to enjoy an evening at the theatre and dinner in a café along the river. After almost two decades in a boom and bust cycle, Melbourne has found its niche, in a world of special cities. Spend a day roaming three parks and numerous art galleries, then head for something to eat, outside, where there is a view of the river. This is Melbourne.

Hobart Tasmania: Port Arthur and the Transportation Era

Port Arthur Prison in Tasmania

In 1775, English King George III was faced with a problem, related to rebellion, but more pressing to city authorities in London. In the wake of rebellion in the American colonies, convicts could no longer be sent to North America as settlers, to relieve over-crowding in the jails of London. A new repository destination was required. A solution was made available, by the voyage of Captain James Cook in 1770, with his exploration of Botany Bay, in the Southern Continent. Henceforth, convicts would be transported to Australia. Thus began, the Transportation Era in the history of Australia, with prison sites in Botany Bay, that is Sydney, and Hobart in Tasmania.

Layers of History

The first chapter in modern, English, habitation of Australia, began in the streets of London, where few options available to the poorest of the poor in the city, pushed even moral humans to crime, to feed their children. What began as a simple solution, to put out of sight and mind, those whom society failed, grew into a pipeline to slave labor for wealthy Australian landowners. Once begun, it was too tempting to end.

The prisons built in and around Sydney, and on the Australian island province of Tasmania, were run as the most extreme form of punishment for men, women and children, whose crimes were most often of economic circumstance. The edifices remain, although the practice of transportation has long since ended. The prisons are places of ghosts and reminders of history.

Descendants of transportees of the Transportation Era, focus today on the strength of character of their ancestors. It is said, that England sent away criminals and received back soldiers. The strong and independent character of Aussies today, is often attributed to their ability to persevere through adversity, a trait that was fostered in the first days of English occupancy of Australia.

This is a short story of the Transportation Era, set in the context of eighteenth-century England. It was a time of display of the worst and best in human nature. It is also a story of the prison site in Hobart, which is a popular cruise ship shore excursion today. History and humanity unite in telling the history of Australia, in the Transportation Era.

England in the Time of Transportation

The streets of London were dismal environments for eighteenth century residents, with no societal connections, and those devoid of resources. Even people with social standing, who were overwhelmed by creditors, found themselves in debtor prison, with the unwashed poor of the city. Factory workers, which included young children, worked and lived in crowded circumstances, where disease and fire frequently erupted. Gin was a great distraction to poverty, although drinking made life when sober, even more bleak.

Crime was widespread in London. Although roving youths in gangs, as portrayed by Charles Dickens, were not common, petty theft necessitated by hunger led to desperate acts. The rule of law in England, allowed for a fair trial and swift hanging, even for petty offenses.

By the end of the eighteenth century, public hanging lost public appeal. The humane upper classes preferred deviants be housed in prisons, out of sight of respectable people. Prisons quickly became overcrowded warehouses of rot and disease. People could not simply be crammed into barges, left to float on the Thames. The incarcerated population became too large, not to be seen.

Banishment was not a new concept. At the end of the sixteenth century, Queen Elizabeth I banished from her kingdom, those not worthy of living under the crown. In the seventeenth and eighteenth centuries, need for plantation labor in the American colonies, made it a convenient venue for deportation of criminals. England populated its vast, open, untamed wilderness, with slave labor from the streets of London.[31] When the American colonies began to revolt, by refusing to pay tax to the king, they also refused to pay the king for a supply of British slaves sent to colonist land owners. A new outlet for overcrowded prisons, and relocation of undesirables in England, including political prisoners, was required.

As the eighteenth century ended, the American colonial effort for independence was not England's only critical problem. The French, always a rival in world trade, were challenging the English in primacy in the Caribbean and across global shipping markets. In 1770, Captain James Cook claimed the known area of the Southern Continent for England, which he named New South Wales. Potential of the new land for cash crops was not yet known, but if the land was of interest to England, then it needed protection from encroachment by France.

The best means to protect a nation's claims to newly discovered lands, was to quickly occupy territory. Landing a garrison of soldiers was a quick means to display occupancy. Founding settlements gave an aura of permanence.

---

[31] Few Americans realize that *indentured servitude* was slave labor. The land owner paid for workers, housed and fed by their owner, at no cost to the crown. Some servants held an illusion of buying their freedom.

Proliferation of settlements, under the king's law, would provide control of crops exported to the motherland. If the American colonies wanted their independence from England, England would replace them with plantations in New South Wales.

For the Term of Natural Life

Church Street in Prison – An Illusion of Normal English Life

The American model of selling convicts for slave labor would not work in Australia, where there were no free settler land owners clamoring for workers. Officers of the New South Wales Company garrison, with an entrepreneurial bent, were adept at obtaining land, which provided an early capacity for slave labor.[32] Initially, need was insufficient, to the supply of convicts available.

---

[32] The New South Wales Company became an entrepreneurial force in the extreme, controlling the government in New South Wales, until recalled to England. See: The Real Captain Bligh, this Itinerary.

Parliament enthusiastically discussed options, to relieve the burdensome prison population, while bringing home income from timber and other raw materials, to be produced in Australia. They could see all sorts of lovely possibilities. England would build a thief colony in Botany Bay. Royal loyalists displaced by the American revolt, could relocate and begin new plantations in Botany Bay. Moving people around on paper, looked simple and neat.

Captain Arthur Phillip was chosen to lead a convict settlement, to be established in Botany Bay, in 1786.[33] His convict labor group was chosen not to include violent criminals, or prostitutes. Most inmates were convicted for theft. They included people who stole a can of snuff, a book, or a pair of socks. Some were children, while others were of advanced age. One convict set for transportation, was an eighty-two-year old rag-seller, who had been convicted of perjury.[34] None of the transportees appeared to have farming experience. In fact, most, if not all, of those chosen for the experiment, had never been farther afield than within a small section of London.

The ships crossed the Atlantic to Brazil, and from there to Cape Town, until they reached Australia, making it a fifteen-thousand-mile journey to a barren landscape. The welcoming committee consisted of a few Aboriginals, who told them to go away. Captain Phillip named their new home, Sydney Cove.

A convict colony was established on Norfolk Island, one thousand miles off the coast of Sydney. Those convicts not made so ill by their journey, and lack of food, tried to farm from seed. Farming was as foreign a concept to the convicts, as their new home, where winter arrived in June. To the extent they were able to raise crops, the abundant supply of rats, ate what they grew.

Phillip had little concern, that his convict band would try to escape. The former city-dwellers feared Aboriginals in the bush and had no ability to live on the land. They could not swim the distance to the mainland, assuming they knew how to swim. Ironically, it was the Aboriginals who feared the newcomers. The English brought mysterious disease, devastating to locals.

---

[33] Botany Bay is the Sydney Harbor, so named by Cook, for the work of his botanists on the expedition.
[34] Robert Hughes, The Fatal Shore, Knopf, New York, 1987, p. 71. This book is often cited by historians.

Starving convicts looked forward to relief ships. More frequent were ships carrying more convicts. In a few years, there were thousands of convicts, few farms, and few land owners to utilize the labor. The convict system was distant from London, yet still a financial burden.

The New South Wales Company (NSW) knew how to govern. Their military training instilled organization and hierarchical management. The lead officers of the company smoothly transitioned into *de facto* government of the colony. Officers obtained personal land grants. As resident land owners, they chose the most able convicts to work their land.

Voluntary settlers came to Australia, seeking land and an opportunity to build a life, unavailable to them at home. They also employed convict labor. Those freed convicts desirous of remaining in Australia, or unable to purchase a return ticket to England, became farmers. The free and freed settlers became the foundation of modern Australia. The need for convict labor soon reduced the pool of healthy, able convicts, bringing civilian land owners in conflict with the NSW Company.

To supply the Australia workforce, the NSW Company encouraged judges to order transportation for more convicts. A minor theft offense, could result in the imposition of a sentence, for the term of natural life, to be served in Australia. Convicts received a one-way ticket to the unknown. Once sentenced, spouses and parents never saw their family member again.

Some of the transportees lived with farm families, whose circumstances were little better than their own. They had lives free of disease and squalor, that they would have experienced living on the streets of London. Other convicts suffered in work-house prison, subject to physical and mental abuse. Some convicts, so abused, lost the ability to talk, while others went insane, and some committed suicide.

Back in London, transportees were out of sight, but not out of mind. Social justice advocates, such as Jeremy Bentham, argued against transportation. He urged that large penitentiaries be built to reform convicts. Reform advocates argued the city poor needed jobs, more than incarceration.

As more jobs became available, in the growing industrial age, so too did more people migrate to the cities from rural areas, keeping the population of poor in city streets constant. To reduce crime, more police were employed in London. This did little to halt crime. Instead, increased arrests increased the number of convicted criminals, which added to the prison population.

Eventually, Parliament lost patience with domination of local politics and control of the economy in Australia by the New South Wales Company. The Company was recalled, in full, to England. British anti-slavery laws of the 1830s, were applied to convict labor in Australia. Fewer convicts were given terms of life for minor offenses. By 1835, transportation of convicts began to diminish. All convict transportation ended as a matter of law in 1868.

In the Transportation Era, from 1787 to 1868, one hundred and sixty thousand convicts were sent to several locations in Australia; notably Norfolk Island, Sydney and Hobart in Tasmania. Of those, twenty-four thousand were women.[35] The high point of transported convicts was from 1831 to 1835, just prior to abolition of slavery. The last group transported, were Irish Fenians, the first group of political prisoners subjected to transportation.

Hobart and Port Arthur

Of all the transported convicts, sixty-four thousand were sent to Van Dieman's Land, the island now known as the Australian province of Tasmania. French explorers were seen making frequent stops at the island, so there was an English imperative to establish residency. The main settlement at Hobart was named for the English Home Secretary for the colonies. Across the island, the prison colony was established at Port Arthur, an otherwise bucolic setting. It was named for the New South Wales head of the military police, who devoted his career to austere incarceration.

Life on Tasmania was difficult, even for free settlers. Free settlers, unsuccessful in establishing food crops, often lived off kangaroo meat. Roaming bushmen, who were often former convicts, or military, or survivalist hunters, competed

---

[35] Prostitution was not a transportable offense.

with local Aboriginals, for increasingly smaller herds of mammals. Aboriginals exposed to English diseases, for which they had no immunity, suffered high mortality. By 1821, more than half the population of Van Dieman's Land were convicts. By 1825, the island was made a separate colony from New South Wales, with its own administration.

Beaucolic Setting for a Prison

Port Arthur was begun as a work camp for convicts. Sir George Arthur decreed seven levels of punishment, to assure people in London, that convicts in Australia were not enjoying themselves in the fresh air and pine forests. Convicts earned advancement, and lost status, for infractions of rules. Rules were many. Arthur wanted there to be no doubt, that incarceration was punishment. Reforming, or training convicts in work skills, if it occurred, was coincidental.

Convicts who did not attend church, or otherwise broke the rules, were sent to the prison-within-the-prison, the solitary confinement area of total silence. Cells within the prison of silence were dark and small. Irish Fenians were the final residents. Some men survived the treatment, and returned to the general prison population, in the dormitories. Others left special confinement and moved to the adjoining hospital building for the insane. Port Arthur could break a man.

Prison of Silence within Prison

Cell Yards Inside Prison of Silence

More than two thousand boys, from ages nine to eighteen, were sent to Port Arthur. They were taught to read the Bible, sew uniforms and build pulpits. They were punished, with the lash and solitary confinement. A cemetery on a small island, within the bay of Port Arthur, was reserved for boys. It is not known how many died, while incarcerated. Records were not preserved.

Desolate Boys' Island

Sir Arthur had equal disdain for local tribesmen, as he had for convicts. As military practice in New South Wales had been to drive tribesmen from their land, and grant the land to settlers, or officers of the military, Arthur sent troops out to shoot tribesmen. He posted signs warning tribesmen to stay away from Port Arthur. Since the tribesmen could not read English, the signs had no effect. In retaliation, tribesmen burned houses, on the periphery of the prison.

Sir Arthur was replaced by George Augustus Robinson. In the post-slavery era of England, rehabilitating convicts, and Christian conciliation with waring Aborigines, were made priorities. When the press reported smiling convicts, having a day off, Sir George was recalled.

Commandant's Cottage

Street View for Prison Officers

Any progress that Robinson may have made in improving conditions for inmates was undone, when in 1843, transportation to New South Wales ended. All new transportees were deposited at Port Arthur. The prison was soon overloaded. Cramped conditions led to fights. Fights among inmates, led to severe punishment. Clergy visiting the prison wrote articles on horrific torture inflicted on prisoners. Punishment so far outweighed the crimes for which they were sentenced, that the cadre of voices advocating an end to the system grew louder in London.

Although transportation of new prisoners ended in 1868, Port Arthur was not closed until 1877. Naturally occurring fires in the area caused some of the unmaintained prison campus buildings to burn. Settlers were allowed to purchase bricks from ruins, repurposed to building homes and town shops. The site became a curious relic of a history, Australians did not wish to remember.

Records of prisoners were destroyed by the government. Former prisoners, living as respectable area residents, did not need to preserve evidence of their traumatic past. Even prior to ending the transportation system, free and freed residents of Van Dieman's land wanted to shed association with the prison. In 1855, the name of the province was changed from Van Dieman's Land, named by the Dutch explorer, Commander Abel Tasman, who arrived in 1642, and rechristened as Tasmania, in his honor.[36]

Legacy of the Transportation Era

Although the English envisioned the convict transportation system as a cost-savings to the crown, in housing and maintaining inmates, in reality, the Transportation Era was a crown subsidized beginning to the new economy of Australia. People with a dim future in England, had a possibility of a better life in Australia, if only they could survive the hardships of the convict system, and the uninviting perils of the landscape.

---

[36] Tasman sailed for the Dutch West India Company, a publicly traded commercial company in Amsterdam. Tasman sailed the northern coast of Australia and determined that the continent held no trade opportunities. He did not recommend colonization. He went on to explore New Zealand and Fiji.

Prison Hospital Repurposed to Town Hall

Those who persevered as farmers, sheepherders, or found jobs in the service economy, built lives, where social status was of no consequence in the open society. Anyone with grit and determination had an opportunity to succeed financially, to build a family life on privately owned property, unimaginable in England. An individual's past was not a distinguishing factor in business, or social life. The new elite of Australia were owners of sheep, timber and farms.

Women not married in the church were considered harlots by English standards. In Australia, a church wedding was frequently unavailable to couples. Australia became a civilized, civil society, beyond strictures of the church.

When the convict system ended, prisons were opened and people were cast out to survive on their own. Convicts "rented" to landowners, became labor for hire. The economy grew. Australia quickly became an attractive option for any healthy person in Britain seeking opportunities.

By 1828, there were more free families in the population of Australia than convicts. Dispelling English presumptions of inherent proclivity for crime in the lower classes, the lowest incidents of crime in Australia was seen among children of former convicts. Regular meals, and availability of jobs, produced fewer criminals.

In 1987, the Port Arthur Historic Site Management Authority was organized. Plans were executed for historic restoration of buildings and adaptive reuse of structures. The Commandant House and Junior Medical Officer's residence became small hotels. The former asylum became a town hall. Other buildings are open shells, where the marks of the past can still be seen on the walls. The prison-within-the-prison is still eerie, although long empty.

So many individual histories of inmates at Port Arthur have been recorded, that staff have associated past events to reports of mysterious sightings, such as a man in a suit in the Commandant's House. In 1989, park employees began offering ghost tours.[37] In this place, where so many souls merged in close quarters, under harsh conditions, even a cynic might feel an aura of those, whose histories are part of the beginning of Australia.

Relic of History

---

[37] *In Their Words; Ghost Stories from Staff and Visitors of the Port Arthur Historic Site*, Port Arthur, 2015.

Hahndorf Signs

Hahndorf Hotel

Hahndorf: A Little Bit of Germany In South Australia

Hahndorf Brewhouse

Along the coast of South Australia, a thousand miles west of Sydney, and the modern Australia capital of Canberra, is the city of Adelaide. Through this small port town, begun in 1836, German immigrants came to Australia in 1838. They came of their free will, to preserve religious practice. A decade later, they were joined in Australia by Germans fleeing rising militarism in their country.

Unlike the history of eastern cities of Australia, which began as settlements in the Transportation Era of forced exile, settlers in Adelaide, and the interior town of Hahndorf, came of free will to build a life. Life was hard. The possibilities were open. Among arriving Germans were farmers and craftsmen. In Australia, they replicated their German community in Europe, in a traditional style.

Hahndorf developed as a little bit of Germany in south central Australia. Named for the Danish ship's captain, who aided his German passengers to find a piece of land for a settlement, the community remained German-speaking, and separate, from the port community of English settlers in Adelaide. Until 1917, Hahndorf grew prosperous, expanded, and developed a commercial relationship with Adelaide. In the twentieth century, the main national highway ran outside Hahndorf. The little German community became part of Australia history.

During both world wars, German heritage of Hahndorf brought the town derision and isolation. The name was changed to Ambleside in 1917, to distance the town from its Germanic name. Residents were not immune from detention in camps, a thousand miles distant from home, regardless of multigenerational presence in Hahndorf, and all signs of loyalty to Australia.

Many visitors pass through Adelaide, on the way to Hahndorf, without stopping. Adelaide has history to add, as a free-town of working-class emigres, thrilled to arrive in Australia for an opportunity to build a life. The free spirit of Adelaide remained strong through its history. It was here, that labor unions were legalized and women could vote and stand for election to Parliament in South Australia, ahead of other states. South Australia led the country to decriminalize gay sex and abortion. Racial and gender discrimination have long been against the law. The German community was not excluded from Adelaide, rather they built a place for traditional farms.

Neither Hahndorf, nor Adelaide, were uninhabited when Europeans arrived. Aboriginal Australians lived for millennia across the landscape.[38] As Europeans moved in, Aboriginals were pushed further to the interior. Aboriginal Australians have their own story.

---

[38] Kaurna and Peramangk people were indigenous to the South Australia landscape. Their language endures today only in place names. By 1850, their food and water sources were altered by farms on the landscape.

Hahndorf was populated by more than two waves of German immigrants. Germans came individually to Australia, where some were drawn to South Australia and Adelaide. Artist Hans Heysen, born in Adelaide, painted across the world and returned to Australia and the hills surrounding Hahndorf. He was drawn by the light. His story is bound with Hahndorf's story.

This is a short story of German history in Australia and its successful community of Hahndorf. It is also an opportunity to tell the other story of settlement in Australia, that of arrivals, who came out of self-initiated purpose, to find a peaceful life, not available in England, or Europe. Adelaide sits in the quiet Gulf St. Vincent, surrounded by national parks, including Kangaroo Island and Port Lincoln. On the other side of Mount Lofty Ranges from the port, is little Hahndorf. Vistas in transit between main port city of Adelaide, and German hamlet, are an enjoyable shore excursion.

Free and German in South Australia

German Arms

At the turn of the nineteenth century in Germany, the bulwark of Lutheranism, times began to change. In 1817, in the city of Brandenburg, traditional Old Lutherans were alienated by the Prussian Union. So deep was the rift in communities, that some felt persecuted by the Prussian king. It was time to leave Germany. Thus, began a German diaspora, some of whom went to Australia.

In 1838, a large group left Brandenburg, Germany, with the aid of an Emigration Fund, set up by the British director of a South Australian investment company, George Fie Angas. Adelaide was established two years earlier, and the prospect of luring of free, industrious settlers was attractive to Angas. Angas learned of the plight of Old Lutherans in London, when he happened to meet their pastor. For Pastor Kavel, the opportunity to fund travel, with a loan to start an Old World community, in the New World, was ideal for his flock.

Thirty-eight families, totaling one hundred and eighty-seven people, boarded the *Zebra*, captained by Danish seaman Dirk Hahn. They arrived in Adelaide at the end of December, then looked hopefully at the coast for the next week, from the deck of their ship, waiting for tide to come in and allow their disembarkation. Years later, Adelaide built a dock capable of overcoming tides.

Pier Adelaide

Over the weeks of travel, the captain became fond of his passengers. While in port, Captain Hahn negotiated with the South Australian Company in Adelaide, for one hundred acres of land, given the settlers, rent free in the first year, to enable them to establish crops, with which to pay their debts. Also, on credit, the community purchased seeds and livestock, as a community obligation.

Land for the German settlers was inland from the port, in the Adelaide hills. The effort of the Brandenburg group so impressed German migrants in Adelaide, that fourteen additional families joined in the community. They named their settlement Hahndorf, or Hahn Town, in honor of their patron. At the central park of Hahndorf today, Pioneer Memorial Gardens, the names of fifty-two original families are inscribed on the entry gate. In the center of the park is a bust of Captain Hahn.

Pioneer Memorial Gardens

Hahndorf Memorial

Hahndorf town was laid out in a horseshoe shape, with the Lutheran Church at the center, from which emanated two main streets. Land was divided among families, in plots, to provide a home, garden and small farm in the town. Homes on the street-facing side of the plot, enabled residents to turn their homes into businesses. Shops, cafés, an inn and a blacksmith fronted on the street.

Working together, the industrious community of Hahndorf soon paid off their debts. Woman of the community brought produce into Adelaide for sale, to the extent that the city dwellers depended on Hahndorf market days. The two communities were interdependent, yet separate. The Germans of Hahndorf fled politics of Germany, which invaded the church. They wished to remain outside of any possible politics of the English in Adelaide. It was a mutual arrangement.

Back in Germany, community life continued to evolve. Germany of the mid-nineteenth century became increasingly militaristic. Young men were conscripted into the military. In 1848, another ship brought German migrants to Adelaide. This time religion was not a factor. In March 1848, a failed revolution left those on the wrong side of politics, the *Forty-Eighters*, in need of a new home. Hahndorf was known to them. It became a quiet port in the growing European storm.

Still, the 1848 migrants to Australia traveled as free Germans. They sought a peaceful life in a traditional, German, rural manor. They were welcomed into Hahndorf. When Germany was united in 1870, more Germans came to Australia, although few to Hahndorf. The relatively small community, remained small and farm focused. Neighboring Adelaide grew in size and diversity.

Accommodating additional families required acquisition of additional land. A single straight extension of Hahndorf was called Strassendorf. The two hundred and fifty residents were a unified community by the end of the first decade of the settlement. The project was a success.

The Lutheran community was sufficiently prosperous to enable building St. Paul's Church in 1890, which stands today. The new church replaced the mud-brick church, built in the first year of establishment of Hahndorf. At that site, St. Michael's Church stands today.

Main street Hahndorf was a fully forged town, by the end of the nineteenth century. The three hundred trees planted along the street reached an attractive height to shade shoppers walking along in front of the continuous commercial district, that main street became. Always frugal, Hahndorf homes were places of business and residence. Residents were joined by culture, religion and communal efforts to build a functioning town.

Houses on Main Street

In the twentieth century, when Germany was at the inception of two world wars, the German community of Hahndorf continued in their characteristic peaceful mode. Culturally German, they were nationally and politically Australian. Appreciative of the environment and welcome afforded them in South Australia, the Hahndorf community was patriotic and aligned with Australian sentiments, in both wars.

Non-alignment with Germany's military objectives, did not spare residents of Hahndorf anti-German prejudice, which grew to a fervor during the wars. Living separate from mainstream Adelaide, allowed suspicion to grow. In total, Germans were the largest non-British Isles ethnic group in Australia. By the First World War, known as the Great War, there were over one hundred thousand ethnic Germans in Australia. Hahndorf was conspicuous for its culture. German-Australians were subject to incarceration in prison camps, along with prisoners of war.

Hahndorf changed its name to Ambleside in 1917. Any trouble-makers taking the train to the Ambleside train station, looking for Hahndorf, could be lost in the Adelaide Hills. The German Arms Hotel in Hahndorf changed its name to the Ambleside Hotel.

In 1935, South Australia planned to celebrate its first centennial as a state. Hahndorf joined in the historic mood and reverted the name to Hahndorf. The move was shortsighted. The Ambleside Hotel did not revert to its original name until 1976. By that time, Ambleside train station business was reduced by the superhighway, built outside of Hahndorf in 1974.

Hans Heysen: Capturing Australian Light on Canvass

Hahndorf School and Art Center

The Louis and Maria Heysen family emigrated from Hamburg, Germany to South Australia in 1883. The family of seven settled in Adelaide. Among the children was six-year-old Hans.

Hans attended school in Adelaide, until he was fifteen. He was expected to work at the family produce carts in the city. He had already begun to paint. By age sixteen, he sold his first canvass.

Tromping around the Adelaide Hills, Hans painted landscapes and scenes of turn-of-the-century life in Hahndorf. His work attracted patrons willing to finance his art education in Europe, in exchange for eventual repayment in finished works. Hans studied painting in Paris and Italy.

At age twenty-six, in 1903, Hans sailed home to Australia. The light reflected by St. Vincent's Gulf, in the approach to the Adelaide docks, struck him as an artist and as a homecoming. Europe expanded his talent. Australia was his muse. Hans Heysen, so immersed in landscapes of Australia, stayed close to home in the Adelaide Hills, as his career came to fruition.

Parklands and hills around Adelaide provided ample subjects for paintings. The city did not have the caché of an art gallery community of note, among major collectors. While Heysen was a prolific painter, and his personal life was enhanced by his marriage in 1904, he needed a worldly venue to sell his art.

Melbourne exhibitions of Heysen's art in 1908 and 1912, established his credibility as a substantial landscape painter. Commercially, his art enabled the purchase of The Cedars, the large estate home outside of Hahndorf, where he lived for the remainder of his life. Artistically, the Melbourne shows placed Heysen's art as collectable for museum collections.

During World War I, Heysen was subject to derision as a German and as a resident of the Hahndorf area. He was a man opposed to war, feeling nationally Australian and most at peace in the Adelaide landscape, with his painting kit. The war years were hard on his spirit and his art.

After the war, Heysen repeatedly garnered national prizes for his work. Major galleries sold his efforts. His water colors, oils and sketches, in charcoal and crayon, were in museums and private collections. Heysen was knighted for embodiment of Australian life and landscape in 1959. Other artists paid the compliment of seeking to emulate his style. Heysen's art was so imbued with his sense of Australian light, his admirers and students could never replicate his works.

As the Adelaide Hills became subject to development, Heysen was an advocate of environmental preservation. Although he did not consider himself part of the Hahndorf historical community, his effort to protect his art, preserved their lifestyle. He is remembered as Heysen of Hahndorf, with the honor of burial in Hahndorf cemetery, in 1968.

Free Spirited Adelaide

Historic Adelaide Today

Adelaide was founded in 1836, in the province of South Australia, which boasts of being the only freely settled province in the early days of Australia. Freedom of religion brought early settlers. The general open atmosphere of inclusive society, brought many more settlers to a starkly beautiful landscape, not otherwise plush and inviting for farmers and gardeners.

Colonel William Light, of the South Australia Company, characteristic of the military/business arrangement in the early development of Australia, had ambitious plans for the city named for Queen Adelaide, consort to British King William IV. The street grid, with wide boulevards, squares and room for parks, was intended for grand buildings and stately homes. The original city has the advantage of the River Torrens running through town. Selling attractive lots to wealthy investors, was intended to organically grow the city.

Although Adelaide is the fifth largest city in Australia today, it lacks the caché of the larger cities. The population is dispersed into tech, health and educational centers, beyond the port. Business grew slowly in Adelaide. More churches than grand estate homes were built. What the city lacked in commercial development, it compensated with an inviting spirit.

Light failed to plan for infrastructure and government buildings. The South Australia Company was a profit-making scheme, not a bureaucracy. When Parliament took oversight of Australia, governors were assigned. The first governor clashed with the Company over priorities. The governor sent in 1838, George Gawler, commissioned a governor's house, jail, police barracks, hospital, customs house and wharf for Port Adelaide. No longer would arrivals sit on deck of their ship, until the tide came into the bay.

Silver discoveries around the state, beginning in 1841, helped grow the population of Adelaide. Silver also created an economy, which helped fund civic construction, committed to by Gawler, on the hope an economy would follow expenses. By 1856, when South Australia was a self-governing colony, there were over one-hundred thousand residents in Adelaide.

In the post-gold and silver rush, drought and economic depression years of the 1890s, which saw Sydney and Melbourne falter as economic and population centers, Adelaide too went into decline. After World War I, the general post-war economic boom experienced throughout Australia, aided development in

Adelaide, fulfilling dreams of Light. During World War II, Adelaide became a war industry city, chosen for its non-strategic location.

When the economy of the Adelaide area continued to grow, after the war, preferred sites for industry were in suburbs, not the center city area. Lack of a discernable city core of government and cultural venues, transportation and infrastructure, has always plagued Adelaide. Flinders University and the Medical Center, the campus of which has icon architecture, sits south of the city. Multinational manufacturers came to Adelaide for its workforce, in the suburb of Elizabeth.

Visits to Hahndorf and Adelaide Today

Flinders University Medical Center

Today, the South Eastern Freeway, built in 1974, runs outside of Hahndorf, leaving the town geographically isolated. Isolation enabled preservation. Hahndorf has retained its mid-nineteenth century, German farm town structure, historic buildings and charm. The blacksmith shop is a museum. The German Arms Hotel dropped the wartime name of Ambleside Hotel in 1976. Hahndorf is a State Heritage Area of South Australia, a defined place on national maps.

Germans in Australia today, comprise less than five percent of the population. At around one million people, many of whom still speak German, the population is a notable ethnic minority. Many more people, culturally, or ethnically German, regard themselves as simply Australian. Germany counts a sizable Australian-German population today.

Hahndorf's German ancestry is a point of pride, every bit a little slice of Germany, in the expanse of South Australia. The main street houses are gabled wood, just like a little town in turn of the nineteenth century Germany. Homes are now shops, cafés and inns. The menu in the coffee shop is simple fare, with excellent strudel. German in tone, language of the town is now English.

When visitors arrive in Adelaide today, they will pass a low-key frontier town, of historic wharf-side buildings, promoting an arts district, festivals and eateries. Nearby, elements of construction of a major city are finally apparent. The visions of Light are being executed to arrive, almost two centuries after he drew his ambitious street plan.

By the second centennial of the founding of Adelaide, it may possess a revitalized Victoria Square, anchored by the historic Torrens Building, housing universities. An upgraded Adelaide Oval is planned to invite football, on a grand scale. Most important, tramway upgrades and extensions will enable suburbanites of Adelaide to travel downtown. If city planners are successful, there will be bright lights and reasons to make the trip.

Hopefully, as Adelaide obtains a grand city center, the few historic buildings will be enhanced, in a manner to invite visitors to come into the River Torrens district and linger. Soon there may be more to Adelaide, than a pass-through on a shore excursion, to Hahndorf and the beauty of surrounding parks. Still, a visit to Hahndorf is an opportunity to wander in a little bit of Germany, in South Australia.

Fremantle Street Art

Wild West of Australia in Fremantle

The focal point icon of Fremantle, in far west Australia, is the Round House. It is appropriate that the signature building, at the top of main street, visible from harbor and inland hills, is the first building of the town and now the oldest, intact building in Western Australia. Round House Prison housed prisoners, who built the city outside its gates. Prisoners remained joined with settlers to build a city, that became the major port of west Australia; the gateway to the state capital of Perth.

West End Fremantle preserves the frontier spirit, the transportation legacy and prosperity of the short gold rush period in western Australia, all of which contributed to building the town enjoyed by cruise visitors today. There are two hundred and fifty-two historic buildings in Fremantle. History at the port was spared urban renewal, while inland Perth grew as the state capital.

Begun as a settlement to receive convicts during the notorious Transportation Era, the eight cells of Round House were soon inadequate. Fremantle Prison opened in the 1850s, and closed in 1991. Today, the history of incarceration is celebrated in freedom of expression in art and music, for which Fremantle is world famous. Fremantle is a living city, not a mere tourist attraction. Walking its streets today, is an authentic step back in time, not a museum reconstruction.

Any story of Fremantle must include its prison tales. Most notable are repeat escapees, such as Moondyne Joe, who was a legend in his own time. Final transportees to Australia were political prisoners, including members of the Irish Republican Brotherhood, forerunner to the Irish Republican Army. Their escape from Fremantle Prison, or rescue, depending on perspective, is an adventure tale, set on the shore of Fremantle.

Today, affectionately dubbed Cappuccino Strip, on South Terrace, off the pedestrian walkway, leading to the main street and Round House, is filled with locals as much as short-term visitors. In a world of large corporate franchise operations, Fremantle retains a low-key existence. Small venue musicians in Fremantle, have become national and international stars. This is the story of the end of the English-speaking world, begun as a prison destination, that is inviting and fun.

Cappuccino Strip

History of Australia's Western Port

Charles Fremantle gave his name to an outpost in the British Empire, in which he stayed just a few months, long enough to begin a camp station of adventurous settlers and claim the entire west coast of Australia in the name of King George IV.[39] Charged with rape in England, when he was twenty-six, it is unknown whether Fremantle was judged an asset, or liability to Britain.

---

[39] Sir Charles Fremantle was born in 1800 and died in 1869.

He was sent on several long-distance missions to choose base stations. After west Australia, he landed in Sri Lanka and later chose the site for Hong Kong. He then served in the Crimean War, as a Rear-Admiral. Redeemed in the mind of the admiralty, he was knighted.

Market Street

Fremantle landed at the site for the town in May 1829. By June, the first settlers arrived. The land was the traditional home of Noongar people, who revered a site, now the Round House hill, as a ceremonial place. If the ceremonies were of their dead, the aura remained in the prison. The new residents quickly became competition for fish and game in the area. European farming practices eclipsed native traditional land use. By August, settlers wandering inland, established Perth.

More settlers arrived in September and October. So anxious were farmers in Britain to establish themselves as land owners, without the requirement of noble title, that the prospect of unknown and unsettled landscape was still attractive. Merchant vessels made regular stops at Fremantle.

The first convict ship to land in Fremantle arrived in 1850. By this time the town was thriving as a market center, in the farthest reach of the British southern continent. It was a town of free settlers. Round House jail, in Britain spelled goal, was completed in 1831, on top the slight rise known as Arthur Head. It was intended for the occasional, local miscreant.

Inside Round House

Round House had only eight cells and housing for the jail-master. The center of the round tower-shaped prison was, and is, a courtyard. The number of unexpected convicts on the first ship quickly overwhelmed capacity. Sitting in the harbor was the hulk of a grounded merchant vessel, which sat for twenty-years, without breaking up, or floating out to sea. The hulk became auxiliary prison space.

Between 1850 and 1868, thirty-seven convict transport ships arrived in Fremantle, some with over two hundred transportees. Within just a few years of the first arrival, a new prison was begun, outside of town. Prison and town grew in population, in parallel lives. Now both are historic sites.

Prison labor was used to build Fremantle, particularly the West End, that is the main street as it moves down from Arthur Head hill. It was income from gold, that paid for the buildings, in rapid succession. The gold rush of the 1880s and 1890s created quick and often short-lived wealth of miners, much of which was spent on buildings in the town.

Available funds and labor in the late nineteenth century, resulted in harmonious development of the core of Fremantle, in colonial Victorian and Edwardian style architecture. In four years, from 1891 to 1895, the population of Western Australia doubled to one hundred thousand. In the next six years, the population almost doubled again. Fortunately, for the historic treasure that Fremantle is today, much of the growth impacted Perth. Fremantle served as the port town, to the capital city. Urban renewal of the twentieth century, evident in Perth, is not a factor in Fremantle.

Victorian Freemantle

Fremantle Territorial Pub

By the end of the nineteenth century, Fremantle Harbor was dredged to accommodate large commercial ships. In this vast country, of little water, some gold miners brought camels, with their Afghan camel drivers. Imagine an early street sign in Fremantle advising pedestrians to beware of camels crossing.

Fremantle Town Hall sits at a pivotal point on the square, looking like a church with its bell tower, Palladian, tall arched windows and false-column façade. Also built in the 1860s, of local quarried limestone, by convict labor, is the Victorian Gothic styled lunatic asylum, now the Fremantle Arts Center. Internal courtyards, safe places to watch inmates, are exhibition spaces.

Main street, leading to the Round House, was the place of several hotels, welcoming merchants, government officials and travelers from Perth, as they waited to board ships. National Hotel, Norfolk Hotel, Sail and Anchor Hotel, built by convict labor, stand today, somewhat repurposed as inns, shops and a microbrewery. The Fremantle Market building opened in 1897, to house stalls, where the merchandise is current fashion and the building function is continuous.

Notorious Prisoners and Escapees

Freemantle Prison (by Gnangarra Creative Commons 2.5 Australia)

Housing a population of transported prisoners, intended as slave labor, in addition to local criminals, disenchanted military and prisoners of war, plus British political prisoners from Ireland, Fremantle Prison was, from inception, a powder keg waiting to blow. Few prisoners in the initial populations were violent offenders. Many locals and transportees had short sentences, at the conclusion of which they were free to wander.

The transportation era began in the mid-eighteenth century, as a convenient means to put prisoners out of sight, far away in New World colonies. When North American colonies revolted and became the United States, a new site was necessary. That site was Australia.

Quasi-military companies, managing the colonies, found convict labor so attractive that transportation for petty offenses outstripped violent offenses. Once non-violent prisoners were held, for long periods of time, in abusive restraints, in long periods of isolation, overworked and underfed to physical depletion, prisoners either went mad, died, or became combative. In Fremantle, where convict labor was utilized to build the town, at least until about 1911, there was an opportunity to learn a skill, be out of restraints, and have a semblance of normalcy. At the least, the climate in western Australia was warmer and drier than London.

During the final decades as a prison, Fremantle housed fewer and more violent, long term offenders, who originated from the resident population. Disaffected Aboriginal people, unprepared for the onslaught of new lifestyles, became a disproportionate prison population to European-Australians. Several riots marked life in the twentieth century prison.

In 1991, Fremantle Prison closed. It is now a World Heritage Site and visitor destination. The story told in the prison today, is prison life in the nineteenth century Transportation Era. This is also the story of the people who built Fremantle.

In the nineteenth century, after two months or more at sea, inmates arrived at Fremantle Prison gates, which looked like something out of medieval Europe. Limestone pillars, with guard towers were ominous, if not overstated, for a place from which escape beyond the immediate area was impossible, even without walls. Today the guardhouse is an inviting coffee shop.

The thirty-six-acre prison held only men, when it first opened. The main cell block for men, intended for one thousand prisoners, was always overcrowded, unhealthy, and lacked fresh air and sanitation, until the end of the era. New transportees, received from England, ended in 1868. By the late 1880s, there were less than one hundred men in the prison. In 1887, women were sent to the women's section of Fremantle Prison, from the jail in Perth.

When the Transportation Era ended, Perth sent its male jail population to Fremantle Prison. Crowded conditions returned. Fremantle Prison was the location for executions from 1888, to last execution in 1964. One woman and forty-three men were hanged in Fremantle. The women's prison closed in 1970. The men's prison closed in 1991. Remaining prisoners were transferred to a new maximum-security prison, with new plumbing.

The first prisoners, in the 1850s, were assigned to dig a tunnel through limestone to reach an aquifer, which fed the prison water supply. Water from the tunnel was also pumped to a town reservoir, for the Fremantle population. Prisoners worked incessantly, to hand-pump water up from the aquifer, through the tunnel, to the reservoir.

Prison philosophy of management evolved over the period of the Fremantle Prison. Although initial prisoners were caught in a ruse to supply labor for free to the colony, prison wardens used punishment to display to British back home, that there was a legitimate need for a prison. As the population evolved in the twentieth century, to inmates convicted of major crimes, often violent crimes, prison reformists of the 1960s developed programs, designed to rehabilitate prisoners.

Improved prison management practices of England, came late to Fremantle. In 1988, a riot resulted in management inquiry and substantial damage to the prison. The prison closed in 1991.

Tales of Moondyne Joe

Freemantle High Street

Most notable of escapees from Fremantle Prison was Joseph Bolitho Johns, known to locals as Moondyne Joe. Johns was born in Cornwall, in 1826. When he was twenty-two, he and another fellow stole bread and cheese from a house, for which they were sentenced to ten years in prison. Never the compliant fellow, Johns was relocated to various prison facilities, until he landed on a prison hulk, one of the rotting prison ships in the Thames.

After the prison ship was destroyed in a fire, Johns was sent to the penal colony of Western Australia, for the remainder of his sentence. He arrived in Fremantle in 1853. Rather than be sent into the prison, Johns was given a ticket of leave, that was a term of probation. In 1855, he was pardoned. Johns began his new life in Australia, in a rugged area the Aboriginal people called Moondyne. Johns worked repairing fences and returning loose cattle to their owners.

Johns could not keep himself from stealing. In 1861, he caught a stallion and branded it with his mark. Police soon arrested him for horse stealing. In Western Australia, it was a serious offense.

Johns was older and wiser than in his bread-stealing days. He broke from jail, found the horse, and cut his brand from the hide, in the process killing the horse. Police were unable to prove he intended to steal the horse, since the evidence was lost. Johns was convicted of jail-breaking and given a sentence of three years in prison. He was a compliant prisoner, earning early release.

After troublesome early years, Johns worked quietly as a farmhand. He was surprised, when he was arrested for stealing a steer. Despite his protestations of innocence, he was guilty by history, convicted, and given ten years in prison.

Intent on achieving justice by self-help, Johns escaped during a work party. For a month, he remained on the run, surviving by stealing food. During this time, he earned the name Moondyne for the area in which he ran. The authorities employed Aboriginal trackers to follow his footsteps. When caught, Johns spent the next twelve months in irons, in Fremantle Prison.

Johns tried a different approach to protest his wrongful conviction. He appealed to the court. The Chief Justice was so impressed, that the sentence was cut in half. Half an unjust sentence was not satisfying, so Johns cut the lock from his cell door and ran out into the wilderness around Perth.

Other escapees joined Johns in the bush. He stole supplies from the store of a former accuser and set off for South Australia, hoping for anonymity, in another territory. By the time the police caught up with the band, they traveled one hundred and ninety miles from Perth, through an unforgiving landscape.

Picture Johns, in a tiny, airless cell in Fremantle Prison, tethered by the neck to the bar of his interior window. Five years of hard labor was added to his sentence. He was let off the tether to break rocks. Since he was to be kept out of the general prison population, rocks were brought to his tiny corner of the prison yard. Given a mallet to break rocks, undetected, Johns took alternating swipes at the prison limestone wall, behind his pile of rock.

The governor of Fremantle Prison told Johns that his situation was escapee proof. He promised Johns to forgive his sentence, if ever he were to break out again. The governor was later called upon to remember that promise.

In 1867, Johns slipped through the hole in the wall. For two years, he was at liberty. Since he committed no crimes, his whereabouts could not be traced. Then, his luck literally ran out.

Johns was in the cellar of a winery, enjoying a bottle of wine, when the cellar owner came to the winery. The cellar owner was entertaining a group of law enforcement he befriended, as a member of the citizens posse, to track prison escapees. Johns had no idea this was a random party. He thought he was cornered. He made a run for it, from the cellar, into the arms of police.

Back in Fremantle Prison, four more years were added to Johns' sentence. Johns told the new warden of the promise made to him. After all, he had been a model escapee. Other than the wine, he kept out of trouble and was never violent. The new warden confirmed the promise made. In May 1871, Johns was free.

From a twenty-three-year career in prison, Johns progressed to occasional brief jail time, for minor offenses. Then he married and became a gold prospector. As he aged, Johns was committed to the Fremantle Lunatic Asylum, where he spent his last years. He died there and was buried in Fremantle Cemetery, in 1900. The legend of Moondyne Joe lives on in books and the Fremantle saloon named Moondyne Joe's Bar and Bistro.

Catalpa Rescue of Irish Republican Brotherhood 1876

Freemantle Beach

In 1868, thirty-two prisoners arrived in Fremantle Prison from Ireland. Half of them were Irish Republican Brotherhood members, or supporters. The other half were British soldiers, who failed to stop rebellious acts of the Brotherhood. All were treated as Fenians, political prisoners.

In the first year of imprisonment, John Boyle O'Reilly escaped on a whaling ship, with the aid of a local Catholic priest. He went to Boston, where he became a newspaper editor. Two years later, another Fenian, John Devoy, was given amnesty and exile. He went to New York City, where he worked for a New York newspaper. Several others of the original group were pardoned in 1871. A small group remained incarcerated.

In 1874, Devoy received a letter from a prisoner, still in Fremantle Prison, begging for rescue from a life of walking death in prison. Devoy contacted O'Reilly and other former prisoners. They made an audacious plan to sail to Fremantle as merchants, join with others of their group on a whaling ship the *Catalpa*, purchased for the rescue, and steal away the remaining incarcerated Fenians.

Plans made by the group were like scenes from a spy novel. One man was responsible for cutting telegraph wires from the prison, so authorities could not be alerted. Other men posed as merchants and other businessmen. The big day was chosen in April, when the Perth Yacht Club regatta distracted many townspeople and held the interest of prison officials.

Conveniently, seven Fenians were working that morning on a detail outside of the prison walls. Six of them were able to run from the detail, for twelve miles to the pier. Their rescuers had a whaleboat, which they quickly rowed away to join the *Catalpa*.

The drama continued, when a storm came up and the whaleboat was tossed about in the waves the whole night. Meanwhile, a government steamship approached the *Catalpa* and was refused boarding to look for escapees. The *Catalpa Six*, as they became known, were at that time laying low in the whaleboat approaching the ship.

As those on the whaleboat rowed to the *Catalpa*, they were spotted by a police boat. Both boats rowed in a race to reach the *Catalpa*. The men rowing for their freedom moved a bit faster than the able-bodied policemen. The whaleboat reached *Catalpa* first and the occupants quickly climbed aboard. The police boat rowed back to shore.

The government steamship spent the night on shore, loading a cannon on deck. That morning, as the police rowboat returned, the steamship sailed out to the *Catalpa* and ordered it to surrender the prisoners. When the captain of the *Catalpa* refused, the government fired a warning cannon shot. In response, the *Catalpa* captain hoisted the American flag. The ship was in international waters. The Western Australia government steamship had orders not to create an international incident. *Catalpa* sailed away.

In August 1876, the *Catalpa* arrived in the New York harbor. O'Reilly printed the story, as soon as he received news of the escape. When the ship entered the harbor, it was greeted by celebrations. When the ship's captain retired from the sea to become a harbor master, the Fenians gave him a gift of the *Catalpa*.

Visiting Fremantle and Perth Today

Perth Harbor Square

Fremantle is a wonderful, walkable port destination for cruise ships. After crossing the port grounds, a harborside thoroughfare and businesses, the old town of Fremantle unfolds, just as it did for visitors to the port a century ago. Today, the Fremantle railway runs to Perth, the modern capital city of parks and government buildings. Short-stay visitors will enjoy wandering deeper into the historic port city, toward the West End. Mark the Round House as the end-point, just as arrivals did in the 1860s.

Commendable, is the University of Notre Dame Australia occupancy of historic buildings in the West End, rather than choosing to build a new structure. The student population keeps the streets occupied and the town continually alive. There is no shortage of good coffee and treats found in old town.

Fremantle Prison is a World Heritage Site, as part of the Transportation Era story in Australian history. The prison has been restored back to the nineteenth century. Newer, non-conforming structures have been removed. The gallows room is also recently restored. See art work left on prison walls by internees and see Moondyne Joe's cell, then visit the Fremantle Arts Center, where he spent his last days. Spend your final hours in town in the bars and bistros of West End Fremantle with locals, just as visitors have been doing for almost two centuries.

Perth Harbor

Indigenous Australians Greet Europeans (public domain)

Aboriginal Heart of Australia

When Captain James Cook encountered Aboriginal people in eastern Australia, he was vexed by an inability to negotiate a treaty. Australia is the only continent in which treaties between Europeans and locals were not instigated.[40] Aside from language differences, no tribes asserted dominant presence. Several groups of people appeared and dissipated. Unlike Cook's prior experiences, no unified people appeared, nor did an asserted king appear, so he took that as an indication of *terra nullis*, the land of no one. He guessed wrong. Two hundred years later, the High Court of Australia had the opportunity to review Cook's decision.

Cook's experiences led him to believe there were kings of clans and unified armies of warriors everywhere. People of Australia were unique. His predecessors wrote of few people and no identified tribes, living a wretched existence. In his observation, people moved quickly and without baggage. Their touch on the land was light. Existence was a constant search for food. Cook's description of people was accurate. His faulty assumptions on land touched off centuries of conflict. The story of land and European conquest through to reconciliation is a separate story.

Aboriginals of Australia, prior to European contact, lived a simple existence. Food was valued. Personal items besides spears were excess baggage. People traveled light. Men hunted and women swam for fish and collected seeds. North coast Australians had exposure to people with agricultural skills from Indonesia. That connection brought disease and death, with few innovations in cultural practices adopted by Aboriginals. At the time of European contact,

---

[40] Josephine Flood, The Original Australians, revised, Allen & Unwin, Crow's Nest, NSW, 2019, p. 22.

Aboriginal Australians, one of the oldest civilizations of the world, lived as they had since their arrival on the Australian continent.

Aboriginal Australia is a story of a people with a highly organized social structure, an understanding of their cosmos, and a developed sense of land rights, despite outward appearances to Europeans. Assumptions of European settlers in Australia disrupted life as it was known from the time of the cradle of humans. Over two centuries of co-habitation of the Australian continent, relations between natives and settlers have traversed through stages of hostility, interaction, and paternalism, to reach a point of understanding through Two-Ways learning.

Two-Ways learning in Australia is a primary school philosophy of teaching traditional European and Aboriginal knowledge. When practiced by government and community leaders, it is a means to reach mutual understanding though consultation. Most effective in bridging cultural understanding have been Aboriginal artists. Their story is one of presenting a safe space for healing. This story has a deep beginning and no ending.

First People of Australia

When the first humans left Africa and turned east to India, some eventually entered Australia. The date for arrival in Australia has been pushed back a few times upon new discoveries. Cave painting and footprints in dried mud of Mungo Lake, put the date of arrival at more than sixty-five thousand years ago. Ice Age land bridges brought people as far south as Java. From there, adventurous explorers crossed the sea to Arnhem Land, an arm of north-central Australia.

Early arrivals in Australia were not sailors. Simple reed rafts provided a one-way voyage and were then forgotten. People spread through the landscape, over thousands of years, developing languages in tight clans. Last to be occupied was Tasmania. Once on the island, people remained an isolated group, not venturing back to the mainland, nor trading with mainland groups.

Testament to isolation of groups, not only on Tasmania, also on the main continent, is the number of languages, without relationship among them. The closest root language detected is recorded as Sanskrit, although that may be thinking influenced by migration theory. Sanskrit is ancient, although not so ancient as arrival of humans in Australia. People of the continent had no known contact beyond Australian shores, until just prior to European arrival, except for islanders from New Guinea, who came to collect sea urchins, not deemed edible by Aboriginal Australians.

Cook was correct when he noted that there were no chiefs, and no unified tribes, with which to offer a treaty. Where his powers of observation failed him, was not recognizing there were tribes of a sort and there were identified land areas of tribal habitation. Six hundred family/clan/tribal groups have been identified on the continent. Tribe connotes an organized relationship. The hunter-gather groups of Aboriginal Australians could be best described as a people. They were extended family groups, with informal leaders, not actual chiefs. No group was dominant.

In the seventeenth and eighteenth centuries, when Europeans came to Australia, the people of the continent were hunter-gathers in the primitive sense. North coast people were introduced to farming by Macassans people from New Guinea, who also brought small pox to Australia. Half the Aboriginal population died from the disease, prior to European introduced diseases. The concept of farming did not ignite Aboriginal people to abandon their lifestyle.

The warm climate left Aboriginal Australians no desire to wear garments. They wore shell necklaces. Men wore elaborate hair cylinders, in which sacred items were carried, leaving their arms free for spears. Men were hunters. Women were gathers.

Women kept the hearth fires burning, gathered seeds to eat and caught fish by hand. Large sea creatures were caught by men fishing with spears. Women raised children and prepared meals. Food was shared by the group. If a husband died, the wife married another in the group. No woman and no children were left without a husband, support and connection in the group.

Women were chosen as mates from outside family groups, most often taken by force. Women were regarded as a community asset for their food gathering skills. Competition for women sometimes escalated to violence. Women bore scared heads as part of the courtship ritual. When British colonists arrived, they were appalled by the treatment of women. The Aboriginals were appalled by British treatment of convicts during the Transportation Era. That is a separate story.

There were no houses, no boats and no mats, or household goods, to move around. People appeared migratory. Actually, they moved around a well-defined territory. They also knew where their territory ended and that of another group began. Trespassing on land of another group was the same as stealing food. It was cause for war.

Competition for food harvesting area and for women, critical to collecting food, were the two main reasons for conflict. In the nineteenth century, when British governors of Australia considered moving Aboriginals to reservations, the idea of consolidating peoples to land of another was a death sentence.

Argument is often made, that Aboriginal Australians did not farm as they had all they needed on the land, without cultivation. This is true to a point. A number of groups were known for their distended stomachs, a sign of malnutrition. Archaeological examination of burials disclosed that males stopped growing three times prior to reaching adulthood. Food was always scarce.

Two exceptions to the natural use of land existed. Aboriginals burned grass lands to promote new grass shoots, which attracted game for hunting. In the north, Torres Strait Islanders, who are also Australians, had some domestic animals and gardens. They were influenced by Indonesians.

Cosmology, Stories and Art

In this large continent, of diverse people, with only a common ancient root, tens of thousands of years past, cosmology of being is somewhat consistent between peoples. Local practices developed, characteristic of a single group, or region. Hairstyle is an example of within group similarity, that readily identified a people, unique from other peoples of Aboriginal Australia.

Warriors in Aboriginal Ceremony 1920 (public domain)

A rite of passage for men in some groups was removing two front teeth. Aboriginal people did not tattoo, as did Polynesians, although they used patterns of scaring. Skin, cut with a sharp stone or shell, in long parallel lines, was made to raise a scar by putting ash, mud, or clay in the wound. Young girls in some groups have successive scars on their backs, for which they endured great pain. Scaring on men was a sign of contending with pain. It is not known why girls were marked.

For Aboriginal Australians, living on the unadulterated landscape, except for burning grass, nothing was random. Great forces put everything in its place. Boulders are eggs of the serpent force, the slithering bodies of which cut great valleys. People believed that so long as people live within their given environment, the world is unchanged. Continuity in life was sacred.

To reduce Aboriginal cosmology to gods and deity concepts, is to translate world view of Aboriginals into Christian concepts. Doing so aids people of a religious society to understand people of a vision tied to their land. Early Christians of Australia were not interested in understanding natives, or viewed

Aboriginal ancient ritual with suspicion. Missionaries in the eighteenth century sought to replace Aboriginal cosmology, by teaching that native ways were sinful. Suicide was prevalent among young Aboriginals, who were accepting of Christianity and could not deny themselves innate knowledge of world order and their place in the environment.

Ancestral beings kept the land productive and women fertile. At birth, children were imbued with totems, the aura of their land, clan and physical surroundings, inhabited by spirits of ancestral beings. They carried their totems within, as a part of their identity and connection to society. To remove, or deny totems, was spiritual death. When the spirit dies, the body cannot function.

In the Aboriginal creation story, the great creator put a hand on the ground and out came kangaroo. Moinee, the great creator of man, fashioned humans from an animal by removing the tail. Two men of the sky, identified today as the constellations Castor and Pollux, rubbed their hands and fire was thrown down from the sky for man. Gagadju people look to Imberombera the Ancestral Being, who came across the sea bearing children and carrying tubers of plants.

Rainbow Serpent is an import force in Aboriginal cosmology. The serpent appears in the sky after a rain. Without this life force, the land would be parched. People wear effigy of Rainbow Serpent in shell necklaces, in the north continent, and carry quartz as a serpent symbol in the south.

Great forces created the world, given to people for their use and care. Sorcerers brought evil. Death of a young person is the work of a sorcerer. Places where evil acts occurred were avoided.

Death was celebrated, in the most elaborate ritual, in the sparse life of Aboriginals. The body of a deceased person, laid on a platform for several months. Bones, painted with ochre, were burned or buried. Wearing the bones of a lost loved one, as a nose ornament, or rolled into a man's hair, was a sign of remembrance and respect. The name of the deceased was never spoken.

In a society without buildings or pottery, foot prints hardened and preserved in Mungo Lake for centuries were an immense find, in dating existence of ancient Aboriginal people. It is also consistent with how Aboriginals identified people in their sphere. Toddlers were taught to identify footprints of their parents. Footprints were as identifiable as faces. Medicine men had feather boots for people to travel incognito. In the era of British prisons in Australia, Aboriginal trackers were hired to locate escapees, based on footprints.

Boomerangs are found in Australia, as well as on other continents of the world. Made of finely crafted wood, a scarce resource in many areas, and thrown by an expert hunter, birds and small game are snared. The skill of a sideways throw, timed to reach small, fast-moving game is taught from childhood. Children are taught to throw a spear, although spearing large game is for men.

Typical in Aboriginal ceremony, are slap sticks. Two honed sticks, struck against each other, create a rhythm for dancers and are used to accompany chants. Early European artists recorded ceremony, with male dancers and women sitting around the dance area with slap sticks.

The earliest example of art in Tasmania, are pecks and dots in rock art. On the continent, there are flat stones arranged in lines, set over charcoal. Stone arrangements have been dated to be seven hundred and fifty years old. They are not so old in the history of people in Australia, although well prior to external influences. How they were used in ceremony, or as markers of ritual is unknown. Older stone alignments may have existed, which are no longer in place.

Ancestral Beings journeyed through the world, on their path of creation. Dots in art follow lines of creation stories, known as Songlines. Ancestral Beings marked their progress by a waterhole here and there. Dots on cave paintings, in face paint and dance ground ritual, tell stories of Ancestral Beings through their Songlines. Stone alignments are ancient Songlines.

Dot painting is iconic of Australia. Dots are pathways of the spirits. Circles drawn around dots are the sun and moon. Body painting and mosaics of stone and seeds on the ground tell stories of life. During festivals, when red and white paint is used to paint faces and bodies of dancers, the dance ground is covered in a mosaic. Dancers step through the mosaic; dancing away the pattern.

Digby Art - Songlines

Dreams are real to Aboriginal people. Totems appear in dreams. Lessons of the ancestors return in dreams. The land is full of signs of the ancestors. In dreams they appear and tell stories of life. Dreams are evidence that though Ancestral Beings are not actively apparent on the landscape, they are still present.

Aboriginal Australians in a Modern Nation

Early British settlers of Australia dealt with Aboriginal Australians by ignoring them, if they went away, by giving them food, and in the case of missionaries, trying to convert them to European Christianity in thought, dress and deed. When competition for land and food was acute, violence broke into open warfare. Competition for land is a separate story. Europeans evolved in attitude toward Aboriginals, replicated toward native people in nations around the world, in paternalism, containment, assimilation and, eventually, respect in self-determination.

Recent statistics, backed by archaeological and other evidence, fault violence for twenty percent of Aboriginal Australian population decline. Eighty-percent of population decline is attributed to diseases. Either vector was a path to societal destruction of one of the oldest, if not the oldest, ongoing people on the planet.[41] Aboriginal people suffered from yaws, diseases that caused blindness and some had stopped eating fish, due to proliferation of a poisonous algae, known as Ciguatera. These maladies predated European contact.

Whether the hunter-gatherer lifestyle could continue, given arrivals of several European nations and incursions for fishing and gathering sea life by New Guinea groups, is debatable. In recent years, a hunter-gather group emerged from the out-back. They were just as bewildered at what they saw, as city-dwellers they encountered were surprised by them. Hunter-gather groups exist in the outback today. Numbers are unknown.

Australian government policies today promote retaining culture, cross-cultural respect and Two-Ways learning, in which Aboriginal children are taught native, as well as European traditions. To be a unified and co-existing national community, all children of Australia may benefit from Two-Ways learning. Stories, dreams and cosmology of Aboriginals, taught within the family group, is the traditional method, perpetuating for Aboriginal children a depth of culture uniquely theirs.

Amid rancor of the twentieth century, and into the twenty-first century, addressing racism and debates over Australia Day legitimacy, Aboriginal artists have shown a path to cultural understanding, in a non-controversial space. By creating art, they preserve Aboriginal culture and traditions. Acceptance of their art, by the general public and the world, fosters cultural respect.

Albert Namatjira is often identified as an artist, who exemplifies perseverance of an Aboriginal artist in the European/Australian world, who gained international acceptance for his art and recognition for Aboriginal art. His art is joined by several other Aboriginal artists in galleries and museums of the world today, notably in Melbourne, where his paintings were first acclaimed.

---

[41] See generally, Flood and Richard Broome, Aboriginal Australians, 4th ed, Allen & Unwin, NSW, 2010.

Namatjira was born in 1902, within a mission. He was educated as a Christian in school, and in Songlines by his elders. Forbidden to marry a woman from a taboo group, he eloped and lived with her in the desert, as they began a family of the first three of their ten children. When he was thirty-two, Namatjira saw an exhibition of watercolor artists. Two years later, the artists invited him to join them on a painting expedition. The trip changed his life.

In his first solo exhibition in 1938, of forty-one water color landscapes, Namatjira sold all his works in three days. He is regarded as putting Aboriginal art into modern mediums and mainstream acceptance. He died in 1959, of a heart attack.[42] His legacy is a path in the world for other artists.

Albert Namatjira Northern Territory Library (public domain)

Creating dot art today, is a medium for serious Aboriginal artists, a community project where elders use art to teach stories to young people, and elementary art training in Two-Ways learning. Dots are deceptively simple. The brush in the hands of young and old are guided by Ancestral Beings, as they have been for tens of thousands of years. Through art, ancient Aboriginal people preserved lifeways. They do so today. European arrival has not chased away the Ancestral Beings. Dormant or not, they are there.

---

[42] Albert Namatjira received full Australian citizenship in 1957. Aboriginals were not regarded as full citizens as part of disenfranchisement and to control access to alcohol. There are no medical studies to show that Aboriginals have body chemistry that causes rapid onset of alcoholism. Rather, drinking is a factor in despair.

Broome of Pearls and Poets

Along the North Coast of Australia, from Broome to Thursday Islands in the Torres Strait, lie a wealth of *pinctada maxima*, giant pearl oysters unique to the South Seas. Ancient mollusks, holdovers from a primeval world, hold beauty inside rough and unattractive exteriors. They were known to Aboriginal peoples of northern Australia, for mysterious appearance of the inner shell, which was made into amulets, hung from hair-rope necklaces. Known as mother-of-pearl, when used for buttons, the inner shell became ubiquitous in Europe in the nineteenth century. The real prize was an occasional pearl found in one oyster out of a thousand. Pearls, an aberration of nature expelling an irritant, became currency of international commerce, intrigue and the occasional good story.

For Aboriginal Australians, oysters were one among many gifts of the creators of abundance in their world. Oysters, like Aboriginal people, never overpopulated their environment, moving to separate turf when necessary. When oysters were discovered by outsiders, from China, Japan and Europe, they were heavily harvested for quick returns, by people having no need for continuity in the landscape. As harvesters scooped beds clean, they moved west along the Australian coast.

Today, sea coasts of Broome, Darwin and Thursday Island are host to a cultured pearl industry. *Pinctada maxima* reproduction, and production of pearls, is a farm industry. Still, only an oyster can produce a pearl. South Sea Pearls are a local industry of north coast Australia, which supports several communities. Randomly natural, or cultured, pearls are still prized as gems. Visitors to north coast Australia communities have the opportunity to choose their prize on location.

Aboriginal Pearl Pendant

Like the perfection of a controlled production pearl, pearling stories of locals are no longer as colorful. In the days when Japanese divers, former gold miners, and some former convict transportees, the old salts of the sea, collected oysters, as hunter-gathers of a nineteenth and twentieth century world, stories of pearl divers were exciting, intriguing and fun. Pearling was muse to such writers as Ion Idriess, who wrote the novel *Forty Fathoms Deep*, about theft, murder and execution of players in the story of a single pearl.

Idriess is one of a bevy of Australian authors, for whom northern Australia informed their writing. Australians prize home-grown writers. They panned *Kangaroo*, the work of D.H. Lawrence, as written by a day-tripper, due to his short stay in Australia. Lawrence looked at young, ambitious Australians as shallow and materialistic. No doubt, rather like people of the same demographic, elsewhere in the world, of the same time. Critics of Lawrence might increase credibility by focusing instead, upon a wealth of pearls in Australian authors, such as: Aboriginal Australian Bruce Pascoe, or Thomas Keneally, Ernestine Hill, Roby Davidson and Edwin Colin Simpson. This is an incomplete list of pearls on paper, found in Australia.

This is a short story, of the long history, of the pearl. Prized by royals and debutants, this story goes to the source and stays close to the north coast of Australia. Sitting on a north coast beach, contemplating a pearl purchase, is also a good time to pick up a good book, the pearls of prose by an Australian author. Like gem pearls, pearls of prose are a personal preference, among so many choices available from Broome to Thursday Island, while on the north coast of Australia.

Pearls of *Pinctada Maxima*

Only mollusks, such as a clam, can make a pearl. Salt water oysters do it best. Only one in a thousand do so voluntarily. Oyster pearls are prized over clam pearls, for their shiny iridescence. Pinctada maxima, the giant oysters of North Coast Australia, are known for great size and round perfection. It seems fitting that in the great geological space of Australia, oversize is normal.

Pearl divers aboard a lugger in 1953. Photo courtesy Broome Historical Society.

Mollusks appear stationary. Actually, they part their shells just enough to allow water to stream in, through which they extract nutrients. Occasionally, a particle passing by remains to become an irritant. The mollusk immune system goes to work, to isolate the particle from interior organs, by covering it with an encasement. The casing grows over time, layer upon layer. This is the pearl.

Oysters are products of their environment. Oysters found in volcanic sands of Bora Bora are known for their black pearls. Pearls may also be pink, gold, or green. Most common is white, or whitish-blue. Perfect round pearls of South Sea oysters of North Coast Australia, born of giant oysters, classified as *pinctada maxima* of the species, are often iridescent white.

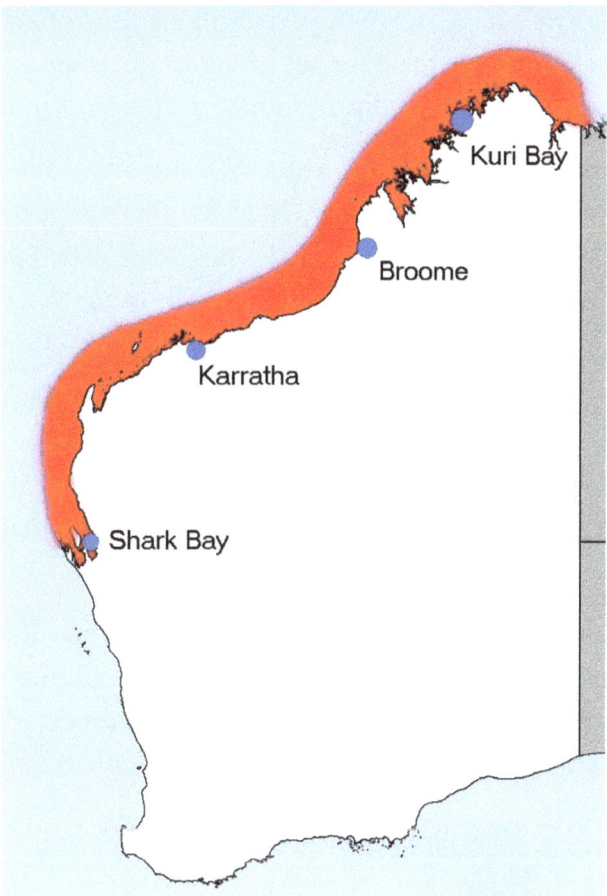

Western Australian Pearling Areas

Sometimes the pearl forms on the shell wall, causing one side of the pearl to be flat. These are known as half-pearls. They fit nicely into rings. Sometimes pearls form in irregular shape, or are multiple pearls together. Irregular pearls have value for their uniqueness. Most valuable on the pearl market, are very large, perfectly round, iridescent white pearls, with no flaws.

Oysters left behind in low tide, or after a storm, were easily collected by Aboriginal gatherers, or later beachcombing survivalists. Shallow diving came next, and was easily accomplished. When shallow oysters were less numerous, deep diving became necessary. Commercial pearl merchants employed Japanese divers, or conscripted Aboriginal divers, to go as deep as humanly possible.

In the late nineteenth century, when popularity of pearls from the Australian North Coast was at its peak, the business became ugly. Chinese and Aboriginal divers were conscripted as slave divers. Going deep was at much personal risk.

Although few oysters held a pearl, oyster shell held value in Europe, for the interior shell, from which buttons were made. Mother-of-pearl, as it was called, was a fashion statement in jewelry and artistic pieces. When plastic became an inexpensive option for buttons, the value of shell dropped. Diving for oysters was all about the pearl. Oyster for shell, or meat, was cast off in waste.

By the 1850s, sailors docking in Broome, Darwin, or the Torres Strait islands, found they could make income quickly by harvesting oysters. Oyster beds were picked clean. Even worse, shovels full of oysters were harvested, destroying habitat for young oysters. Not only were mature oyster populations decimated, the habitat was being lost at an alarming rate.

In 1875, the Australian Parliament passed a Pearling Act. The Act prohibited females from pearl diving. Depth of diving was limited to thirty-six feet. Pearling business owners were prohibited from beating divers, and were required to return Aboriginal divers to the place of conscription.

Diving Helmets

Advent of the copper diving helmet, in 1828, to which air was pumped, extended the depth of pearl diver reach. Fewer divers need be employed, to harvest a larger haul of oysters. By 1883, the diving helmet was standard equipment. From 1909 to 1917, when diving was in hiatus, about one hundred fifty divers worked from Broome. More divers worked from Darwin and other ports.

Pearl diving was always a dangerous job. Divers were at mortal risk of sharks and sudden cyclones. Diving helmets, which extended diving depth and length of dives, brought new hazards to divers from the *Bends*.

The bends received its name from debilitating pain in extremities, felt by divers, after a day of diving. Some divers awoke in the middle of the night, in searing pain. Some divers died. Others lost eyesight, or limbs.

Diving helmets were developed for the Royal Navy in Britain. Research in the bends disclosed that, under pressure, nitrogen in oxygen, normally expelled in breathing, was instead retained in the blood. The more pressure under which a diver was put by depth in the water, and over longer periods of time, the more nitrogen remained in the blood. Upon slowly surfacing, nitrogen in the blood is slowly released into the lungs, as external pressure on the body is reduced. If the diver surfaces, before nitrogen is fully released, a sudden and total release of nitrogen will stress blood vessels and lungs, causing extreme pain, blindness, or death.[43]

Pearl divers learned to hang below pearling boats, for hours into the night, after a long day of diving. The Broome Museum has an early decompression chamber, which saved many lives. Today hospitals along the north coast have modern equipment and experienced operators. Even after the advent of SCUBA, copper helmets were used for pearl divers in Australia, until 1975.

In the first decades of the twentieth century, Kochichi Mikimoto was a pearler in Ago Bay Japan. Faced with over-harvesting of oysters, and slim chances of finding a pearl in an oyster, he experimented with growing oysters, under controlled farming circumstances. He manually introduced pearl instigating irritants to oysters. After years of trial and error, he perfected pearl farming. At the time of Mikimoto's death in 1954, he was the wealthiest man in Japan.

---

[43] See generally, Hugh Edwards, Pearls of Broome and Northern Australia, Western Australia Press, 1994.

Initially, pearl merchants and diving operators dismissed Mikimoto pearls as of lesser quality. In reality, the only way to tell a farm pearl, from a wild pearl, is to destroy the pearl, to examine the core. Farmed or wild, all pearls are natural. Today, wild pearl diving continues, even as pearl farms proliferate along the north coast of Australia, from Broome to Darwin, and into the Torres Strait Islands, near Thursday Island.[44]

Mikimoto, reviled initially by north coast Australia pearlers, saved the Australia pearl-based economy. At the turn of the century, Broome supplied Europe with mother-of-pearl for popular buttons. Plastic decimated the pearl button market, almost overnight. By farming pearls, pearl divers and merchants revived use of over-collected oyster beds, increased pearl production, and supplied a world-wide growing demand for pearls. North coast Australia is still home to *pinctada maxima*, the giant oyster of the largest pearls found in the world, farmed, or wild.

Making Mother of Pearl Buttons (credit Hemis Almay)

---

[44] Freshwater pearls are a separate story of interior rivers. The concept is the same. The result is unusual pearls of irregular shape. Freshwater pearls have a distinct beauty. They are usually of much less cost.

Pearler Stories

Pearler Lugger (credit Manfred Gottschalk)

In the mid-nineteenth century, when errant adventurers, unsuccessful gold miners, and sailors escaping the sea, came to north coast Australia, they brought nothing with them, but a need to live off the land. Less resourceful than Aboriginal occupants of unforgiving terrain, who mastered hunter/gather techniques over thousands of years, new arrivals scrounged for a basic living. Beachcombing for oysters was one of very few options available to men, living low on the land.

Occasionally, a beachcomber found one dreamed of gem in an oyster. Some sold their pearl to fund purchase of a ranch, or business, and moved up in the world. Others spent their profits at the bar. Their days were spent dreaming of the next big find, and their nights were passed at local bars, telling pearling stories, to anyone who would listen.

Stories often told among pearlers, and by locals of north coast beaches today, include one of a man, who found his prize pearl, while opening his harvest of the day on the deck of his lugger. Luggers are the small, double-mast sailing vessels of pearlers. The man held up his new-found pearl, still covered in slime of the oyster, so his friend on the next lugger could marvel at his lovely large pearl. As the two men looked in horror, the pearl slipped from the man's hands, bounced on the deck, and plopped into the sea. The old pearler regained enough of his senses to mark the spot with a float, find a Japanese diver, and hire him to look for the pearl. The diver dropped down to the floor of the sea, under the float, and retrieved the pearl.

In another story, a woman pearler, with a crew of Malay divers, was informed by one of her divers that one of her crew stole a pearl and sold it. She enlisted Interpol to find the pearl, which sold for three times the initial price in Paris. Reunited with her pearl, the woman sold it for the initial price. Pearlers lived in an isolated world, where their catch was sold to intermediaries of dealers. The concept of retail sales outlets, at the source, came later.

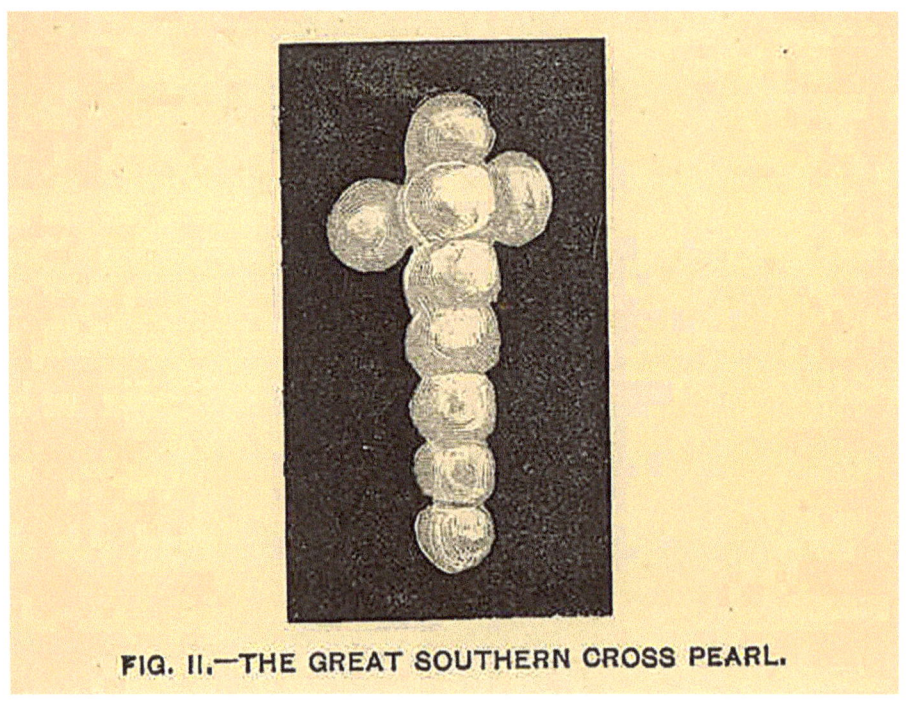

Great Southern Cross Pearl (Edwin W. Streeter 1886)

Other than knowing that very large pearls held high value, pearlers had little idea of market value. In 1883, a salty old pearler found a cluster of small pearls in an oyster. He sold it, on the beach, for a small sum to a pearl buyer, who resold it for four times the amount, still less than $100. The second buyer knew about marketing pearls. He gave the cluster a name, *Southern Cross Pearl*, for the cluster glued together as a cross. The worthless aberration on the north coast beach, became a gold medal exhibit in Paris in 1889. The last known whereabouts of the *Southern Cross Pearl*, was in 1933, when a marketeer encouraged Catholics to donate funds, to gift the pearl to the pope. Substantial donations were collected. The Vatican has no reports of such a gift.

Most notorious of pearl stories, is the mystery of the *Roseate Pearl*. Found at the turn of the twentieth century, near Broome, the single, large, rose-hued pearl, became the source of mystery and paranormal fascination for the next century. Its story is central to the book, by Australian author Ion Idriess, *Forty Fathoms Deep*, a novel of murder and passion for pearls.

The non-fiction story of the *Roseate Pearl*, is worthy of its fictionalized legacy. The story began with the common occurrence of a pearler, who passed out drunk celebrating his find of the day. The diver stole the pearl from his employer, and showed it to his friend, another Asian diver. The friend stole the pearl from the first thief, joined with his friend, and the pair decided to find a white man as an intermediary, to sell the pearl to a broker in *snide*, that is, pearls of questionable provenance.

Charles Hagen, owner of a saloon in Chinatown at Broome, was well known to locals as a purveyor of snide. The threesome agreed to sell the pearl to Robert Liebglid, a pearl dealer, who would ask no questions. They asked to be paid in gold coin, of a substantial amount. Later, investigators speculated that Liebglid was shown the pearl, or he would not have carried so much gold in his pockets, on the night of his murder.

Late one night, several locals heard a man yell, *Murder!* They ran toward the sound, coming from near an old wreck of a lugger on the beach, and found nothing. In the morning light, townspeople located Liebglid. He was hit on the head, fell into shallow water and drowned, under the weight of gold, still in his pockets. As the story goes, foul play was suspected.

Second thief of the pearl, Robert Marquez, confessed to the murder. He told the tale of theft and attempted sale. Their idea was, to knock out Liebglid, take the gold and keep the pearl. After the first blow, when Liebglid yelled out, the threesome ran away. Liebglid passed out and drowned.

The three co-conspirators were hung in Fremantle Goal, on December 14, 1905. By this time, the finder of the pearl and the first thief died in weather related diving accidents. A pearl merchant purchased the *Roseate Pearl*, locked it in the ship's safe of the *SS Koomba*, and sailed for Adelaide.

As the *SS Koomba* sailed down the north coast, in 1912, a cyclone suddenly hit the area. The *SS Koomba* and all on board were lost at sea. Neither the ship, nor the ill-fated *Roseate Pearl*, were seen again. Everyone involved with the pearl, legitimate, or not, met an untimely end.

Pearls of Australian Prose

Broome Monument to Pearlers credit Robert Harding

David Herbert Lawrence, known as D. H. Lawrence, British playwright and author of *Lady Chatterley's Lover*, traveled across Australia, in the early twentieth century. He wrote disparagingly of young, upwardly mobile Australians he met in his travels.[45] Australians show equal lack of regard for Lawrence, as a day trekker, a non-Australian, who assumes they can write about the Australian psyche.

Australians need no visiting British to tell their story, with a wealth of pearls in Australian prose, by home-grown authors. Ion Idriess, born near Sydney in 1890, wrote fifty books based on Australian history, by the time of his death in 1972. Contemporary of Idriess, also prolific, was Brisbane travel writer Ernestine Hill.[46] Her *Peter Pan Land and Other Poems*, won a prize in 1916, and earned Hill a job as a typist. She traveled Australia, as a syndicated newspaper travel writer. Hill's, *The Great Australian Loneliness,* of a trek across Australian bush country, published in 1937, was given as basic reading to American troops in Australia, during World War II.

Other Australian writers, trekked across Australian landscapes to encounter Aboriginals, still unaffected by modernization of coastal Australian cities. Robyn Davidson[47] trekked seventeen hundred miles on camels, to write her account in *Tracks: A Woman's Solo Trek Across 1700 Miles of Australian Outback*, which became a movie script in 1980. Edwin Colin Simpson attacked the notion of Social Darwinism, foretelling extinction of Aboriginals, in his 1951 account of enduring Aboriginal culture in Arnhem Land, *Adam in Ochre*.[48]

Bruce Pascoe, an Aboriginal Australian, born in Melbourne in 1947, and educated at the University of Melbourne, first wrote under *nom de plume*. Prolific and well-known as a novelist, non-fiction writer, poet and writer of children's literature, his notable non-fiction work *Dark Emu: Black Seeds: Agriculture or Accident?* in 2014, seeks to fill gaps in knowledge of Aboriginals,

---

[45] D. H. Lawrence, *Kangaroo*, 1923, a novel set in Australia, was adapted as a movie script in 1986.
[46] Mary Ernestine Hill was born in 1899, and died in Brisbane in 1972.
[47] Robyn Davidson, was born 1950, in Miles, Australia.
[48] Edwin Colin Simpson, was born 1908 and died in 1983, in Sydney. Not to be confused with Australian musician Colin Edwin.

perpetrated by white academia through history.[49] Impact of Pascoe on Australian writers, is noted by famed author of *Schindler's List*, the prolific Australian author, Thomas Keneally, who said of his novel, *The Chant of Jimmie Blacksmith*, written in 1972, that if he wrote the story again, he would do so as a white observer, and not presume to know the Aboriginal mind.[50]

Visiting Broome on North Coast Australia Today

Broome Pearl Store in the Style of Old Broome (credit Richard Cummins)

Broome remains a quaint pearling town, on north coast Australia. Cruise guests disembark here, to walk the short commercial street, and buy pearls, or ride camels along Cable Beach. This is the port to look for footprints of

---

[49] See also, *Dark Emu: A Truer History*, published in 2019.
[50] Thomas Michael Keneally, born in 1935 in Sydney. See his *Book of Science and Antiquities*, 2019.

dinosaurs, and rock paintings of Aboriginal people, in neighboring Arnhem Land. Pearl farming, and wild pearl harvesting, are still done from luggers, as was done a century ago. Local descendants of Greek pearl merchants, Paspaley is the largest local purveyor from company stores, begun in 1956. Pearls take time to form. Farmed pearls are informed by science. Still, only an oyster can make a pearl.

Broome benefited from relocation of the Adelaide telegraph line to Cable Bay, Broome, after submerged volcanic eruption disrupted cable connection to Darwin in 1872. The historic Court House in Broome today, occupies the pre-fabricated Cable House, sent to accommodate cable transmissions. The Beagle Bay Church, modest from the exterior, holds a prized mother-of-pearl altar. The graveyard of the church holds stories of Japanese pearl divers, who supplied the shells.

Broome population of fifteen thousand, swells to forty-five thousand, during tourist season. A third of the permanent population are Aboriginal Yawuru and Torres Island Strait people. Many more are descendants of Asian pearl divers, relocated gold miners of the last century, and pearl merchants of the world. Broome is closer to ports of Indonesia, than main cities of Australia.

The first governor of the territory, Sir Frederick Napier Broome, was appointed by Queen Victoria to bring civilization to a Swan River Colony of the outback. Founding town leaders drew a street plan and sold lots of sand, in an imagined dummy townsite. Governor Broome begged the Queen to remove his name from the farce of a town. She refused. Today, the town is still small and undersized, to the reputation desired by its namesake. For cruise visitors, it is a piece of pearling heaven. Small, distant to large metropolis, and mired in pearling tradition, Broome is inviting.

Darwin Cullen Bay Marina, courtesy Darwin Northern Territory

Darwin of the Air

Sitting at the top and center of the Australia Continent, in the Northern Territory, it is difficult to imagine the town of Darwin was the dream child of city fathers in Adelaide. From south-central Australia, Adelaide's ambition to run a road directly north, through the continent, to a port of Darwin, known as Palmerston from inception in 1869 to 1911, was a means to capture trade from Asia. The sea route around the west coast was subject to weather. Plans were well founded, in a time prior to air travel. The road built from Darwin to Adelaide, runs through the Red Center of Australia, the open, red rock desert.

Despite the relationship to Adelaide, Darwin remained small and insignificant in world events, until the advent of air travel. When the era of flight came, Darwin proved its worth as an aviation center. For a century, Darwin has attracted flyers testing their range. During World War II, when Darwin was an airbase, heavily bombed, it was the valor of residents that was tested. Darwin was rebuilt four times. Three times due to cyclones and once after bombing in World War II.[51]

Darwin's critical place in world history is its geographical axis point, at the epicenter of primeval and modern worlds, both seeking to survive, with the oldest and newest of technology. Aboriginal people of Australia, original residents of Arnhem Land, today Kakadu National Park, have their own story. This is the story of Darwin of the air; those who flew to Darwin of choice and necessity, in peace and war.

---

[51] Hurricanes, cyclones and typhoon are the same weather occurrence. Cyclones occur in the South Pacific and Indian Ocean. Hurricanes occur in the Atlantic and northeast Pacific. Typhoons occur in the northwest Pacific.

Route from Adelaide to Darwin Australia (Digby art)

Frontier Town to Air Base – A Little History of Darwin

Browns Mart Theatre (credit Dietmar Rabich)

In December 1868, recently appointed Surveyor-General George Woodroffe Goyder left Adelaide to sail for the north coast. Sailing with Goyder were one hundred and thirty-seven men, a dozen of whom were trained surveyors. All were hand-picked by Goyder and well supplied. Five prior attempts to found an outpost on the north coast of the continent failed. Goyder studied those failures and was determined to succeed in his assignment.

Prior attempts to found a settlement were focused upon British need to display a presence in the face of possible Dutch and French desires for land holds on the continent. To the north in Java, Dutch had plantations, the wealth of which funded a sea-faring empire. France was invested in southeast Asia, French Indochina. Both nations utilized slave labor to make operations viable.

Unknown to British agents in Australia, was just how tenuous Dutch and French colonial hold was at the time. Both ended in disaster. Slaves in Java revolted against the Dutch. France became invested in a long-term war.

Britain colonized Australia coincidental to housing criminals, which evolved into indentured labor, to satisfy commercial aims of the quasi-military companies, that held land and ran ground operations. Interests of these companies was commercial trade in England, through export of farm output. Trade with Asia, through a port on the Indian Ocean, was a new goal.

The first three British attempts to found a colony on the north coast were fashioned as military posts. As such, choice of site was strategic, not agricultural. Site choice did not consider needs of long-term residency. The fourth attempt was intended as a civilian settlement, still mounted as a military expedition. Needs of a town were still not considered.

Of early attempts at a settlement, the expedition of 1839, produced no more than a tenuous encampment. A Northern Territory Expedition in 1864, devolved into a survivalist camp by 1866. People chosen to lead the expedition, were of the mind of quasi-military companies, which for so long controlled New South Wales, and to some extent Queensland and Southern Territory.

Government House Darwin (credit kenhodge 13)

In 1863, when city leaders of Adelaide had the idea to found a northern port, South Australia controlled the central continent, and what became known as the Northern Territory of South Australia. Later, the territory split and the Red Centre became part of the north, with Darwin as the capital. As history of the first five attempts at founding a port city evidence, founding Darwin was not organic, as a trade, or traffic center. Founding a port city in the north was an imperative of Adelaide, the capital city of the south, for trade with Asia, to gain profits for investors.

An open-ended goal, to establish a viable town on the north coast, became a critical financial need for Adelaide city leaders, held to produce on advertisements of land in the Northern Territory. City leaders presold lots in Palmerston, prior to existence of a town, based upon assumed success of the Northern Territory Expedition of 1864. Failure to create the town by 1868, brought buyers forward, wanting real titles, or refunds. Adelaide did not retain funds to enable refunds. Goyder was on a mission to save the souls of the government of Southern Australia.

Goyder was a man of talent and action.[52] He was not a politician, and held no desire to remain in Darwin as a governor. Father of nine children in Adelaide, he was anxious to complete the assignment and head home. Goyder was born in Britain, trained as a railroad engineer, and came to Sydney at age twenty-two. Connections with a church society in Adelaide brought him to the town, where he met his wife and built a home.

The life lesson Goyder learned in Adelaide was the tenuous nature of water supplies in Australia. He was led to believe that Adelaide sat on a lake. He learned that the lake was seasonal. Enduring cities require a year-around water supply. When Goyder arrived on the north coast, his priority item was to establish a well. In survey for a town, he was sensitive to water flows and access.

Goyder's team surveyed 500,000 acres of bush country in eight months. They mapped roads and a townsite. Most important, they established a well. The focus of Goyder was a townsite of long-term habitability. His legacy is the enduring existence of Darwin. Upon Goyder's return to Adelaide, he was greeted as a hero.

The name Darwin, assigned to the port in 1839, and to the town in 1911, came from John Clements Wickham. Wickham was second in command of HMS *Beagle*, when Robert FitzRoy took command on the first voyage of HMS *Beagle* to map southern hemisphere coasts and returned in 1832, with Charles Darwin. Darwin, a recent college graduate at the time, was intended to provide biological data collection and intellectual conversation on the voyage. Wickham succeeded Fitzroy as captain of the HMS *Beagle*, when Fitzroy became governor of New Zealand.[53]

As Goyder sailed home to Adelaide in 1870, government workers were busy building roads, grading subdivision streets and planting poles for telegraph lines. In the process of digging telegraph lines, workers struck gold. The telegraph line shortly thereafter moved to Broome. Income from

---

[52] See generally, Derek Pugh, Darwin 1869, 2019 edition.
[53] FitzRoy assumed command of HMS *Beagle* upon suicide of Pringle Stokes. On the second voyage of FitzRoy on HMS *Beagle*, John Lort Stokes, no relation to Pringle Stokes, shared a cabin with Darwin. John Stokes was a successor captain of HMS *Beagle* to Wickham. Stokes biographers give him broad credits for naming Darwin.

the short Gold Rush of 1870 built Darwin. Gold mining hopefuls sailed to Darwin from London in 1872, adding to a growing population of three hundred by 1875.[54]

Lines of the Australian Overland Telegraph Line ran almost two thousand miles from Darwin to the Adelaide port of Port Augusta. Several surveyors on the telegraph line were Goyder veterans. Running along the telegraph lines was the Adelaide to Darwin Railway. The railway was completed from Adelaide to Alice Springs by 1929, and all the way to Darwin in 2003.

Darwin fulfilled dreams of city fathers of Adelaide by the 1930s. At the beginning of World War II, the population of Darwin swelled by ten thousand, as a military post of Australian and other Allied troops, in defense of the Australian north coast. In February 1942, the same Japanese aircraft that bombed Pearl Harbor, joined by additional bombers, dropped an even greater number of bombs on Darwin.

In the history of Darwin, the town begun in 1839, was rebuilt four times. It was rebuilt after World War II, and after each of three cyclones. The storms of 1897 and 1937, were devastating, although not to the extent of cyclone Tracy in 1974. Seventy-one people died in Tracy, and three-fourths of the structures of Darwin were lost. The death toll would have been greater, but for the airlift evacuation of thirty thousand people, from the city to safety, in record-setting time. The inland city, which housed people of Darwin during city recovery and rebuilding, holds the ironic name of Palmerston.

Darwin – Aviation Center of the World

Darwin presents visitors with a unique and intimate view of the beginning of aviation history, when crossing the Atlantic by air was as exciting as following the path of a rocket to outer space. Darwin Aviation Heritage Center houses early aircraft, as well as exhibits to the history of some great names in cross-oceanic air flights. The museum is in an historic aerodrome, which survived bombing during World War II.

---

[54] One third of the population of Darwin perished in 1875, while sailing to Adelaide, when caught in a storm.

Bank of New South Wales Damaged in Bombing (public domain)

Palmerstown Town Hall After Cyclone Tracy (courtesy Tourism NT)

1921 Hovercraft at Darwin Aviation Heritage Centre (courtesy Tourism NT)

In 1919, The Australian government sponsored a challenge for any flyer, who could transit from London to Australia, in under thirty days. Sir Ross Macpherson Smith was aged twenty-six, when he and his brother Keith took the challenge and won the ƒ10,000 prize, for their one hundred-and-thirty-five-hour flight, accomplished in twenty-eight days. They flew a World War I era Vickers Vimy, to land on what is now central Darwin. Ross piloted T. E. Lawrence across Arabia after the war, previously earning a Military Cross, twice, and Distinguished Flying Cross, three times during the war. He died in 1922, while testing a Vickers Viking amphibious aircraft.

Amy Johnson was the first woman to fly solo, from London to Darwin, achieving the distinction in 1930. Born in 1903, in Yorkshire England, her father purchased her first plane. Her flight to Darwin was eleven thousand miles, in nineteen days. Her bi-wing de Haviland DH60 Gypsy Moth, was named Jason, for her father's company. Johnson married two years later, and either solo, or with her husband, continued to set flying records for timed non-stop flights and long-distance records.

Keith Smith's Vickers Vimy biplane 1919 (State Library of Queensland)

During World War II, Johnson flew as a civilian, in the Aircraft Transport Auxiliary. In January 1941, while delivering aircraft, under poor weather conditions, she was forced to bail from the plane. She landed in the Thames, where she was spotted by ships, that came to her rescue. Unable to reach her with a rope, a sailor dove into icy water. Both he and Johnson perished in the cold. Johnson is remembered in Britain, as the Queen of Flight. Planes, a runway and a building at the University of Sheffield are named in her honor.

American Queen of the Air was Amelia Earhart, who in 1932, flew solo across the Atlantic, from Newfoundland to Derry, Ireland, in under fifteen hours, in a single engine Lockheed Vega. Other crowd stirring, non-stop flights, such as from Mexico to New York City, followed. In 1937, she flew east from Oakland to Miami, where she announced plans to circumnavigate the globe.

The circumnavigation route took Earhart from Miami, down the coast of Brazil, and across the Atlantic, to West Africa. From there, she flew over the African continent, to India. Earhart then flew south, down the Malay peninsula, to Darwin. From Darwin, she flew to Lae, New Guinea. The next intended stop from Lae was Howland Island, just southwest of Hawaii. Finding the tiny island, in the open sea, was a task of orienteering perfect navigation. Under low cloud cover, historians believe the plane ran out of fuel, and was lost in the ocean. There are many mysteries, and several conspiracy theories, yet remains of the national darling aviatrix have never been located.

Australian flier, Sir Charles Edward Kingsford Smith flew across the Pacific, from the United States to Darwin, in 1928. Born in Brisbane, Smith served in Gallipoli, then transferred to the Royal Flying Corps in 1917. After the war, he traveled as a barnstormer in the United States, flying as a performer at fairs. Returning to Australia in 1921, Smith became one of the first, licensed, commercial airline pilots.

The plane flown by Kingsford-Smith, across the Pacific from Oakland to Brisbane, in 1928, was a Fokker Trimotor, he named *Southern Cross*. Kingsford-Smith, knighted in 1932, left Australia too late to participate in the 1934 England to Australia air race, so instead he flew from Australia to the US. He completed the east-bound air flight, which was fatal to Amelia Earhart, two years earlier. The next year, Kingsford-Smith disappeared over the Andaman Sea, while attempting to break a speed record, for a flight from Allahabad to Singapore. Later, wreckage of his plane beached in Myanmar. The *Southern Cross,* not flown on the fatal flight, is housed in a memorial to the famed flyer, at the Brisbane Airport.

Famed as the Australian Lone Eagle, was flight pioneer Herbert John Louis Hinkler. He began as a glider, then airplane engineer. In 1913, he worked in England, designing the Sopwith Camel, for Sopwith Aviation Company. During World War I, Hinkler served as a gunner, in the Royal Naval Airforce, earning a Distinguished Service Medal. After the war, Hinkler was a test pilot. In 1933, when attempting to break the speed record for flight from London to Australia, Hinkler crashed in the Italian mountains. He is honored in England and Australia, in a monument and airfields.

Wealthy confection magnate, Sir Macpherson Robertson, underwrote prize money for the MacRobertson Trophy Air Race in 1934. Organized by the Royal Aero Club, founded in 1901, the London to Melbourne race had fuels stops in Baghdad, Allahabad, Singapore, Darwin and Charleville, Queensland. Billed as the World's Greatest Air Race, the sponsor requested safety equipment be carried on all planes. The race was to be thrilling, fast and safe.

MacRobertson Air Race Poster 1934 (public domain)

Of the twenty planes beginning the race on October 20, 1934, twelve eventually finished. The winner was a British team in a de Havilland DH 88 Comet, a duel engine plane, purpose built by the aircraft company for the race. Last to arrive, was on November 24. The race was made famous in a 1991 television series: the *Great Air Race*. The trophy was melted down in 1942, for its metal in the war effort.

Air Race Trophy Melted by RED CROSS 1941 (photo public domain)

Visiting Darwin Today

Kakadu National Park (credit Dietmar Rabich)

Today, Highway 87 runs through the Red Centre of the continent, from Adelaide to Darwin, through Alice Springs to the Top End. Most ground travelers hop between cities by air. Cruise travelers ring the coast, as founders of Darwin did a century and a half ago. Ships today travel in optimum seasons, aided by weather equipment, unknown a century ago.

Cruise ships on the circumference of the continent, travel the green fringes, while guests fly inland to the Red Center, to visit Alice Springs and Ayers Rock. For many cruise visitors to Darwin, the port is access to Kakadu National Park, where Aboriginal life seems unaffected by events of the world beyond. Step through Darwin into an ancient world in Arnhem Land.

In Darwin, original wood buildings of Goyder's team long ago succumbed to termites, the giant habitat of which is a visitor attraction. Fort Hill is no longer a hill, and no longer has a fort. To have a sense of the town as originally surveyed, take the elevator to enter Goyder Park, and see the foundations marked by poured cement, showing where development began.

Stone buildings of the 1870s which remain standing are Government House, the Courthouse, Police Station and cell block, all of which have been restored. The Town Hall building, destroyed by Cyclone Tracy, sits in its unrestored condition, lending perspective to the original townsite. Victoria Hotel, built in 1890, a gold rush beneficiary, sits on the Smith Street Mall. Brown's Mart, the original 1885 gold exchange, now Solomon's Mart, evolved from market to bank, then military storage during World War II, to post-war government use. It is now a theater.

Two favorite indoor sights in Darwin are the Darwin Aviation Museum, where an American B-52 is on display by permission of the United States, and the Museum and Art Gallery of the Northern Territory. The Museum holds an impressive display of Aboriginal culture and arts, as well as the local icon, Sweetheart, a sixteen-foot-long preserved crocodile.

Darwin today, welcomes visitors to the last stop of *Priscilla Queen of the Desert*, shot in 1994, and the gateway of *Crocodile Dundee*, to numerous adventures. Natural landscapes seen in films still exist. Even with cruise ships in port, the landscape is never crowded.

Darwin was built to connect Australia to the world, by telegraph. It gained world-wide attention, as an airfield. People of Darwin credit their pilots, for their airlift to safety in a cataclysmic cyclone of 1974. Darwin of the air endures, through people of the land, and from tourism from the sea.

Darwin Waterfront (credit Dietmar Rabich)

Brisbane Lighthouse (credit Chris Grienke)

Independent Queenslanders of Brisbane

Great cities have time depth, that is, heritage told in street names, buildings and choice of monuments. Cities are built by people, who have at their best a few decades of influence, while their buildings, monuments and legacies endure for centuries. Brisbane, capital of Queensland, Australia has only two centuries of existence, yet it has indicia of a great city.

In Julius Caesar, Shakespeare gave Brutus the punch line, that the good that men do die with them, and their evil lives forever. Was Shakespeare so jaded by Southwark docks, that he could not see London, beyond its sixteenth century grime? Did he write this line, staring at prison barges in the Thames, or across the water to the Tower of London? From these docks on the Thames, left ships for Australia, two hundred years later. The worst of transportees, or those hardened in transit, were sent north from New South Wales convict settlements, future Sydney, to Morton Bay Penal Settlement. Morton Bay became the cornerstone of the city of Brisbane.

Some historians of Brisbane might argue, that the core of the city began at the Commissariat Building, built by convicts in 1829, on the site of the initial women's prison barracks. Other city historians might urge Fortitude Valley, as the true site of the beginnings of the city. Free settlers moved into the valley in 1849, when land and building space near Morton Bay was refused to them. In Fortitude Valley, newcomers built a life, as did waves of newcomers thereafter.

Brisbane today, is a city that has kept its historic core of the first century of existence, added a civic core in the second century, and continued to evolve, within a sea of high-rise steel and glass. Arguments over site of the city core, are relegated to the beginning of the twentieth century, when city council members argued for over a decade, over the site of the new town hall, to be located in Fortitude Valley, or a swampy area near the site of Morton Bay. Council members had personal stakes in both locations. The mayor held swamp land. The swamp won. Fortitude Valley is considered an inner-suburb.

Today, people of Brisbane have a shared history, even if it is not a personal history. Half of residents were born in Australia, and half were born out of the city, or out of the country. For future city leaders, to not know from whence the city has come, is not to know where it may go.

This is a short history, of the short life, of the accomplished city of Brisbane. The story is told from the convict era, that began in 1823, to becoming capital of Queensland in 1860, through an era of World War I, to the post 1960s, surviving of urban renewal, into a time of organic urban growth. In many ways, the history of Brisbane is iconic of a history of Australia. Brisbane tells its story well, in its streets, buildings and monuments, which reflect the good of what men and women have created, even though they may be imperfect humans. The city today, forms a perfect prelude, to what the next generation will add.

Morton Bay Convict Settlement Era (1823 – 1859)

Brisbane River (credit Greg Obeirne Creative Commons)

In 1823, Governor of New South Wales, Sir Thomas Brisbane, looked north to his vast territory, encompassing the eastern half of the continent, and sent forth explorers to seek a site for a satellite prison. They located a lush paradise north of Sydney, with fresh water from the Brisbane River, as it snaked down to the ocean. A site was chosen in the inner bend, with water on three sides, for Morton Bay Penal Settlement. The site was easy to reach by boat, yet any prison escape attempt could be openly seen. On land of Turrbal and Jagera peoples, Governor Brisbane established his repeat offender prison.

Across the river from the base point, on a thumb of land that pokes into the river, now Kangaroo Point, sandstone cliffs were quarried, for stone to build a penal settlement. Two hundred, to a thousand, convicts hollowed out cliffs for stone blocks. Those cliffs remain, on the east bank of the Brisbane River, facing the historic Customs House, backed today, by Bradfield Highway.

Tents and wooden shacks of the penal settlement are long gone. The initial women's barracks was replaced in 1824, with a Commissariat Store, built by convicts of stone from Kangaroo Point. Stone was ferried from Kangaroo Point, to the far side of the inner thumb of land, opposite kitchen gardens, tended by convicts, to grow vegetables. Convicts cleared mangroves along the river, to create their garden. That garden is now Brisbane City Botanic Gardens. Commissariat Store, now a museum, is separated from the river by the Riverside Expressway.

Inland and uphill were more gardens, to grow staples for the convict settlement. Albert Park and Wickham Park maintain open space, in a now dense city. A windmill, built by convicts in 1828, at the base Wickham Park, never functioned as initially intended to mill grains. It became a convict treadmill, which stands today, as an odd monument of the Transportation Era, in contrast to the present beaucolic setting.

Morton Bay was an attractive setting for settlement, regardless of its intended purpose. In 1837, free settlers started to pressure New South Wales government, to allow establishment of homes and farms. Within two decades of laying stones for the Commandant's Cottage, in 1825, Morton Bay was opened to free settlers. The prisoner population dropped to a couple hundred. No new prisoners were arriving. In 1859, when Queensland was carved out of New South Wales, the Commandant's Cottage was rebuilt as a home for the first governor, of the new state of Australia.

Wickham Park (State Library Queensland)

Chinese workers began arriving in Australia in 1818. Representative of the times, Mak Sai Ying came that year, to Sydney, as a carpenter.[55] He moved up to Morton Bay in 1848, purchased land, and built a building. Prohibited from building too close to the Morton Bay Settlement, Ying's land was across Brisbane River from the tip of Kangaroo Point. As more Chinese came to the area, they became a community, that became Chinatown Brisbane. Those who worked for British land owners, closer to the core of Morton Bay, were paid in British and Spanish coins, plus flour, rice, meat and tea.

Hopeful leaders of a self-governing state, independent of New South Wales, built stately homes, well beyond Morton Bay Settlement and Chinatown, employing Chinese labor. Captain John Wickham, second officer to Captain FitzRoy, when Charles Darwin joined them on the HMS *Beagle*, retired from the Royal Navy to become Police Magistrate, then Governor Resident

---

[55] See history blog, John Oxley Library, guest essay of Rutian Mi, Chinese Business History in Queensland, Pre- Gold Rush 1840 to 1850, last accessed March 26, 2020.

of Morton Bay Colony. Newstead House, the home Wickham purchased in 1847, is now a museum.[56]

In 1859, the year self-governing Queensland was established, with Brisbane as its capital, two-hundred and fifty free settlers boarded the *SS Fortitude* for Australia. They arrived with expectations of free land, promised to them in the town. Immediately upon arrival, they were disappointed at being held away from the still-existent penal colony. The new arrivals moved next to Chinatown, and built an adjacent community of Fortitude, named for their ship. The trans-Atlantic cruise brought the travelers together as a cohesive group. They built homes, farms, businesses and a school in Fortitude Valley. Their community became the welcoming place for new arrivals, over the next century.

Old Museum Building Fortitude Valley Brisbane 1926 (Queensland State Archives)

---

[56] Newstead House was made a historic site preserved by Act of Parliament in 1939. Wickham mapped the north coast of Australia, when he named Darwin Bay for his famous former ship's guest.

Brisbane: Capital of Queensland (1859 – 1959)

Brisbane, the new capital city of Queensland, was laid out on a perfect grid, emanating north from the original Morton Bay Colony. In proper British fashion, north to south streets were named for kings, and east to west streets were named for queens. Civic center was designated between the Botanic Garden and Commissariat, at the southern tip of land, surrounded by river.

On a perfect government common green, Parliament House was placed at the north end and a government house, now Old Government House, was placed at the south end, overlooking Brisbane River, with 180° views of the river. Old Government House, completed in 1862, was the center of high society events in Brisbane, until 1910. Since 2009, it has been an art gallery. Parliament House took longer to build, from 1865 to 1868, in a French Baroque style. Over the almost twenty years taken to complete a civic core of the new capital, botanist Walter Hill transformed convict gardens, to a botanical garden of pines, fig trees and floral landscape, to grace the capital city.

A gold rush, and development of coal mining in the vicinity of Brisbane, drew more residents and a source of funds, with which to build the city. Elegant government and private structures were built, in the final two decades of the nineteenth century. The General Post Office was built from 1871 to 1879, of materials imported over time, and employing scarce labor. It has been in continuous use since completion.

Additional government projects included the 1886 Customs House on Queen Street, now an event center, and the 1880 Coal Board Building. The governor's home was repurposed to a Government Printing Office in 1884. The building is now a Public Service Club. On an open grassy square, of the former convict lumberyard, the Land Administration Building was opened in 1899, as an administrative center, for adjudicating land rights of displaced Aboriginals. Today the building is the Treasury Hotel, recognizing the building's initial purpose, as the 1886 Treasury Building.[57]

---

[57] The Treasury Building was on Queen Street at number 21. Today the Treasury Hotel Casino has a prominent spot on the corner of Queen and (King) George Streets.

In 1880, Morton Bay Penal Colony convict barracks were demolished, making room in the center city for business buildings along Queen Street, indicative of a capital of enterprise. Buildings seen today on Queen Street, built from 1881 to the end of the century, include: Colonial Mutual Chambers (no. 62); Palings Building (no. 86); Manwaring Building (no. 110); Gardams Building (no. 114); Hardy Brothers Building (no. 116); and Edwards and Chapman Building (no. 120).

Knowledgeable residents of Brisbane expect high water in their city, during the wet season. Classic Queenslander architecture, seen around Brisbane, employs high pitched roofs, to drain water, raised foundations and external entry stairways, for accommodating wet season. Verandas overhang porches, to cool air entering the many large windows, placed on opposite walls, to draw cooling ventilation through rooms, keeping them habitable in warm months.

Queenslander Architecture (credit English Wikipedia Commons)

Despite taking high water in stride, Brisbane floods in wet seasons of 1893 to 1897, surprised many residents of the city. The city center, Adelaide Street, was turned into a swamp. Business owners looked toward Fortitude Valley with envy, at small streets of high and dry newcomers.

Floods came at an inopportune time for Brisbane. City leaders planned to build a new city hall, to begin the twentieth century, with a showplace of a grand and prosperous city. In anticipation of a center city location, numerus members of the city council purchased land in the vicinity. Other council members purchased land in Fortitude Valley, in anticipation of moving the city center to high ground. For two decades, a battle for the site of city hall waged in city government chambers.

1893 Brisbane Flood Queen St (photo public domain)

Charles Moffatt Jenkinson, mayor of Brisbane in 1914, cast the decisive vote on a city hall site. He chose the swamp. In 1930, a new City Hall opened on Adelaide Street. It still functions today, as the city looks toward its bicentennial. The building also houses the City Museum of Brisbane.

Self-serving acts of the city council a century ago, are now seen as fortuitous for Chinatown and Fortitude Valley, left preserved in a wealth of late-nineteenth century gems. The site of the never-built city hall was gifted to a church, for a never-built grand cathedral. Left preserved from the era are: the 1885 Wickham Hotel, 1887 Jubilee Hotel and 1888 Empire Hotel. The 1887 Fortitude Valley Post Office still stands, as do a number of cottages and small nineteenth century buildings.

City Hall Brisbane 1930 (State Library Queensland)

Brisbane River Story Bridge 1934 (public domain)

In the 1930s, Brisbane envisioned itself as a commercial harbor. In 1934, the City Wharves were built, as well as the Fortitude Valley Police Station of 1935. The Queensland Brewery building was completed soon after, in 1940. These buildings all still stand. In 1935, construction began on the Story Bridge, named for city leader John Douglas Story. The bridge took five years to complete, connecting Kangaroo Point and Fortitude Valley. Today the old bridgeworks are preserved. They are a fun two-hour climb, led by enterprising city tour guides, who tell stories of city history as visitors view the built, historic landscape, on both sides of the Brisbane River.

Brisbane River Kangaroo Point 1939 (State Library Queenland)

Celebrating ANZAC in Brisbane

Proof positive, that someone is a native Australian, or New Zealander, is their reverence for ANZAC Day. ANZAC is the Australian and New Zealand Army Corps, which served valiantly in the disastrous Gallipoli Campaign, in the First World War. In that campaign, British military commanders underestimated the ability of their ANZAC troops, to battle Turkish troops, on the Gallipoli peninsula, in late April 1915. Acting on the military blunder of Winston Churchill, Kemal Ataturk rose to prominence as a war leader, who became the first president of modern Turkey. In protecting the cemetery of the ANZAC war dead in Turkey, Ataturk once said: *They are all our children*. Today, ANZAC Day is commemorated on April 25, in remembrance of all Australian and New Zealand troops, who gave their lives in service to country.

ANZAC Square Brisbane (State Library Queensland)

Most cities, in Australia and New Zealand, have ANZAC Remembrance monuments. In Brisbane, the modest ANZAC monument in Toowong Cemetery served as location for remembrance ceremony, until unveiling the stunning, neoclassical arched, circle arcade in the city center on ANZAC Square, adjoining Post Office Square. The Brisbane ANZAC Remembrance monument was inaugurated in 1930. Impetus for ANZAC Remembrance in Queensland, was Anglican Church Cannon David John Garland.

Garland was born in Dublin, in 1864. He arrived in Brisbane in 1886. He was then sent to Perth, where he ministered to soldiers leaving for the Boer War, from Fremantle. By 1900, Garland was Canon of Perth. In 1903, he returned east as archdeacon of North Queensland. Garland was next sent to New Zealand in 1912. There, he founded a Soldier's Help Society. In Garland's travels to bolster military recruitment and foster aid to returning soldiers, he returned to Brisbane in 1915.

Garland led non-denominational ANZAC memorial services in 1916. A tribute of silence, replaced prayer, to keep the ceremony non-religious and thus all-inclusive. He began ANZAC Day marches, laying of the wreath, and a lunch for veteran soldiers, returned from conflict. He held annual remembrance services at Toowong Cemetery, until the ceremony was transferred to the Brisbane city-center ANZAC Memorial in 1930.

With Church of England funds at his disposal, Garland founded several Clubs for Soldiers at the front of conflicts, including for Australian troops serving in Egypt. Garland was knighted as an OBE in 1934. He died in 1939, and is interred at Toowong Cemetery.

From 1960 Forward: High Rise Metropolis

In the 1960s, several historic buildings met the wrecking ball, in the name of urban renewal. Brisbane suffered the era of the automobile, in a diminished city core, in favor of suburbs. Fortitude Valley became a shabby extension, of an empty business district. Longtime retail icons of Fortitude Valley, including McWhirter's and TC Beirne Department Store, closed.

Queensland was experiencing a financial boom, from mining in coal, silver, lead and zinc. In the old city, former military barracks of Morton Bay, became a high-rise office building on Elizabeth Street, as a new neighbor to the Post Office Building, and the 1874 Gothic gem, Cathedral of Saint Stephen. Across the Brisbane River from the historic city, grew a forest of high-rise steel and glass. Brisbane became metropolitan. The historic city, on the peninsula of the Brisbane River, was framed by concrete freeways.

Brisbane took back its identity, in the first decade of the twenty-first century, by investing in its core. Historic buildings were restored, and some restored buildings were repurposed to museums and commercial space. Most effective for urban resurgence, was establishing the forty-two-acre cultural park, on the point across the Brisbane River, from the historic city to the west. The 1895 institution, the Queensland Art Gallery, moved into new space in the cultural park, joined by the Gallery of Modern Art. The Queensland Performing Arts Centre, State Library of Queensland and Queensland Museum and Science Center, home of dinosaurs, complete the resident family and visitor entertainment venue of a revived Brisbane.

As an organic response to city investment in its future, moving into the center city is once again attractive to residents. Once sought after, then shabby, buildings in Fortitude Valley are prime real estate. Brisbane residents take the ferry across the river, from wharf to beach, and from office buildings to entertainment venues. They enjoy bike paths and open space, against a backdrop of high-rise steel and glass.

Visiting Brisbane Today

Brisbane Cultural District (Queensland Heritage Register)

Today in Fortitude Valley, Chinatown has a pedestrian mall, parallel to Fortitude Valley shops on another pedestrian mall. In center city, Queen Street, along the water, forks at the Customs House, to a smaller street of nineteenth century business buildings, along the Queen Street pedestrian mall. The original Brisbane city grid is a walkable tour of city history. Across the river, in the cultural precinct, is Queensland Maritime Museum, containing ships featured in Brisbane history, including pearling luggers, common along the river, into the early nineteenth century.

At Brisbane, cruise guests disembark for shore excursions to the Lone Pine Koala Sanctuary, or the Brewery Museum. Many visitors will find much to enjoy, in a short walk through town, from the historic core of Morton Bay Penal Colony, to the free-settlers first neighborhoods of Chinatown and Fortitude Valley. Small shops and eateries line the streets of these quaint neighborhoods.

Brisbane is a vibrant living city, that has grown from its past, while preserving memories. The past is as full of Shakespeare's caution of bad, as it is a place for inspiration of the good, that humans can endow on a city. The history of both is preserved in Brisbane streets, buildings and monuments.

NEW ZEALAND

Maori Strong and Resilient

Aotearoa

Prior to 1200, New Zealand was the last uninhabited island of the globe, able to support human settlement. In 1250, Polynesian people made the journey from Hawaii, they called Hawaiki, to the land of the long, low, cloud-covered island, they named Aotearoa. This was New Zealand.

In coming south to New Zealand, people were completing the Great Migration of Polynesian people, from the islands of Malaysia, east and southeast, in which they populated islands of the Pacific, over the period of a millennium. Usually migration was fostered by tribal antagonism, in which a leader felt compelled to seek a life elsewhere. Successful habitation of an island, and population growth, often created a society, in which rights to scarce land became contentious. The migrating Polynesians, reaching New Zealand, were the Maori.

Flotillas of Maori canoes arrived in New Zealand, in several waves, over the space of a few years. Each group had a tribal leader, who established his people in an area not yet claimed. Maori trace their lineage to the canoe, on which their ancestors arrived in New Zealand. Lineage confers status.

As Maori tribes became established in communities on the east and west coast of North Island, or South Island, often competing for resources, and fighting inter-tribal disputes, they held in common certain Maori traits. In common, were the ability of Maori to traverse the sea in canoes, expertly navigating by following stars, ocean currents, and birds; develop communities under a chief, who kept order in ways of Maori tradition; regard territorial rights, including rights to fish and hunt; and evolving forms of cultural expression, in the new landscape. For five hundred years, until arrival of Europeans, the Maori derived their strength and resilience from cultural tradition.

This history of New Zealand begins, with arrival of Maori, to the time of European contact, a period between 1250 and 1750. Once European disease, religion, weapons and domination of land impacted the order of Maori life, the Maori adapted to survive, in their changed world. That Maori tradition is a vibrant part of New Zealand culture today, is a tribute to Maori resilience.[58]

Maori Society

As each group of canoes arrived in New Zealand, boundaries of tribal territorial areas were established. Within the boundaries of tribes, or *iwi*, families, as sub-groups of a tribe, had their *hapu*, or home turf. Several hapu might join to build a *paa*, that is a fortified area, easily seen on ridge-tops, surrounded by a palisade fence of poles.

A paa might be found uninhabited, while residents went to hunt, or fish, on a seasonal basis. A tribe defeated in an intertribal war, could be chased from their paa, to return, when tensions cooled. When Europeans arrived in New Zealand, and assumed that Maori had no designated land rights among their own societal order, they were mistaken. Occupation of land established ownership among Maori. Seasonal use, was not abandonment of land.

---

[58] An enlightening source on culture and meaning in Maori society is: Anne Salmond, Two Worlds, University of Hawaii Press, Honolulu, 1991.

SHERRY HUTT | 179

Tauranga

Maori Paa (New Zealand Archives)

The first canoe group was led by Kupe, and his companion Ngahue. It was Ngahue, who called the land Aotearoa, when it appeared to her as, Land of a Long White Cloud. On their canoe, were food sources of sweet potato plants and rats. Once on land, the people discovered shell fish, berries and flightless birds of New Zealand; the giant moa and tiny kiwi. Large moa were soon hunted to extinction. Nocturnal kiwi were elusive.[59]

More canoes arrived in close succession. Chiefs Tainui, Te Arawa and Aotearoa landed on the northwest coast of North Island. Fortunate were tribes, that went east, overland to Tauranga, where they found ideal fishing bays and prime land for crops. Chiefs of the three canoes soon disputed turf and mana, that is, primacy of leadership. Although they had ancestors in common, competition for land started with the first arrivals. Some canoes brought tribes, who were enemies in Hawaiki. Those rivalries continued in New Zealand.

A chief was a man, or woman, who possessed *mana*, the internal strength to lead, granted by the gods. Mana was lost, when a chief's authority was compromised. Insult to a chief, or the tribe, required a response. Usually that response was a war party, that killed one, or a few, of the offending tribe, and ate their captives. Cannibalism was the means to denigrate a foe, by reducing them to mundane food. The victor exalted their mana, by making their enemy insignificant. Bones of an enemy were made into fishhooks, adornments, or culinary items.

Maori society operated under commonly known rules. Chiefs determined *tapu*, that is, enforcement of sacred laws. For instance, it was tapu to fish in a place, where a warrior drowned. Fish are prone to nibble on bodies. Eating the fish from those waters, was tantamount to eating the dead hero. European arrivals, unknowing of this tapu, fished in waters, to their peril.

Maori Cosmology in Poetry and Song[60]

Maori had no written record, prior to English. They preserved their creation story and history orally, in stories taught to the young. Feelings, loves, tributes to heroes and trials of life were expressed by men and women in poems, sung to audiences and repeated as popular expressions.

---

[59] Plural of Moa is Moa. Plural of Kiwi is Kiwi.
[60] See: Anthony Alpers, Maori Myth and Tribal Legends, Longman Paul Ltd, Auckland, 1964; Margaret Orbell, Waiata: Maori Songs in History, A Raupo Book, New Zealand, 1991.

Maori Carving

Left: Maori God (Auckland Museum) Middle and Right: Maui

Maori creation stories came with them from Hawaiki. Father Sky and Mother Earth came from darkness. Their son Tane, god of forests and birds, separated his parents, to allow light to shine through. Another of the children, Tawhiri was troublesome. He was the god of wind and storms from the sky, that thrashed the earth. Tawhiri caused the seas of his brother Tangaroa, to have waves. The god of cultivated food was Ronga. The god of raw food and reptiles was Haumia. From red clay, Tane created woman and named her Hine.

Tu was the war god. He could not render the children of Tawhiri, that is, the wind and storms, into food. Man could not control, that which was not food. Tu could eat the fish in the sea; children of Tangaroa. Children of Tane; man, birds and plants, could be rendered as food by Tu.

Another of the god siblings was Maui. He was a man, who was the youngest sibling. Maui lacked fear, becoming a great warrior. Maui fished up the land.

Once there was only Hawaiki. Then, new lands appeared. Maui created New Zealand, when he fished up North Island from the sea, with the fishhook of South Island.[61] Maui tricked his siblings into putting fire in the trees, where any mortal man could have fire, to use on the land.

Unfortunately for Maui, his father blessed him with an incomplete prayer, rendering Maui a mortal man. Wishing to be immortal, Maui came up with a plan to re-enter his mother, and exit her mouth. He turned himself into a caterpillar. His mother felt the irritation of the caterpillar and dispatched it, not realizing she caused the death of her youngest child.

The gods gave greenstone to the Maori. Carving stone into fishhooks, brought luck in catching fish. Greenstone was carved into adornment, particularly an earring, or pendent. Pendants in the likeness of a god, or the children of a god, are lucky talismans.

Hinepare of Maori Ngati Tribe Wearing Greenstone
(Alexander Turnbull Library)

---

[61] North Island has the shape of a fish. The north of South Island has a hook-shaped barrier bay.

Maori believe that upon death, the soul leaves the body. Cape Reinga, at the northernmost tip of New Zealand, was the optimum point for the spirit to leap from the body. After the death of a chief, his, or her, goods were rendered utilitarian, by using them to prepare, or serve food. Once made common, the goods could be distributed, rather than burned as sacred property of a chief.

People came together at funerary ceremonies, to sing the spirit out of the body and send it on its journey to the sky. Songs of mourning were composed in tribute to the dead, and to unite the living. Referenced in song, were ties of the deceased to their lineage and history, thus also reaffirming the history of the tribe.

Not all Maori songs are sad. Women poets were adept at expressing maltreatment of their husband, loss of respect by being made a second wife, or casting off unwanted lovers, and sending messages of desire to men, to whom they were attracted. A popular poem, often re-sung across the islands, told of a woman at her lookout place, next to a waterfall, from where she could see the men she wished to attract, where they were living and working. *Here I am*, she sang, *in this lovely, seductive place, waiting to be found.*

Often poets were women. In one popular song, the story of a young woman, who desired a man from another tribe, unacceptable to her parents, was told as a warning to parents, who interfered in matters of love. She sang, *am I food to be kept?* Another woman sang out a song of love to her daughter, who married a man from a tribe farthest away on North Island. The comforting song was repeated across the island, until it reached the lonely, young bride.

Arrival of Maori people in New Zealand, came at the end of the Great Migration of Polynesian peoples. When the English settlers came, crowding the Maori, and pushing them out of prime fishing and cultivation areas, there were no new lands waiting to be discovered, which could receive traveling canoes. The Maori sang, *we will become like the moa, extinct.*

Artfully Maori

*Wahanui Reihana Te Huatare Carrying a Mere by
Gottfried Lindauer 1839-1926*

Artists traveled with early explorers, to document the landscape, prior to photography. Preserved are drawings of Maori, wearing feather cloaks, greenstone ear pendants and extensive body and facial tattoos. Weaving mats of grasses, intricately laced, with thousands of feathers, was a skill and style of a chief's mantle, brought with the Maori from Hawaiki. Greenstone was a new find in New Zealand. The stone was a gift sent by the gods.

Surviving feathered capes can be seen in museums. The birds that gave their feathers are, in some cases, gone from the landscape. Greenstone is found in abundance, and continues to be carved today, by expert Maori craftspeople. Originally, Maori used greenstone for fishhooks, and to make wood-carving tools. Metal later replaced stone for carving wood. Greenstone became precious.

Greenstone is most often seen in pendants, in large, rounded figures, hung from a leather cord, for wearing around the neck, or carved into long, slender designs, to be hung from a pierced ear. The figures are usually of a god, worn as a talisman of good mana. Popular styles were repeated across the islands and can be seen today in contemporary work. Although basic concepts derived from Hawaiki, the designs as evolved, are uniquely New Zealand Maori artful expression.[62]

Maori Marae

---

[62] Maori art is so integral to New Zealand identity, that protecting art and traditional designs of Maori has been problematic, as seen in the 2002 New Zealand trademark protection act. Maori fern symbols are seen in the New Zealand flag and jerseys of the All Blacks, New Zealand rugby club. The buyer should beware, when purchasing greenstone, or other items made by Maori, that in fact, the artist is Maori.

Carving and decoration extended from personal wear, to tribal meeting places. *Marae*, tribal meeting houses, show the ability of tribal artists to bring living nature to the wood beams and standing poles, planted in tribute to leaders. Long, curving shapes of the fiddle-leaf fern, growing all through the islands, is a frequent design. Every exposed inch of the wood support beams is usually carved, extending interior designs to the exterior. Today, restored marae replicate historic designs, while original beams are preserved in museums. The New Zealand fern design is ubiquitous in flags and in field jerseys of the All Blacks, New Zealand rugby team.

Tattoo, the art of impressing dye under the skin, did not originate with Maori. They have raised their designs to an art form, now seen around the world, impressed into visitors to New Zealand, with souvenir tattoos. Maori tattoo, as an enduring vision of culture, is another testament to Maori cultural resilience. Tattoo designs replicate carvings in marae, representations of gifts from gods.

Maori by Sidney Parkinson artist with Captain James Cook in 1770s

(NZ gov archive)

Some Maori tattoos are known as *moko*. First recorded by Europeans, moko are spiraling lines around the eyes, across the forehead, or across the nose and cheeks. No two designs are identical. Most popular were swirling design of ferns, which grew throughout the islands. A man was made handsome with his tattoos, and was known by them. Popular also, with north island tribes, was a spiral on each buttock, with lines flowing down the thighs. In a *haka*, the power stance, tattoos added to visions of power and strength. A chief displayed elite mana by his tattoo.

Early English and French explorers recorded tattoo on Maori, whom they encountered. The older the man, the more tattoos on his face and body, as if additional moko was added each year. Women also bore tattoos, often blackening their lips. Tattoos on young men were observed to be less numerous, and of less depth. Tattoo is a painful process. Tolerance to pain built with age.

The first recorded tattoos of warriors, seen by Europeans, suggest that some tribes had similar designs. In some instances, groups of warriors had only blackened lips and no body art. Some tribes had tattoo designs, that fully covered their buttocks with spirals. Other tribes reserved designs for their face. Further south in New Zealand, people had neck tattoos, and body, or forehead tattoos, of long lines.

Maori men and women mixed red ochre powder, with oil, and painted their face and body. In *hongi*, rubbing noses in greeting, Englishmen found themselves sporting tell-tale signs in red.

War and Dispute Resolution

Maori were not anxious to kill. Cannibalism was not a means to obtain food. Rather, it was the ultimate insult to reduce an enemy to the utilitarian level of food. Maori preferred a haka, that is, a dance performed by warriors, to display strength and to issue threats. Haka was a way of communicating that those approaching, who appeared threatening, should be made afraid.

In a haka, warriors display their strong, healthy bodies, roll their eyes upward menacingly and extend long tongues, then shout the ultimate insult: *bother us and we will make you food.* If the infringing group is impressed with the show, they will leave without losing mana. If the group advances, the next step is a display of arms.

Actors Demonstrate Haka

The short wooden club is a *wahaika*. The long club is a *taiaha*. Spears were also made of wood. Maori would twirl and toss weapons in a haka, as a display of skill, capable of deadly force.

If a chief determined that an insult required vengeance, a war party would seek out offenders, or members of the offender's tribe. A simple insult, like a death between two warriors of different tribes, might require a death of a tribal member. This was *utu*, the principle of equal return. The greater the insult, the more avenging deaths were required. Vanquished prisoners were eaten. Once vengeance was achieved, the war party returned home. Utu might require reciprocal vengeance, and so on.[63]

As tribes flourished in New Zealand, and tribal populations grew, jealously over prime land, or fishing areas, resulted in inter-tribal warfare. One such instance occurred, on the east coast of the North Island, in the area of Tauranga, home of the Arawa. Arawa people had ideal fishing waters and land for cultivation of crops. Their prized canoe was secured in a protective structure, whenever they left the village to go hunting. Once, Tainui people from the west of the north island, long jealous of Arawa land, came to the Arawa village and burned the canoe. Though the chiefs in Hawaiki instructed the Arawa to begin with peace in the new land, they could not excuse the Tainui act, without being thought of as weak, so they waged war on the Tainui.

Dutchman Abel Tasman sailed quickly by New Zealand in 1642. In the two decades after 1750, European explorers began arriving in New Zealand and interacting with the locals. Their stay was short. They were there to evaluate existence of resources to exploit. Prior to the arrival of English Captain James Cook, who mapped the islands from 1769 to 1770, Spanish and Portuguese explorers made brief stops. About the same time as Cook was in the area, French ships sent sailors on shore to obtain fresh water. The French enjoyed contact with Maori ladies.

The Maori referred to Europeans as *paakeha*. Paakeha brought trade goods. They also brought death, in the form of disease. The Maori thought the paakeha had strange mana, as they had the magic ability to put words on

---

[63] To some extent, in becoming Christian, Maori were pleased to pass the responsibility for utu to the vengeful god of Europeans. They were thus relieved of mortality in traditional utu, without losing mana.

paper. Paakeha also had the ability to make a loud noise and kill a man from a distance. Introduction of guns, robbed chiefs of mana. The new world of the Maori after Captain Cook, is the story of New Zealand History, Part III and the Treaty of Waitangi.

Tauranga Beach & Marina Today

Maori culture did not dissipate, even after years of education in English schools. Maori nationalism, in the 1840s, ended in a bloody war, where British troops interceded. The war is the story of New Zealand History, Part IV - Wairu, from War to New, New Zealand. Maori culture was never defeated by European action. Maori culturalism replaced nationalism, which endures today.

Today, Maori children have the option of attending Maori schools, where Maori language is taught. Even in English schools, all children learn of their joint past. Maori still meet in marae, to sing and dance the old poems, keeping the beauty and meaning of the past alive. In 1888, an all Maori rugby team toured England, winning most of their games. Perhaps it was the haka performed prior to each match, to intimidate the foe, which helped to win the games.

Landing in New Zealand

Travels with Captain Cook in New Zealand

In the sixteenth and early seventeenth centuries, when the New World was a familiar land mass, although not fully mapped, there still existed unknown portions of the Pacific. Routes frequented by merchant ships, of Spanish, Portuguese, Dutch, French and English origin, sought the most direct course across the Pacific, to the Spice Islands of Malaysia. Small islands, not deemed of importance for development of plantations, were noted on maps as sources of fresh water, or ports for safety in a storm.

Among maps of the great unknown, Dutch cartographers indicated a Great Southern Continent. In a pun on the burgeoning Austrian empire of Europe, they called the imaginary continent Terra Australis. Captains of other seafaring monarchies well knew, that the Dutch were infamous for proliferating maps with false information, as a means to keep their intelligence on world travel secret. Still, empty space on the world maps was too vast, not to include land. Seeking the Great Southern Continent, if only to disprove the Dutch maps, became a priority for explorers.

Captains of Spanish and Portuguese ships may have been first to land on Australia, or New Zealand. They were interested in seeking new ports for trade. Finding none, their curiosity did not extend to mapping the extent of land. Another reason for a dearth of records indicating Spanish or Portuguese landings, was the possibility that, sailors did not survive contact with the natives.

Dutch captain Abel Tasman sailed along the south of Australia in 1642. He mapped the island province named for him, Tasmania.[64] Next, Tasman sailed

---

[64] Tasman named the island Van Dieman's Land in honor of his homeland governor. The island was renamed Tasmania, in the nineteenth century, to remove the taint of association with the Transportation Era in Australian settlement history.

east to New Zealand, where hostile reception from natives, chilled his desire to land. He sailed northward and homeward, along the western coast of New Zealand, noting a single island mass on his charts.

In 1769, Captain James Cook was sent from Britain, to determine whether the Dutch reference to Zeeland, was the same land mass as Terra Australis. It was his secret mission, to follow the route of Tasman, map the lands, and resolve the question of the existence of a Great Southern Continent. If such a land mass existed, Cook was ordered to claim it for England. Cook was also to observe the passage of Venus over the sun in the southern ocean, as an aide to navigation.

Instructions given to Cook, on behalf of his king, set the tone for the British relationship with New Zealanders from their first interaction. Cook was to make friends with the islanders. His ship included botanists and artists, with few soldiers. His task was to make complete maps, and bring home information on people, the landscape, and resources. Locating sites for forts, from which Britain could mount a military conquest, was not part of Cook's mission.

James Cook mapped the circumference of the north and south islands of New Zealand. He discovered that the island was two land masses, separated by the strait, now named for him. At each landing, he made attempts to engage the locals on a friendly basis. The impact of Cook's sailors on the locals, the vast information brought to England about the islands, and his contribution to completing the picture of the known world, are legendary. At each place in New Zealand where Cook landed, there is a monument, a land feature named for him, or some other recognition of his travels. The story of Cook's travels in New Zealand, is integral to the history of the country.

James Cook: The Man, His Times and His Travels

James Cook was born in Yorkshire England, in 1728, to a family of modest means. As a child, scrounging for food to survive, he showed promise as a student. A family friend paid his school fees, enabling him to complete school. At seventeen, Cook was a shop assistant, who slept under the counter, as his only lodging.⁶⁵ Such a beginning, was hardly predictive of the career of the man, who captained three extensive sea voyages for the Royal Navy, from the Antarctic, to the Arctic; mapped Hawaii, and several Pacific Islands, including New Zealand; and searched for the elusive Northwest Passage and Great Southern Continent.⁶⁶

*Official Portrait Captain James Cook by Nathanial Holland
in National Maritime Museum UK*

---

⁶⁵ See generally, Frank McLyn, Captain Cook, Yale University Press, New Haven, 2011.
⁶⁶ Cook's instincts were excellent. He determined that there was a southern continent, covered with ice. As to the Northwest Passage, over the top of Alaska and Canada to the Atlantic, he determined that it could not be done. The first such passage, in the twenty-first century, has not become a regular event.

Tall, handsome and reserved, Cook had the appearance of an English gentlemen. His lack of social status, in eighteenth century England, where status trumped ability in career advancement, meant that Cook accepted assignments, at lesser pay and position, then gentlemen of his age and experience. He confounded his supporters, when at age twenty-eight, having worked his way up the ladder to master of a merchant ship, he turned away from financial success, to join the Royal Navy. In the navy, Cook began as an able seaman, returning to below officer status.

In eighteenth century Britain, a sailor joined the Royal Navy, to either distinguish themselves in battle, or in discovery of new lands and routes, to enable foreign trade. James Cook had the opportunity to do both. His skill as a master's mate, earned quick promotion to master of a ship, although no exception was made for his advancement to captain of a battle ship, until he served six years in lesser status. As master of a 64-gun ship, Cook sailed from Portsmouth, to serve with valor in victories over the French.

Had he never gone to the South Pacific, Cook would have been known for his excellent maps of Canada and Newfoundland. His meticulous work was relied upon for centuries. The maps enabled Britain to expand fishing ventures. Appreciated during his tenure with the Royal Navy, the accomplishment was insufficient to earn a knighthood for commoner Cook.

Cook was fortunate, that within his era at sea, Britain enjoyed times of peace, where exploration for the purpose of advantaging trade, took precedence over military use of the Royal Navy. British Captain Samuel Wallis discovered Tahiti in 1768, with the French following close behind. Britain lost the advantage of a presence in the south Atlantic, where Spain established a colony in the Falklands, off the coast of Argentina, and in California, on the west coast of British north America.[67] If there was a Great Southern Continent, Britain did not wish to arrive second to any power.

The eighteenth century, was an age of the appreciation of science. Discovery of new lands was accompanied by a curiosity about the people, animals and flora of distant places, for more than commercial interest. Wealthy men in England

---

[67] See Cruise through History, Itinerary IX Ports of South America- Falklands, for the story of a Little Bit of Britain in South America.

collected libraries, with cabinets of curiosities.[68] James Cook was given the position of captain of the HMS *Endeavor*, to seek out the existence of new lands, chart Zeeland island, placed on Dutch maps by Tasman, and observe the transit of Venus as an aid to navigation. His was a mission to advance knowledge, not military advantage.

In 1768, when he was forty years old, Cook was vindicated in his choice to leave the merchant marine for the Royal Navy. As captain of HMS *Endeavor*, Cook was assigned to resolve the most pressing and vexing issues facing his country, in the South Pacific. The square-rigged *Endeavor* was outfitted for a science expedition at sea. The 369-ton ship was 106 feet (30 meters) long and 32 feet (9 meters) wide. The ship was just a little longer, although heavier and deeper in draft, than the Maori canoes the ship would soon encounter.

The HMS *Endeavor* had six large and twelve small cannons on board, for defensive purposes. Cook made it clear to his crew, and those they encountered, that fire-power was for demonstrative purposes. Of the one hundred and six men on board, fifty-five were sailors, twelve were marines, and the remainder were officers and gentlemen scientists. There were no women on the ship.

Sir Joseph Banks, a wealthy landowner, served as a naturalist on Cook's first journey to the South Pacific.[69] Joining Banks was Danial Carlsson Solander, a Swedish naturalist.[70] Their task was to *botanize* the bays, where the HMS *Endeavor* dropped anchor, to collect and record the local flora and fauna, as well as geology of the terrain. Their records, and Cook's log, became the beginning of a natural history of New Zealand, relied upon by all subsequent

---

[68] Twenty-first century, post-colonial race theorists paint Cook as a racist for the impact of his journeys on the civilizations he encountered. Academic fashion aside, there is nothing in the factual data to paint Cook as other than respectful of the cultures he encountered. Dutch, French, Spanish and Portuguese explorers landed on these islands and all had an impact, positive and negative, on cultures otherwise existing in isolation.

[69] Sir Joseph Banks was born in 1743, and lived to 1820. Danial Carlsson Solander was born in 1733, and died in 1782.

[70] Cook's naturalists corresponded with Swedish botanist Carl Linnaeus, who was categorizing all plants and animals into a scientific hierarchy of species. Solander went to the British Museum to catalogue the Linnaeus collection. He joined Banks as members of the Royal Society, in London.

scientists. Years later, Banks became president of The Royal Society, which was established in London in 1662, to foster science and discovery. On the HMS *Endeavor*, Banks boarded with two servants, who did not survive cold temperatures of the Antarctic. Cook frowned on having servants.

Of note, among the travelers on the *Endeavor* was Sydney Parkinson, an artist.[71] He became the first artist to travel the South Pacific. His thousand drawings of the landscape, the Maori people, and the abundant flora and fauna, so new and strange to Europeans, are prominently featured illustrations in the literature on New Zealand, rendering an immense contribution to the voyage.

Cook married Elizabeth Batts, in Essex, in 1762. When he boarded the *Endeavor*, Cook left her behind, with two small children. Publication of his maps of Canada, and his captain's pay, were barely enough to sustain the family, during his absence. Upon return, Cook learned that his children succumbed to disease. Over the marriage, the couple had six children, three of whom survived.

Journey Around New Zealand[72]

Natives preserved memories of meeting Captain Cook in poems, describing the first landing of the HMS *Endeavor* in New Zealand, at Whitianga, known today as Mercury Bay, near Auckland. The Maori thought the sailors were goblins, with eyes in the back of their heads, as they watched the English sailors rowing their long oars, facing backward in their longboats.[73] They turned out to be nice goblins, who laughed and greeted them in a friendly way.

On October 8, 1769, Captain Cook made his first landing on New Zealand, near the same spot where one of the first Maori canoes, Horouta, came ashore. The Maori responded to sighting strange beings with a traditional haka, a

---

[71] Sydney Parkinson was born in Scotland in 1745, and died on the return journey of dysentery, in 1771.
[72] See generally: Graeme Lay, Captain James Cook's New Zealand, New Holland Pub., Auckland, 2017.
[73] Anne Salmond, Two Worlds, University of Hawaii Press, Honolulu, 1991, at 87.

threatening dance. The English were unmoved. A Maori warrior threw a spear, a tradition unknown to the English, so a soldier shot the man.

HMS Endeavour replica in Cooktown Harbour (Wikimedia Commons)

The first encounter with Maori, resulted in six Maori being shot, in a display of power, which the Maori interpreted as magic. To make amends, Cook generously bestowed gifts. He did not condone thievery, which occurred when Maori helped themselves to supplies, tools, or weapons, left unattended by the crew. Tension ended, with Cook walking through the surf to press noses with the Maori leader. Word spread through the island, that these were peaceful gods.

The *Endeavor* did not remain long, in the bay of the first landing. Cook named the place Poverty Bay, as it afforded him no fresh water, or other provisions. Obviously, Cook was unaware of the importance of the landing, as an event in the history of England, the islands, and the future of a new country.

Proceeding south along the coast, Cook named the bay, Hawke's Bay in honor of Sir Edward Hawke, first Lord of the Admiralty. Boats were sent out with trade goods of Tahitian bark cloth, to trade for fish, brought in canoes by Maori. In one exchange, Maori tried to kidnap a Tahitian guide traveling with Cook. The Maori thought him a prisoner, who might be eaten by Cook's men. The guide jumped from the canoe and swam back to the ship. Cook named the headlands, Cape Kidnappers, as a reflection on the incident.

In the distance Cook's Cape Kidnappers, foreground, a park in Napier

Turning north, HMS *Endeavor* was met by a large welcoming party in Tolaga Bay. Unknown to Cook, he made another landing, in an area sacred to Maori, further proof to the locals, that *Endeavor* was the transport of gods. It was at East Cape, that the Maori god, Maui, pulled the land from the sea, forming the islands.

As Cook continued to sail immediately northward, along the coast, he noted the abundant fields and larger population, than he observed in Poverty Bay. Cook named the area, Bay of Plenty. This was the Maori settlement of Tauranga, sitting in the shadow of a volcanic mountain.

In the first days of November, Cook sailed into the south end of a deep bay. At the bottom of the bay, was a river. Cook named it Thames River. Around the *Endeavor* war canoes swarmed, filled with elaborately dressed men with weapons. Cook sailed into the midst of a major war, that was brewing between descendants of the two founding canoes; Aotearoa and Tainui. No one on *Endeavor* was in danger, so Parkinson took the opportunity to make numerus drawings of everything around him.

One of the chiefs invited Cook and Banks into a paa, that is a palisade surrounded village, in this instance, the Hauraki paa, one of the most historically significant to Maori. Cook's host gained mana, preeminence demonstrated to his people on the eve of battle, by welcoming men of the strange canoe, into the place where battle for control of this spot occurred, between original arrivals of the first canoes. The Maori chief was aware of history, and of the history he was making on that date. Neither he, nor Cook, could know the future significance of their meeting.

On November 8, 1769, Cook's astronomer, Charles Green, marked the transit of Mercury across the sun. Cook named the bay, where they anchored, Mercury Bay, in honor of the event. The jubilant crew, anchored at the island of Waiheke, then sailed north to the Bay of Islands, missing the opportunity to sail beyond the island, further into the bay, to land at the site of Auckland.

HMS *Endeavor* sailed through the Bay of Islands, where Cook made notes of the villages on hills, with protective palisades. His botanists collected plants, while artists drew pictures of Maori and their tattoos. While the ship anchored near Waitangi, at North Cape, the crew celebrated Christmas 1769.

Cook Monument Cook Strait (NZ archive)

By January 1770, Cook progressed down the west coast of north island, and entered Cook Strait. He named the area Queen Charlotte Sound. To him, it was the most beautiful scenery of the islands. HMS *Endeavor* anchored in Ship Cove five times, as Cook traversed the strait, and charted channels leading to what is today, Picton on the South Island, and Wellington on north island.

Cook mapped the east side of South Island, and then sailed around to the west coast, despite violent storms. This was his opportunity to determine, whether he was sailing around the Great Southern Continent. Satisfied that this was not the unknown continent he sought, Cook finished mapping New Zealand, stopping for water, and to allow botanists to collect four hundred plants.

Maori at Dusky Sound by William Hodges 1770s

In a little more than six months, Captain James Cook charted 2,400 miles of coastline. He was ready to sail west to New Holland, now known as Australia. Cook anchored in Botany Bay, naming the area New South Wales. He returned to New Zealand in 1773, after a brutal sail in the Antarctic, while still seeking the Great Southern Continent. On this second voyage of discovery, Cook did not linger in New Zealand. It was his mission to seek the unfamiliar. He recorded sounds of the south coast, although he feared, that if he spent too much time sailing in, there would be insufficient wind to sail out, and on to his next adventure.

Remembrance and Legacy

Cook Monument Giborne 1906 (NZ archive)

In Cook's meticulous notes, were recorded the population of natives at each landing, description of the terrain, accompanied by Parkinson drawings, suitability of the land for crops, and the local political organization, to the extent he could determine the ruling chief, and the domain of their tribe. Almost a century later, Cook's notes were utilized to determine Maori rights to land. It was an application of the knowledge he collected, which he could not have foreseen.

After 1771, HMS *Endeavor* was put to use as a supply ship to the Falklands; the little bit of Britain in the south Atlantic. It ended up in the Newport harbor, in the United States, where it was exhumed in 2016. A replica HMS *Endeavor* was assembled, to sail Cook's historic route.

Today, the area of Cook's historic first landfall in Turanga, is sparsely developed at Poverty Bay. The area looks much as it did in 1769, with a lovely beach at Te Oneroa, in proximity to vineyards of white wine grapes.[74] Much of the area is preserved as Maori territory. In 1906, an obelisk was erected, to commemorate the landing, in what is now a national historic site. Cape Kidnappers is a shore excursion from Napier, a favorite of birders.

Not far from Tolaga Bay, where HMS *Endeavor* anchored to reprovision, is Cook's Cave, one of several natural features named to sign-post Cook's circumnavigation. In the 1920s, the wharf in the bay was named for Cook. East Cape was the setting for the 2002 film, *Whale Rider*, about the coming of age of a Maori girl, and a favorite whale of the locals.

The cruise port, in the Bay of Plenty today, is Tauranga. From this port, visitors admire the lush vegetation grown by Maori for centuries, climb Mount Mauganui, an extinct volcano, sacred to the Maori, and swim on the beach. This was the site of an early missionary school, the 1847 Elms Mission Station, where Englishmen attempted to Anglicize Maori children.

Cook anchored off Waiheke Island, in Mercury Bay, missing the opportunity to find fabulous anchorage at the site of Auckland. Today, Waiheke is an area of vineyards, a short ferry ride from Auckland. Still, Auckland remembers Cook, with the central wharf named in his honor.

English settlers, enamored of Cook's description of the Bay of Islands, made their first permanent settlement at Russell. Protestant missionary, Samuel Marsdon, established a school there in 1814, where he translated the Bible into Maori language. Near the historic English settlement, a Maori village has been reconstructed, from Cook's description.

---

[74] Distinguish Turanga at Poverty Bay, population 35,000, from Tauranga at Bay of Plenty, population 135,000.

Cook made fewer stops, while mapping South Island. The fjords of the southwest were lovely, although Cook reasoned, that a ship could become trapped in the sounds for the lack of wind. A mountain peak is named for him in south island.

Cook made two further voyages of discovery in the Pacific. He sailed to Australia, French Polynesia, the anything but Friendly Islands, Tonga, New Hebrides and eventually Hawaii. His third journey ended in Hawaii, ten years after his first landfall in New Zealand. Cook's fatal mistake, like that of Magellan, was to involve himself in tribal politics. The remainder of Cook's contributions to knowledge of the Pacific, is another story.[75]

---

[75] See Cruise through History© Itinerary VII Ports of the West Coast of North America, for more on Cook and his travels in the North Pacific.

Treat of Waitangi (original in National Library Wellington - exhibit Te Papa Museum)

Waitangi: A Treaty in Translation

Treaties typically resolve the end of a war. In the British experience in New Zealand, the treaty began the course of events, which resulted in war. The clash was inevitable.

From the sixteenth century forward, British explorers claimed lands on behalf of the mother country, which were brought into commercial control, as British colonies. By the mid-nineteenth century, Britain had its fill of rebellious colonies, and the legacy of colonization on conquered native people. Queen Victoria sought to learn from the past, to establish a relationship with the Maori people of New Zealand, in a spirit of respect. She wished not to repeat the conquest-domination/colonization-rebellion-rift of relationships pattern, seen elsewhere in the Empire.

The Queen was pleased to extend local self-rule and residency on homelands to Maori tribes. She drew the line at a dual monarchy of the British crown and a Maori monarch. Allegiance to the English crown was mandatory, not negotiable. Maori chiefs appreciated the wealth brought to tribes by trade with the British. Maori residency and control of homelands was mandatory, and not negotiable. British and Maori leaders entered into the 1840 Treaty of Waitangi with relief.

In fairness to leaders of both worlds, British and the Maori, meaning given to words is subject to cultural interpretation. The two cultures had no understanding of the contextual meaning each would give, to the desires of the other. Translation was absent from the treaty.

This story of the Treaty of Waitangi covers the history of New Zealand, from the impact and consequence of travels of Captain James Cook, in 1770, to the immediate post treaty period, up to 1850. In eighty years, from Cook's arrival to the prelude to war, between Maori and English settlers, the landscape went from exclusive Maori homeland haven, to the increasing population of English settlers, seeking to build dream homes. Competing interests were irreconcilable. The history of escalation of the conflict, into a war, is reserved for the next story.

The Treaty of Waitangi is still a living document, the meaning of which has been examined repeatedly. An English-Maori translation has been critical to its success. The Treaty evolved from ambiguous, to contentious, to a map to the future, of a multi-cultural New Zealand.

After Travels of Captain Cook in New Zealand

The immediate impact on the Maori, as a result of visits by Captain Cook and other explorers, who preceded, or closely followed him, was to introduce possibilities of trade, the power of strange magic, which could kill with exploding powder, and the stealth magic of disease. Death of key tribal members and many women, including intended wives of future chiefs, began the erosion of tribal social structure. Prospect of trade with paakeha, the Europeans, brought out entrepreneurial spirit in tribal members, who sought their own mana, not directed through a chief. Concepts of wealth in more than land, were introduced to Maori culture.

Profound and lasting alteration of Maori life began, when paakeha arrived to stay. First came the missionaries, with Christianity and schools, where Maori children were required to become literate in English. Then, English settlers arrived directly from England, or from Australia, seeking free access to land, or purchase of vast acreage, for a few trade goods. To English settlers, the Maori were an inconvenience.

Next came British soldiers, sent to keep peace between settlers and Maori, which in large part meant protecting Maori from random killing by settlers. Settlers and soldiers were followed by British government officials. Each addition of Europeans, bound the Maori into increasingly smaller spaces on the landscape, to accommodate the needs of newcomers.

To the Maori, the ability of missionaries to put words on paper, was visual magic. Those Maori, who became early masters of English language, had a competitive edge in business dealings with the British. Their tribes soon became wealthy, as purveyors of goods in trade, masters of mills, and suppliers of goods to British ships and settlers.

Economic superiority of one tribe over another destabilized the system of war and vengeance, while it increased jealousies and competition. Individual tribal members, lent funds by banks to build mills, surpassed chiefs in importance. Chiefs lost control of moral balance in society.

Of greater impact to the Maori tribal social structure, was the trade of guns for field crops and fish. Once some tribes had guns, when others did not, guns replaced clubs and spears as weapons. Performance of a threatening haka, to scare opposing warriors, where no warriors died as a result, was replaced by warrior assaults armed with muskets. Violent death numbers rose. Those tribes with English guns, quickly assumed land and crops of tribes, that did not possess muskets.

An effect of missionaries, converting Maori to Christianity, was cessation of cannibalism. Cannibalism ceased, not as a moral wrong, as missionaries may have thought. The purpose for cannibalism, of reducing an enemy to mere food, became unnecessary, when the Christian god was available to punish sinners for wrongdoing.

In the Maori system of justice, utu, that is vengeance for a wrong, was the island equivalent of an eye-for-an-eye. In the Christian cosmology of a vengeful god, punishing wrongdoers, even in the afterlife, Maori were given an outlet to transfer their vengeance system to the English god. They could pray for their enemies to lose mana, and to have mana bestowed on them for good acts. Maori people did not convert to Christianity. Rather, they fit Christianity into their cosmos.

Before British officials came to a decision, on how to fashion a political approach to New Zealand, whalers, missionaries and bankers had already effected a change on the landscape. Land ownership, central to Maori tribal standing, became tenuous and complex. To Maori, occupancy determined ownership. A seasonal absence from the village to hunt, or fish, was not abandonment of ownership rights. A vanquished enemy could be forced from their land, or battle for return of land. All Maori understood the rules.

Increasing numbers of English settlers seeking land, put greater pressure on tribal leaders to sell land. At first, when a tribe saw paakeha pitch their tents in an area, the tribe packed up their homes, picked their crops, and moved. When the number of new settlers overwhelmed tribes, particularly in prime farm areas, displaced Maori resisted further assumption of land.

Some Maori were initially pleased to exchange use of land for guns, with which to rout their long-time enemies. Too late, they realized rules of land ownership were changing. Paakeha did not want to merely use the land. They sought permanent, private ownership, to exclusion of Maori.

Destabilization of tribal structure, left tribes with disparate authority. Individual tribal members engaged in land deals with settlers, for that which previously was group-owned land. Land purchases were not subject to survey, so what the seller sold, may have been assumed to be a smaller area, than the purchaser assumed to own. Assumptions became a source of contention.

Presentation of the Treaty of Waitangi

Presentation of Treaty of Waitangi 1856 (Alexander Turnbull Library Wellington NZ)

Three factors caused the British to establish a government presence in New Zealand. The initial concern was indiscriminate killing of Maori by English settlers. Deployment of British soldiers to contain violence, pit English soldiers against English settlers. Settlers wanted land. Violence would not end, until a scheme for distribution of land was resolved. Recognizing the need for organization in the midst of chaos, Britain established the beginning of a colonial office.

The third factor was the French. French explorers had contact with Maori, at the same time as Cook. Chiefs of north island requested English king George IV to protect them from the French, who were making plans for a settlement, to anchor a French colony.[76] Although Britain was not intending to claim a colony, protection of English superiority in trade, or whatever else might develop in the new land, meant preempting the French. Administering British interests from the crown office in New South Wales, Australia, was insufficient to resolve matters in New Zealand.

In 1833, James Busby was dispatched, as a representative of the governor in New South Wales, to Waitangi, in the north Bay of Islands. His task was to stand in the midst of unruly, land-hungry settlers, to ask that they desist from violence. Busby had no authority, no soldiers, and no administrative infrastructure, from which to create an orderly existence.

The interests of New South Wales in New Zealand were economic. Trade across the water was hindered by lack of leadership consistency. An arrangement to deliver, or receive, goods at a dock in the Bay of Islands, would dissolve mid-sailing, when inter-tribal wars displaced a chief. Only a British presence, could protect trading rights of supply ships, under a British flag, when there existed no reliable local authority. The British concept of a single monarch, did not translate in New Zealand reality. Newcomers could not grasp, that homogeneous Maori culture, was not a unified political unit. Busby's contribution to New Zealand, and to Britain, was his recognition of cultural differences.

---

[76] See, Claudia Orange, The Story of a Treaty, Bridget Williams Books, Wellington, NZ, 2013, at 12.

In 1835, Busby brought together thirty-five chiefs of tribes, leaders of tribes and sub-tribes, of north island, to establish a confederation. The existence of thirty-five, or more, chiefs in just the north island, evidenced the erosion of tribal cohesion, since the arrival of Captain Cook. The ambitious plan for a declaration of independence of New Zealand, a nation of united tribes, was unsustainable from inception. Britain did not support Maori independence. Among the tribes, leadership was fluid. The settler population was rising. Violence against Maori increased.

While Busby was making attempts to quiet north island tensions, pressure from settlers on the south island was building. Settlers claimed land purchases from individual Maori, without regard to tribal-owned land. Size of the purchase was based upon what the settler claimed. Young Maori men were lured onto ships, as hard-working sailors, only to be abandoned in far-away ports, often without payment of promised wages. Maori death from disease, inter-tribal warfare with muskets, and shootings of Maori by bands of settlers, increased devastation of the Maori population.

For three years, from 1837 to 1840, Busby, aided by British naval officer William Hobson, tried to devise a solution for New Zealand. Their effort was complicated by the shifting British position from: a Maori government, protected by Britain; to a British New Zealand, in which Maori would be protected British subjects. Maori people later realized that being "special" was not favorable.

Defining Terms

Busby and Hobson drafted the Treaty of Waitangi, in January 1840. By February 6, 1840, it was law of the land. The signing ceremony was conducted as a great celebration. Chiefs wore their feather capes and greenstone pendants. British food stalls provided rum, obtained from French purveyors. British dignitaries gave gifts of pigs and flour to Maori chiefs. Eventually, Britain and five hundred Maori signatories, from the north and south islands, officially entered into the treaty. One of the Maori chiefs sent a greenstone pendant, as a treaty gift, to Queen Victoria.

Maori Tribal Land & Terms of Treaty – "Fisheries and Forests"

The treaty was written in English and Maori. Hobson did not read Maori, and the Maori did not read English. Few chiefs read the document prior to signing. It was enough to believe, that the treaty would end the killings and preserve their homeland for their people.

The Treaty of Waitangi had two main provisions. First, of great importance to Maori leaders, the chiefs could keep tribal land, fisheries and forests. Second, in the interests of Britain, Britain was acknowledged sovereign of New Zealand, in which Maori were British subjects.

Chiefs met to debate the treaty for hours prior to signing. Some admitted to selling too much land, a practice they wished to halt. Some chiefs hoped the treaty would be a means to seek return of some land, or at least establish boundaries to English land claims. To the chiefs, being English subjects meant British protection from bands of settlers entering Maori villages, killing their people.

As Hobson traveled the islands collecting signatures, not all chiefs agreed to sign the treaty. Some chiefs had remorse for signing, during the thrill of the ceremony. They returned gifts.

The treaty resolved Queen Victoria, as the monarch of New Zealand. Henceforth, all transfers of land were administered by the crown official. The British land office was the only authorized purchase agent for Maori land. The office resold the land, at a higher price, to settlers. The price differential was justified, as necessary to cover costs of land administration, in a place where government income from tax was not established.

The British land office pressed tribes for more land, to satisfy demands of new arrivals. Officials in positions created to protect Maori interests, found that acquiescing to the insatiable demand of settlers for more land, put them in an ethical bind. The authority of British officials, to keep the peace, was contingent upon their ability to obtain land for resale.

The British flag flew over the Bay of Islands and Wellington. Britain had authority over commerce at the docks. British soldiers enforced the peace, and made vain attempts to protect Maori in their tribal settlements, from incursions of angry settlers, pushing for greater quantities of land sales. Britain had the authority to exclude French trade and residency in the islands.

Maori children learned to speak and write English, in English schools. They sang, *God Save the Queen*. Their parents were employed in public works projects. Roads were being built. Banks loaned funds to Maori-owned businesses. Maori farmers and fishermen supplied food to Auckland and Wellington. General prosperity among Maori and settlers fostered peace.

Queen Victoria's desire that Maori be an included, and not a conquered people, appeared realized. Maori wore British clothes, became Christians, participated in British sports, and eventually, served with loyalty and bravery in the British armed services. A country of culturally Maori and socially British people, appeared to be the result of a successful treaty.

The simplicity of the solution was only successful on the surface. Settlers soon pressed for more, than Maori were prepared to give. Maori realized, they had already given up so much more, than they originally thought. Chiefs were embarrassed. They lost their mana.

Grounds of Contention

Treaty Close-up

From its inception, ambiguous terms in the Treaty were powder kegs of future calamity. When chiefs learned, that sovereignty meant they no longer had authority over their people, they realized, that Maori life, as they knew it, had gone the way of the moa, the flightless bird of New Zealand, hunted into extinction. The Queen, who was to protect them from land hungry settlers, was pressing them to sell more land. Their homes, their family life, and their identity were tied to the land. When disputed land sales were resolved, to the settler's favor, Maori were defeated.

The Maori also learned what it meant to be British subjects. Their assumption had been, that as British subjects they would be protected from slaughter. Certainly, all parties to the treaty wanted cessation of killings. Maori realized that being special actually meant, being neophyte British, in a British society, under British rules of law. A New Zealand government was established to administer the law. Maori chiefs were not players in that government. Although individual Maori, and some Maori tribes, controlled businesses, mills, farms and dock-works, which made them wealthy, they lived in a new world.

The critical point of contention, the issue that engendered war, at the culmination of a decade of disputes, was over land ownership and control. Chiefs signed the treaty, with the promise they could keep their land, fisheries, and forests. Every word of that provision was ambiguous. What land, what fishery, what forest was subject to question, and interpretation by British officials.

Chiefs were mistaken, if they assumed that land use permission, which was assumed by settlers to be transfers of ownership, would be unwound and resolved, with ownership reverting to the tribe. Land surveys established boundaries of large territories, based upon settler descriptions of assumed land purchases. Captain Cook's logs, which described empty settlements, and land areas vacated in inter-tribal wars, was used to the disadvantage of tribal land claims.

The 1852 Constitution Act was a bright light on the status of Maori land rights, and what it meant to be special in Britain. The Act gave the vote to males, over the age of twenty-one, who owned land. Communal ownership of Maori tribal land, did not confer enfranchisement. British citizenship did not come with voting rights for Maori in the new, New Zealand government.

Representations were made to Maori chiefs, that land sales to the government, at low prices, would be reciprocated, with new schools and hospitals for Maori people. When facilities did not materialize, Maori chiefs placed a moratorium on land sales to the government. Banks responded, by ceasing loans to Maori entrepreneurial ventures.

Maori nationalism, and a movement leading toward a Maori king, floated around the islands for a few decades, never achieving united Maori support. After the Constitution Act, an armed Maori riot was met, with British troops being deployed, against the Maori. Maori displayed that they were the better warriors, and the British stood down. Maori spirit was awakened. It was time to avenge the loss of mana. The Treaty of Waitangi became prelude to war.

Waitangi Today

Winery Today former Maori Land

In 1877, the Treaty of Waitangi was adjudicated to be an unenforceable nullity, by courts in New Zealand, on the basis that the Treaty had not been ratified by the British Parliament, nor the eventual New Zealand parliament. The court ruling had the effect of nullifying British sovereignty, prior to the constitution, and establishment of the New Zealand parliament. The Native Land Court, established in 1865, filled some of the void, with its determination of land title on an individual basis. Native New Zealanders, and English arrivals, were conflicted on whether the Treaty should be ratified, and what that meant for the status of land claims. After a century of European contact with Maori, semantics of relationships were still unsettled.

In 1940, New Zealand celebrated the centennial of the establishment of the country, based upon the Treaty of Waitangi. Once the treaty was judicially determined of no effect, it placed a chill on festivities. Maori and settler descendants looked to the centennial, as acknowledging their heritage, however disparate their visions remained.

As of 1975, the Treaty of Waitangi was revived, through the Waitangi Tribunal, a body devised to resolve land claims. The Tribunal recognizes land held in freehold by Maori, lands reserved by the crown to the Maori, and *papatupu*, that is, land that was always Maori, with no clouds of claims to title by a European. Although decisions of the Tribunal are advisory, the government has acted on its recommendations, compensating Maori claims to breaches of the Treaty, to the extent of over one billion British pounds in awards.

The Treaty of Waitangi remains a treaty subject to translation. Disputed land claims are resolving, over time, with the benefit of precedent, and a body of factual determinations. Negotiation and compensation result in restored mana, rather than bloodshed. In a country, that has become an English/Maori hybrid, a new mutually-beneficial translation is possible.

Wairu: From War to New, New Zealand

From the beginning of settlement of New Zealand, the issue of contention, that brought men to war, was land. It was always about land. Two of the founding Maori canoes came to blows over right to prime land, near the best beaches from which to fish. When the crush of settlers from England, became too much for Maori to bear, in the face of settler claims of vested rights, Maori and Englishmen went to war, over which people had rights to the land.

In the 1840s, in the aftermath of English foreign war, there was surplus labor seeking employment in the urban centers of England. Uneducated men, with few skills, and no social standing granting introduction to management, sought entrepreneurial opportunities, in the fringes of the British Overseas Empire. Australia carried the stigma of the Transportation Era, of enslaved prisoners, working for politically and economically entrenched military officers, who controlled the New South Wales Company. New Zealand offered open access to land, and a new life.

Land opportunity, so idealized by incoming boatloads of settlers, did not consider prior occupants of the land, as owners of the land. The Governor of New South Wales, whose career was ruined by his handling of the situation in New Zealand, Captain Robert FitzRoy,[77] saw rising tensions, between settlers and Maori, as socially and not racially motivated. Settler anger toward Maori, stemmed from settler perception of Maori unwillingness to part with their land. Maori and English intermarried, and did business with each other. They became aggressive, each to the other, over challenges to control of land.

---

[77] Captain Robert FitzRoy of the HMS *Beagle*, provided the physical and professional vehicle to Charles Darwin in the Galapagos. When Darwin stayed home, to collect accolades for research published by his professors, FitzRoy went to Australia. Read their story in Cruise through History, Itinerary 9, Port of Ushuaia.

Becoming Kiwi

The great question, in mid-nineteenth century New Zealand, was when circumstances would tilt aggressive attitudes, toward physical expression.[78] All informed sources thought, war would explode in Waitara, in the Taranaki region, south of Auckland, on the north island. Surprisingly, the first gunfire occurred in 1843, at Wairu, at the northern end of the south island, near Picton. Flames of war were unintentionally fanned, by a well-meaning Governor Robert FitzRoy, who stepped into the situation, and tried to make a Solomon-like decision, intended to avert war.

Full scale, bloody war, waged in 1860, with a reprisal in 1863. It was only after the futility of the outlet in argument expressed in war, the Maori form of utu, or hostility in return for hostility, had played out, fatiguing its proponents, did land competition flow to the courts and a land commission. The Land Commission, an imperfect response to the need to resolve Maori land rights and settler's claims, evolved into, at its least, a peaceful method to resolve disputes. Although New Zealand national formation is usually dated from the signing of the Treaty of Waitangi in 1840, the inclusive form of nation, that New Zealand became, dates from 1865, the Native Lands Act, and subsequent improvements to the Act, in what became a peaceful Maori-European nation.

---

[78] The best analysis of this chapter in New Zealand history, is found in Keith Sinclair, The Origins of the Maori Wars, Auckland Press, 1957; 1976.

Prelude to War: Wairu Affray 1843

Site of Wairu Affray

The Treaty of Waitangi, of February 6, 1840, intended to avert war, actually established the grounds for disagreement, which erupted into war. By the terms of the Treaty, Queen Victoria established sovereignty in the British crown, which took primary ownership of all land, made available for alienation and resale, by the crown. The unruly land-grab by settlers, was staunched. Instead, settlers pressed the government, to require Maori to make more land available for sale.

By the deceivingly simple terms of the Treaty, Maori chiefs preserved their homeland and fisheries, in tribal ownership. They were surprised to learn, that land sold comprised a greater area, than they thought. Land survey, after-the-fact of sale, worked against Maori interests.

Tension over land rights was building in the Taranaki area, on the west coast of the north island. It came as a surprise to all in New Zealand, when the first armed conflict occurred in the Wairu Valley, in the north of south island, between Nelson and Picton. In the area known as the Marlborough Valley today, the New Zealand Company claimed a vast area, of about 200,000 acres.

Land was purchased by the Company, from individuals, rather than through the government.

The Company offered land in Wairu, for resale to buyers in England. Problems escalated, when the Company was able to sell more land than they bought, and needed sufficient acreage to cover outstanding obligations. The Company claimed to acquire land from the family of an early European whaler, whose ownership rights were questionable.

Trouble began in June 1843, when tribes noticed survey markers on their land. Maori chiefs Te Rauparaha and Te Rangihaeata organized ninety warriors to burn surveyor huts. At the same time, agents of the New Zealand Company organized and armed a private army, of about sixty men, to remove the tribes. Opposing armed warriors met at Wairu.

A settler soldier fired the first shot, killing the wife of Te Rangihaeata, who was the daughter of Te Rauparaha. Maori warriors demanded utu, reprisal, as they pursued the settler army. By the time the firing stopped, four Maori and twenty-two settlers were dead.

Six months later, the new British governor for New South Wales in Australia arrived. This official had administrative authority over New Zealand. Governor FitzRoy traveled to Nelson, to resolve fears of settlers, that Maori were killing innocent British subjects. Maori chiefs termed the incident a massacre. Land sales came to a halt in England. Everyone looked to the governor for an answer.

FitzRoy was a religious and deeply moral man. He parted company with Darwin, over what to him was Darwin's betrayal of the Biblical description of creation. In his first act as governor, FitzRoy stepped into another controversy, in which he again fell on the wrong side of public opinion. He condemned the killing of settlers by Maori, angering Maori chiefs. He also acknowledged, that the New Zealand Company had assumed control of land, that the company did not own, angering the British company. The Company demanded that the crown recall FitzRoy.

British officials agreed with FitzRoy, that the Company overstepped, in surveying land it did not own. They found FitzRoy's decision practical, since Maori had the force to annihilate settlers and push them from the island, had they chosen to do so. Then they made their own Solomon-like decision. In deference to the British Company, FitzRoy was recalled to England.[79]

In the decade following the Treaty of Waitangi, Maori resistance was sporadic. There was no coordinated effort, to stem land sales, or resist settler development of the land. Some Maori looked at the Wairu incident, as a singular event, in the less settled south island. Other Maori considered it a massacre, which could be repeated anywhere. Maori became divided between those who wanted to sell land and move to cities, where they had business opportunities, and those who wanted to cease all land sale, and reverse sales, where purchasers overreached.

Dissension within Maori came to a climax, with the election of a Maori king in 1858. It was the first, undeniable, expression of unified Maori nationalism. A war could be mounted behind a king.

Land War Part I: 1860 Taranaki

In a government census of Maori in New Zealand, as of 1858, there were less than fifty-six thousand counted. The population of Maori was greatly reduced from one hundred thousand estimated by Captain Cook, almost ninety years prior. Maori were reduced by half, less any accounting for new births, over the period of almost a century. Disease and death by war, intra-Maori and Maori-settler, had taken a significant toll in tribal communities.

In Australia, Aboriginal tribes retreated west into the bush, ahead of settlers. Maori had no place for retreat, and chose not to do so. They were always land-bounded tribal units. In the nineteenth century, Maori were part of the New Zealand economy, in mills and fishing enterprises. Maori were divided, over whether to unite and fight the English, or negotiate a peaceful co-existence.

The king movement toward Maori nationalism, came too late to unite Maori. British officials and settlers viewed those organized behind the king, as a

---

[79] FitzRoy was later made head of the British meteorological office, where he used his skills as a sailor to build the office into the international weather reporting agency that it remains today. Maori erected a FitzRoy pole, showing a cowering British agent under a powerful Maori chief. The Taranaki pole marked a boundary area.

group dedicated to halt all land sale, at a time when pressure was upon the government to provide much more land for sale. In the area of Taranaki, settlers demanded that ten times the amount of acreage, already in settler ownership, be made available for sale.

In 1859, the Maori king opposed a land sale, by an individual Maori, of Taranaki area land in Waitara, near New Plymouth. The new British governor of New Zealand, Gore Browne, was a strong character, who let all parties know, he wanted no obstructions to land sales. Then in 1860, the flu claimed the life of the Maori king.

Supporters of the Maori king erected Camp Waitara, from which to claim the land and disrupt survey. Governor Browne ordered troops into the area, to evict Maori from their camp. Troops fired on Maori settlements, which Maori vacated in the night, without casualty.

The facts of this First Maori War, as it is known in British records, are hard to establish. Maori chiefs assembled five hundred warriors and built several fortified paa, that is walled settlements. British sources, as reported in the press in England, claimed major victories and mounting casualties of Maori, although the paa, upon which British troops fired, was likely vacated in the night prior to assault. One fact is certain: by March 1861, the belligerents agreed to a truce.

Land War Part II: 1863 Waikato

Taranaki, smallest of the original British provinces in New Zealand, had complex ownership claims, made more difficult by the 1839 purchase of Waikato land, by the New Zealand Company. The Company purchased contested land from the Atiawa. The Atiawa tribe of Maori represented the land as theirs, and that they had only vacated temporarily, to go to the coast, to do business with whalers, as they had seasonally done for years. The tribe action was a plan, to sell farming rights to Englishmen, and retain the right to return, without fear of their Waikato Maori enemies. The Company assumed total control of the region, and expected to be rid of native interference.

Governor Robert FitzRoy 1855 (public domain)

The Waikato Maori claimed the same land, in victory over their Atiawa enemies, whom they claimed to have chased from the area. However, the Waikato did not move in and occupy the land, as was the method to finalize land control, under Maori custom.

During his short tenure as governor, Fitzroy tried to resolve contentious claims in Taranaki, by purchasing Waikato rights to the land, and setting limits to settler expansion. The Atiawa claimed compensation from the government, for their rights to the land. The angry settlers argued, that had FitzRoy not offered protection to Maori, neither Maori tribe would have returned to the area.

The new British official in charge of New Zealand, Governor Sir George Grey, employed a different approach to the situation, then had his well-meaning predecessor. He added ambiguity in policy to the mix. Chiefs were told, they could stop sales of land they owned. Chiefs assumed, that if they did nothing, the land remained in tribal ownership. Settlers assumed, that inaction meant assent.

Grey issued an ultimatum to Maori, demanding an oath of loyalty to the Queen. He also made a statement, that peaceful Maori would be protected by the government. Without waiting for response, under the calm of his words, Maori were caught by surprise, when troops invaded Waikato. Grey justified his offensive, by reporting to England, that he preempted Maori attack on Auckland, an attack he provoked, by demanding sale of land in Taranaki. War was inevitable.

The 1863 invasion of Waikato was a bloody affair, involving fourteen thousand British troops, against four thousand Maori. During ten months of intermittent skirmishes, from July 1863, to April 1864, fighting came to within a few miles south of Auckland. When the fighting stopped, the Maori were defeated, the king movement was dead, and thousands of acres of Maori land was confiscated by the government. Wrongful taking of Maori land was not addressed until 1995.

Commander of the British forces, Lieutenant-General Duncan Cameron, learned much about Maori resilience and dedication to their homeland, in ten months of war. Maori fought bush raids, against disciplined, orderly British troops. Eventually, the greater numbers of British troops, overcame the spirit of Maori fighters.

At one point, Maori raised a white flag to open negotiations. Grey's men entered the Maori fort, followed by soldiers, who took all Maori prisoner. There was no honor in the war. War was the culmination of efforts, to remove Maori from the land, in favor of European settlers.

Aftermath of War: Imperfect Solutions – Toward a New, New Zealand

New Zealanders in Foreign War

Once the land was resolved in favor of settlers, the war ended. The divisiveness was about land, not racial distinction. Many Maori were Christian. They were business owners. In 1867, Maori men were enfranchised voters. In foreign wars, Maori fought with distinction, in British uniform.

As testament to the futility of war, and the short-sighted pursuit of land, as a justification for abandoning civility, the area of Taranaki, around which so much blood was shed, is today a small dairy farm. The land of Wairu is open and quiet. A small marker notes significance of the place.

Before Maori could feel beneficial effects of British citizenship, resolution of the actions of Britain, in assuming settlers had rights to land, as if there were no prior owners, needed rectification. Maori defeated in nationalism, never abdicated cultural survival, if not as tribes, as first people.

Various versions of the 1858 Native Territorial Rights Act became law in 1862 and 1873. The laws allowed direct purchase of land from individual Maori, a death blow to Maori communities and the tribal structure. Governor Grey's New Zealand Settlements Act of 1863, was more direct. Under the Act, 1.2 million acres of Waikato-Tainui tribal land was confiscated. Maori evicted from the land, saw their household goods and cattle taken by soldiers.

The Treaty of Waitangi of 1840, was made official in 1975, clearing the document of any legal infirmity, for failure to be approved by Parliament and the crown in the nineteenth century. Under authority of the Treaty, the Waitangi Tribunal was created in 1985, to recommend resolution of Maori claims, under the Treaty, and for confiscation of property subsequent to 1840. An alternate route to redress is available in the Office of Treaty Settlement, a judicial process.

In 2014, the Tribunal determined, that Maori tribes did not relinquish sovereignty, when they signed the Treaty. The Treaty has been given twenty-first century application in property rights, to radio frequency. In the 1980s, the government gave fishing rights to corporations, despite Maori rights to fisheries in the Treaty. The 2004 Maori Fisheries Act, was an attempt to resolve the issue, by giving a lump sum payment to the tribe, to purchase an interest in the fishing company. The government is sensitive to property rights, in private corporations.

Maori underlying rights to land, are still subject to government interpretation, when popular public enjoyment of the land is in conflict with Maori private rights, such as the 2004 Foreshore and Seabed Act, vesting beach land in the crown, for management as public beaches. The government assumes all rights to sub-surface minerals and coal. In deference to the historic significance of Hawkes Bay, the government and Maori have a co-management arrangement.

The area of resolution, having significant healing effect, is the series of recommendations of the Tribunal reflecting acknowledgement, that New Zealand has two founding cultures; Maori and European. Maori language is taught in school. Street signs and government documents are bi-lingual. Notably, the principle museum of New Zealand history, located in Wellington, the capital, is the Museum of New Zealand, Te Papa Tongarewa.

After more than a century of injury to Maori, and resentment, Queen Elizabeth II personally issued the £171 million payment to the Waikato-Tainui tribe in 1995, as compensation for wrongful seizure of their land in 1863. The payment was a gesture of acknowledgement of wrongdoing, and respect for the Maori. The value of the payment represents a small percentage of the value of the confiscated land. About a quarter of land initially confiscated was returned to Waikato-Tainui.

Picton Today

Blendheim

Today the site of Wairu battle, where twenty-six people died, is just outside the tiny town of Picton, known as a cruise and ferry port. Picton is a short ferry ride from Wellington, across the Cook Strait's Queen Charlotte Sound, the area of New Zealand that James Cook found most attractive. The battle site is actually in Tuamarina, a small dairy farming community. Administrative functions of Picton are managed in nearby Blendheim, where the central park includes a war memorial to foreign war. The quiet today, belies the tension of 150 years past.

Today the region is known for the wine industry, largely white wine grapes, of the Marlborough Region. Not far from where Maori first came to the south island to settle, and where English settlers fought a war for farm land, New Zealand looks to a twenty-first century economic future, in wine exports. It is a peaceful, culturally inclusive, vision for the new, New Zealand.

Wine and Coffee in Auckland

When Captain James Cook rounded the north end of New Zealand in 1770, he spent time in the northern Bay of Islands, before charting the east coast of the north island. He was lured by islands of the Bay of Auckland, never venturing inward, to the dual harbor and fertile valley of the city of Auckland today. Had he sailed into the harbor, he would have made note of the successful Maori settlement, with its lush terraced gardens. Auckland would have been an instant hit in England.

Seventy years later, English provincial governor, William Hobson, chose Auckland as the capital of the New Zealand colony, as a default location. The Bay of Islands, so well-advertised by Cook, was more populous, although remote to the north. Otago Bay, the site of Dunedin, was heavily settled by Catholics from Scotland, so it was deemed too remote to the south. Fast growing Wellington, was a good central choice, with which Hobson was not familiar. Hobson chose the place the Maori called the *isthmus of a hundred lovers*, and named it for his mentor and friend, the 1st Earl of Auckland, George Eden. Eden never came to New Zealand. Too bad for him.

Auckland developed quickly as a commercial harbor, although it was eclipsed in 1865, by Wellington, the political capital. Newly freed convicts from Australia, eagerly came to Auckland, as did English emigrants, fleeing a depression in Britain, which left those without resources further disadvantaged. Auckland then, as now, was a new home to the hopeful, with big dreams.

Early Auckland was divided into two sections. The east was quickly purchased by British officials, and entrepreneurs with means and connections. The west side was sold, in small lots, to freemen emigres from Australia, and those escaping poverty in England. Today, it is all prime real estate.

Morning in Auckland

Auckland has blossomed into a cultural capital of New Zealand. It is also the commercial center. Along Queen Street, are still great places to shop. In the quaint side streets, are the cafes and coffee bars, which are the prize of youthful, business residents. Auckland is a foodie heaven.

The islands of the bay, that so lured Cook, now are prime vineyard estates. Waiheke Island is a major visitor attraction for its vineyards. Auckland is the place to wander central town streets, and have the world's best morning coffee, then hop on a ferry, for a wine experience.

Early Auckland – Capital of New Zealand

The area of Auckland today, was a vibrant area of Maori settlement, from the fourteenth century. Fertile land for farming, as the result of years of volcanic activity, was utilized by Maori in terraced gardens, which supported a large population. By the early nineteenth century, what is now Auckland, including fishing bays to the east and west of the valley, was home to tens of thousands of Maori people.

Cook Pier

The history of Maori, in contact with Europeans, is a separate story, not repeated here. Auckland does present an example, of the effects of introduction of muskets and European disease to the Maori culture. Heightened mortality in inter-tribal wars, through unequal access to muskets, and epidemics of smallpox and tuberculosis, reduced Maori population by the 1830s, to less than a thousand inhabitants of the bay.

Credit for being the first Europeans to settle in Auckland, and realize its potential, were John Logan Campbell, and his newly-made shipboard friend, on the voyage from England to New Zealand, William Brown.[80] As fellow Scots they bonded, becoming emblematic of waves of Scotsmen, to this faraway place, who brought their dreams. Their initial act was buying land.

The first battles of Brown and Campbell were not with the Maori. They dealt with aristocratic British, sent by the crown, to hastily organize government, in the island offshoot to New South Wales, Australia. The partners made an initial purchase from Maori, of the volcanic island in the bay of Auckland, they named Browns Island. In a place of few conveniences, both partners soon returned to England.

In Maori culture, leaving the land is abandonment of ownership. The Maori tribe, which at the time dominated the land, as victors in the most recent inter-tribal war, gifted Browns Island to the British governor. The Maori sale to Brown and Campbell was intended, by Maori, to create trade opportunities. In the absence of the pair, Maori looked to crown officials, to engage in trade.

When word of the British flag hoisted on a flagpole on Browns Island, came to Brown and Campbell in England, the business partners quickly returned, to claim their turf. Brown remained on the island, to oversee farm and pig operations, while Campbell expanded business operations in Auckland. The British governor refused government recognition of the Brown and Campbell initial land purchase. Validating purchases made, without recorded documentation and site survey, had become a major headache for officials, attempting to manage the new colony.

---

[80] John Logan Campbell, born 1817 in Edinburgh and died 1912, in Auckland; William Brown born about 1809, in Scotland and died in 1898.

Historic Auckland

In 1844, Robert Fitzroy, previously captain of the famous HMS *Beagle*, came to New South Wales, as the replacement governor, tasked with reconciling the quagmire of entrenched private interests in Australia and New Zealand. Tangling with the New South Wales Company, of newly wealthy, former military, stationed in Australia, was the undoing of FitzRoy's career. In Auckland, FitzRoy acknowledged the land purchase of Brown and Campbell, enabling their further pursuits.

Eventually, Campbell purchased Brown's interests in their partnership. Brown returned to England and Campbell became a founding father of the growing city of Auckland. Campbell left Auckland for an extended Grand Tour of Europe with his wife, Emma Wilson, whom he met on previous travels and married in 1858, and their two daughters.

Campbell returned from travel, with renewed energy to expand into timber, milling and brewery businesses. His time in Europe, imbued Campbell with a sensitivity to art and European culture. He founded a school of art in Auckland in 1878, fostering Auckland as the art center of New Zealand. Then in 1881, Campbell wrote his autobiography of his pioneering life, *Poenamo*, which was popularly received.

Campbell served in Auckland city government in 1855, after making the notable purchase of a thousand-acre parcel, near central Auckland, which he named One Tree Hill. The one tree on the top of the hill is now the centerpiece of Cornwall Park, part of Campbell's 230-acre gift to the city. Two more bequests followed, until half of the initial Campbell purchase became public park and the other half was developed as the fashionable Parnell neighborhood, where the Campbells lived.

Campbell's Italianate mansion was demolished in 1924, and replaced with a rose garden. The oldest home in Auckland, the cottage of Brown, Acacia Cottage, is preserved within Cornwell Park. Campbell is buried on the top of One Tree Hill, next to the 1940 Centennial Memorial obelisk, dedicated to Maori founders of the bay of Auckland, on the centennial anniversary of the treaty, which joined the Maori and settlers into a new nation.[81]

Growing Auckland – Cultural Capital

Freeman Bay and Commercial Bay, several blocks apart, along the waterfront, separated the have nots and haves of Auckland's business and social elite. Leading into town, from Commercial Bay, the creek, that often overflowed, turned the early city center into a swamp. The creek was channeled and covered, becoming the central town thoroughfare, Queen Street.

Today, along Customs Street, where it becomes Beach Road, there are a string of dimples in the sidewalk, marking water levels of the harbor, encroaching into the city, prior to dredging the harbors. By 1955, water frontage of the Auckland harbor looked as it does today. There is a straight line of docks, to the residential area of Freeman Bay, now a highly desirable, residential, historic district. Queen Street is the central city artery, that ends at the harbor and ferry terminal.

---

[81] One Tree Hill, Maungakiekie to Maori of several tribes, was home to about 5,000 Maori at its height. During the Musket Wars between tribes, a victor tribe sold the land to a merchant in 1845, who sold it to Campbell.

Auckland Commerical Pier

At the top of Queen Street, the Auckland Town Hall was constructed in 1911.[82] It is an example of Italian Renaissance Revival, as it is neither columned as a classical building, nor edged with high windows, as were Gothic Revival churches of the early twentieth century. The result is a European style. Inside are Art Nouveau light fixtures, English tiles, stained glass and an organ. It is as if the building was designed by a committee, wisely anticipating multiple uses over time.

The Town Hall building is wedge-shaped, to fit dimensions of the lot when built. Today, with encroaching buildings since removed, the Town Hall anchors Aotea Square, the venue of public events for about twenty thousand people. Town Hall is home to administrative offices of the Auckland Philharmonia Orchestra, and its home venue for performance.

---

[82] The building was designated a Heritage New Zealand property in 1988, and restored in 1998. The original organ was rebuilt in 2010, to discard changes made over the decades from the original, and restore the original power and sound as built by Orgelbau Klais of Germany.

Auckland Town Hall now Symphony Venue

Reaching out from the Town Hall, are other cultural icons of Auckland's central historic district: the 1929 Civic Theatre, 1915 Myers Park, and the 1887 Auckland Art Gallery/Toi Tamaki. Civic Theatre is a classic of pre-depression era movie houses, with its Moorish lobby. The theatre ceiling replicates an open sky of twinkling stars. Civic Theatre is enjoying a revival in the twenty-first century, after a restoration and starring role in the movie remake of *King Kong*.

The entrance to Myers Park from Queen Street, appears as overgrown green space in the center of towering office buildings. The park interior is an open former play space for kindergarteners, attending Free Kindergarten in 1915, in the Arts and Crafts bungalow designed to give children of poor residents an early education and safe place to play. The current park play area is joined by a copy of Michelangelo's *Moses,* installed in 1973, and *Hau te Kapaka,* the *Flapping Wind,* which are three sculptures by modern sculptor Rachel Walters. The 2013 Walters installation is a reflection on negative human impact, upon the natural world.

Art Deco Civic Theatre Queen Street

The building housing the Auckland Art Gallery, began as a free library. The French Chateau style building was one of the first civic institutions in the city. In 2008, central courtyard structures of the chateau were removed, and a two-year, new-build, steel and glass gallery was inserted, that enhances display space, for fifteen thousand objects in the collection, without overwhelming the foundational historic building. Auckland Art Gallery is the largest art institution in New Zealand.

Auckland Art Gallery backs up to Albert Park, the core historic setting of Auckland. Albert Park was the site of Te Horotiu Pa, the walled settlement of Maori, next to the stream, made into a covered canal, over which Queen Street and central Auckland was developed. In 1840, the site became home to Albert Barracks, the British military installation, active during Maori wars and in protecting commerce to and from the islands. Walls from the fort are still visible in the park. Today, a portion of the original fort grounds are the campus of the University of Auckland.

Auckland Art Museum

The history of Auckland and New Zealand, settled by Maori, developed by British officials and entrepreneurs, and expanded by emigres from Asia and the world, is preserved in the Auckland War Memorial Museum. Although war memorabilia are the core of the collection, cultural history is the heart of the museum. Stand up close to a German buzzer bomb, a Japanese Zero plane, and then view a Maori show, performing a haka. In the museum café, enjoy a locally ground coffee.

Enjoying Wine and Coffee in Auckland Today

War Museum Coffee Bar

In a web search for coffee in Auckland, a list of twenty places will appear, all with a five-star rating. All earned their stars, with exceptional coffee. The central business district of Auckland, has by design, or fact of habit, become one of the world's best places to enjoy great coffee.

What makes coffee great, is a matter of personal taste. In Auckland, it is routine for baristas to use more than twice as many beans per cup of espresso, than popular chain coffee spots. Start with quality freshly roasted beans, in clear New Zealand fresh water, and the result is amazing, even for people accustomed to coffee in barista havens such as San Francisco, or Seattle.

Great coffee in Auckland can be found, in posh specialty places, with comfy chairs, as well as hole-in-the-wall, coffee-to-go, spots with no seating. Central Auckland is a high-density business area, with enough coffee aficionados to support a coffee culture. People can be seen everywhere, cell-phones down, talking to each other, and drinking coffee. No wonder New Zealanders are pleasant.

Next to coffee, the best beverage in town is wine. New Zealand has tied its clean industry economy to wine. It is a safe bet, since some of the best, new, white, wines to come on the international market are from the southern hemisphere growing regions of New Zealand.

Winery at Waiheke

There are four wine growing regions in New Zealand. Of the four, Hawkes Bay, Marlborough and Central Otago Valley face south and east, catching cold arctic breezes, warmed over the sea. The fourth wine region of Waiheke Island is sheltered from harsh winds, in the Waitemata Bay of Auckland. Fortunately for visitors to Auckland, Waiheke Island is a short, picturesque, ferry ride from the pier, at the end of Queen Street. On the island, buses take wine tourists on a ride through heaven and wine.

The wine industry in New Zealand is reminiscent of historic business ventures in New Zealand. While large, well-funded, corporate interests own or control vineyards and produce wine, so are there small entrepreneurs, each with their own ideas on producing the best bottle of wine. In an open economy, innovation and quality wine have rapidly made New Zealand a major producer of note to consumers. New Zealand will not be listed among the highest in quantity of national wine producers. The wine houses seek to bottle the best quality wine, sustained over time.

Sustainability and biosecurity are big issues in New Zealand. There is a requirement that vintners use organic growing methods. The national concern over biosecurity and protection of all native wildlife, means that cruise visitors will bring no food, or plants, off ship into ports. Take wine home, if you can resist opening the bottle.

New Zealanders trace a history of viniculture to missionary Samuel Marsden, who came to the Bay of Islands in 1819. Scots emigrating to the South Island, and Otago Bay, in 1840, began growing grapes and making wine. French settlers near Christchurch, brought wine culture with them.

Waiheke Winery

New Zealand protective tariffs protected local producers until 1995. When faced with competition for local customers, New Zealand producers entered the world market in full force. They seek to capture an outsize share of the export market, by proof of consistency and quality, in the tradition of the best French winemakers.

Each New Zealand winery has their own story of origin and success, based on the individual talent and insight of the winemaker. Fortunately, domestic appreciation of wine has grown along with world market recognition of kiwi labels. New Zealand wine is more than a visitor attraction.

Waiheke Island is a fun place to go from Auckland, to sample wine and enjoy the view. The climate protected island, made it a haven for cabernet vineyards, as the island evolved from the brews of the 1950s, to sophisticated winemaking techniques in the 1990s. As of 1997, there were twenty-two members in the Waiheke Winegrowers Association. Growers added Syrah to their vineyards, as the grape grows in popularity.

Waiheke winegrowers are acutely aware that their production accounts for barely one percent of New Zealand production, and that New Zealand has a small share in the world wine market. They depend on a reputation for quality, to keep their wineries viable. In 2007, the local association established a certification program, allowing wines of quality, to carry the mark of Certified Waiheke Island Wine on the label. All visitors need to do, is taste and enjoy.

Wine, coffee, art and history in Auckland make it a wonderful place to linger, at the end of a cruise. Knowledgeable cruise guests know, that a pre-stay in the embarkation port, takes the stress out of transit and any possibility of lost luggage marring a perfect cruise. Wait in Auckland for your luggage to appear, while visiting local coffee spots, and perhaps take a ferry to Waiheke Island wineries.

Winery Views

Art Deco Napier

Art Deco Napier

Napier, the little port town of the east coast of north island New Zealand, is a visitor favorite. The town exists as a time capsule to the worst day in town history, February 3, 1931, when an earthquake struck. In three minutes, one century of development was reduced to rubble.

Napier is not measured by its disaster. Testament to the people of the city was their response to witnessing their city in ruin. Few people held property insurance in 1931, yet most residents were determined to rebuild. The small regional harbor and market town was rebuilt in two years, a tribute to community spirit and cooperation.

Rebuilding Napier in a short time was largely enabled by two factors. First, the four major architectural firms of the city came together, to cooperate in commissions, turning out building designs at an unprecedented rate. The other factor was choice of architecture. A city decision was made to rebuild in a popular style, which could be quickly built. The style choice was Art Deco.

Little Napier rose from disaster, to be an Art Deco gem in the Southern Hemisphere. The small town with so much style, where buildings are sized in proportion to the town and each other, forms a pleasant vista against the green of natural New Zealand. Tourist response was prompt.

Telling the story of Napier begins with its history as an attractive spot on Hawke's Bay for Maori encampments and anchorage for whalers. Instigation of trade by both, began the village of Napier. Putting the coast of Hawke's Bay on a map, to enable trade, was the work of the French explorer, botanist and ethnographic scholar, Jules Dumont d'Urville. Dumont is often left out of history, in the shadow of Captain James Cook. In this story, Dumont receives his tribute.

The story in Napier is all about the architecture. Art Deco is deceivingly simple in design, yet playful in spirit. People of Napier rebuilt their city as an extension of the inhabitants. Today, locals display that spirit, in coffee shops and retail, as well as street names. This is a story of spirit expressed in design, that is Napier.

Prelude to Hawke's Bay Settlement

The first inhabitants of Hawke Bay were Maori. They appreciated the marine life and protected coast, backed by green hills. Otatara, a Maori paa, that is walled fortress, has been reconstructed as an historic feature. Captain James Cook interacted with Maori in Hawke's Bay. Maori captured Cook's guide, thinking he was a slave. Cook named the southern point Cape Kidnappers, for the incident. Today, visitors hike out to Cape Kidnappers to bird watch at a gannet colony.

Cook Arrival Napier Now Public Park

Lesser known than Cook, was the French explorer and botanist, who spent extended time exploring New Zealand and Antarctica, Jules Dumont d'Urville. Born in 1790, often ill as a child, precluded from a military career, he made the most of his studies in Caen. Available to Dumont were maps and logs of Cook, and those of Cook's contemporary in France, Louis-Antoine Comte Bougainville. Bougainville's story is enmeshed with the Falkland Islands, he claimed for France.

The French navy of 1808, when Dumont enlisted, was much reduced by the post-Napoleon period, and domination by Britain of many ports of the world. The young, serious, naval junior officer spent his early naval career studying botany. A high point of his early career, was recovery of the Venus de Milo, discovered by a local fisherman and brought to his attention, while on survey of Greek Islands. The second century Greek statue, likely pilfered by Romans, was lost at sea, after it was taken from an ancient temple site. That statue now sits in the Louvre Museum in Paris.

In his early thirties, Dumont had the opportunity to sail on a mission to South America and the South Pacific, as France assessed territory still available for colonization. As the fleet sailed south around Australia, New Zealand and the Antarctic, Dumont collected thousands of animal and plant specimen, hundreds never before seen in Europe. His notable find of the time was the Antarctic penguin, he named for his wife, Adélie.

Dumont was rewarded for his efforts with command of his own ship, the *Astrolabe*, and assigned a mission to circumnavigate the globe in 1826. While surveying Marlborough Sounds, and the east coast of New Zealand, Dumont was able to improve upon Cook's maps. D'Urville Island is named for his efforts, which Cook determined to be part of the mainland. Dumont's maps of coastal North Island, were later found valuable, by whalers looking for suitable anchorage.

Dumont sailed off from New Zealand, to Fiji and New Guinea. He is credited with locating remains of earlier French explorer, La Pérouse. His extensive survey and analysis of island cultures, resulted in identifying Malay, Micronesia and Melanesia peoples, as distinguished from Polynesians. Clearly, the contribution of Dumont was extensive, not only in credibility of his maps of the southern hemisphere, but also in his early ethnographic and botanical work.

In 1837, Dumont was given a second assignment for the *Astrolabe*, to map Antarctica, in the French race to dominate the most southern continent, and claim the South Pole. He historically crossed the Antarctic Circle on January 20, 1840. The *Astrolabe* was not alone on the Antarctic Sea. American and British ships were seen in the area, at the same time, all part of the race of seafaring nations to control Antarctica.

Dumont returned to France in 1840, where he was promoted to rear admiral and given accolades, commensurate with his vast addition to the body of knowledge of the southern hemisphere. Tragically, Dumont and his family were killed in 1842, while on holiday, when their train derailed in France, resulting in a disastrous incident near Versailles. In addition to his naval and scientific achievements, Dumont's novel, *The New Zealanders: A Story of Austral Lands*, was an early portrayal of Maori. Several points on maps of Antarctica are named for him. He named Adélie Land in Antarctica for his wife. Dumont's legacy to New Zealand generally, and to Napier specifically, was use of points of anchorage along the coast from which trade blossomed.

Early Napier

Early Napier Park Along Marine Parade

Other than name the bay for Sir Edward Hawke, First Lord of the British Admiralty, Captain Cook made no landing on the bay, for fear of hostile Maori. Utilizing Cook and Dumont maps, whalers came to Hawke's bay in the 1830s, where they traded with Maori for food and fresh water. Throughout New Zealand, Maori traded with whalers and merchants. Maori were able traders.

Where there were natives to convert, missionaries were not far behind whaling ships. Anglican missionaries did more to settle new lands to British interests, than military outposts or government sponsored settlements. Missionaries expected little on the landscape, and lived by establishing contacts with natives, whom they could bring to Christianity. From missionary settlements in the Bay of Islands, missionaries came south to Hawke's Bay by the early 1840s.

To the credit of missionaries, they received grants of land by request from chiefs of local Maori paa. In 1843, such a grant of ten acres was received from the chief of Te Awapuni. By 1844, when the Treaty of Waitangi was taking effect, the Hawke's Bay Anglican community of Maori Christian converts was established. Maori looked upon missionaries as preferable, peaceful residents who negotiated use of land, over land grabbing farm settlers, who made assumptions based on European treaty and force of guns. Land issues are a separate story of New Zealand.

In 1854, the little settlement on Hawke's Bay was officially named Napier, by the British governor from New South Wales, Australia, in honor of Charles Napier, a British colonial administrator in India.[83] By 1855, Napier was a British port with a customs house. The farm community of Hastings was established nearby and inland. Today, Hastings and Napier are considered sister communities of Hawke's Bay. Wool and farm produce from Hastings, are exported through the port of Napier.[84]

The town took shape around the multipurpose town council building, built in 1860, that also functioned as a theater, justice courts and church, until various church buildings were built nearby. Within two years, there were three churches in the tiny town for Anglican, Presbyterian and Roman Catholic parishes. Wellington overtook Napier in importance, and grew larger, leaving Napier with a substantial port business from interior farms. The port was improved, and the city benefited from water, street and sewage infrastructure, enabling a permanent city.

By the 1880s, Napier had a significant, seasonal, seaside population. Marine Parade was established along the waterfront, planted with Norfolk pines. The attractive route, with parks, remains today as a city asset. A fire in 1886, resulted in a building code, which required structures to be of brick, or cement. Few early nineteenth century city buildings remain.

As Napier headed to the end of the nineteenth century, the commercial district was expansive. Along Marine Parade, were the Masonic Hotel and grand homes of prosperous merchants, engineers and exporters of wool and frozen meat. The busy port of Napier was home to industry associated with ship building and repair.

---

[83] See Cruise through History© Itinerary XIII Ports of West Africa to Southeast Asia, India Heritage Cities; and Itinerary XV Ports of the Far East and North Pacific, Port Hong Kong, for more on Charles Napier.
[84] Napier.govt.nz for a history of the area. Last visited March 30, 2020.

Seaside Napier Shops Along Marine Parade

From inception, Napier was an attractive, English, seaside resort town. More playfully conceived than many English colonial cities, with classic street names of British royals, in contrast, streets of Napier were dedicated to British poets. Cross streets, which reach Marine Parade in central Napier, are: Dickens, Tennyson, Emerson, Byron, Browning and Shakespeare.

The Napier mayor chaired a Carnival Executive Committee in 1908, charged with fostering tourism. Prime among touted attractions were: parks, restful walks along Marine Parade, and visits to local wineries. In 1912, funds were appropriated to build the municipal theatre, on Tennyson Street. Theater goers attended the first production of Napier's Amateur Operatic Company, *A Greek Slave,* to rave reviews.

Napier achieved, in a few decades, the sort of balanced civic and commercial growth most cities strive to achieve. The small, urban, population was bolstered by a rural population in Hastings. In the 1920s, a new post office and several commercial buildings were added to downtown. Locals took much pride in their city. Vacationers from Wellington, and elsewhere, enjoyed their short stay in the pretty little town. The biggest problem of the time, faced by Napier, was lack of space in which to grow. Bounded by ocean and cliffs, there was little open space to build on the hills.

On February 3, 1931, in the midmorning, new land was created for Napier, in a most unimaginable way. An earthquake, measured as 7.9 on the Richter Scale, and lasting only three minutes, leveled Napier and Hastings. Fire from ruptured gas lines engulfed, that which was still standing. By the end of the day, two hundred and fifty-six people were dead and all buildings were lost. The city sat higher in elevation. New land rose from the ocean, along the coasts.

Eventually, the newly created land was dedicated to an airport. In 1931, new civic projects were not a priority. The priority was cleanup and rebuilding. Among ruins of Napier, a new Napier rose.

Art Deco Design

People of Napier were prosperous prior to the quake, although few were wealthy. Many had mortgages on their land improvements. Fewer than ten percent had property insurance. New structures were needed soon, to restore business income. Building owners wanted quality construction, that would not easily burn, could be quickly constructed, and at low cost.

Residential Art Deco Napier

In 1930, there were four architectural firms, with a presence in Napier, called upon to rebuild the city. To their credit, the four joined forces, to share commissions and expedite the rebuild process. Since at the core of an architect is an artist, with varying visions of a city, the four firms had loyalties to different styles popular in the early twentieth century.

The firm of Finch and Westerholm were devotees of the Spanish Mission style of architecture, seen in numerous commissions around Napier, some on the hills, still standing after the quake. Natusch and Sons were proponents of a modernist style of simplicity and form, while JA Louis Hay was fond of the Wright and Sullivan prairie style, so compatible with mission style. Commissions of these firms, expressing style preferences, were prevalent in pre-quake Napier.

The prevailing voice came from the Ernest Williams firm, a leader in Art Deco architectural style. The four firms settled on Art Deco, as the unified building treatment for Napier. Their decision facilitated construction in time and materials. Their cooperative decision left the city with a harmonious scale of buildings, each unique, yet in a consistent theme.

Streets of Napier

The style name Art Deco, comes from the 1925 Paris *Exposition de Arts Moderness Decoratifs et Industriels*, or Art Deco for short. The style quickly became the rage in Europe, supplanting highly decorative Art Nouveau, with its flowing shapes of goddesses and floral motifs. Art Deco exhibited materials and strong lines of new technology, in industrial goods of the twentieth century.

Characteristic of Art Deco buildings are concrete structures, with clever integration in the design of straight lines and geometric shapes. Concrete, easily produced on site, is less expensive than brick, immediately procured locally, and quickly applied by speedily trained laborers. Gone are ornate, costly and time consumptive, baroque carvings and appliques. Windows have eye shades of concrete overhangs, integrated into design. Decorative treatment of straight lines, sunburst, or stylized Maori designs, are part of the overall architectural style. The key to successful Art Deco design, is in integration of art into architecture. The result is deceivingly simple, yet lovely.

Rebuilt Napier

Art Deco can be used for tall buildings, notably skyscrapers such as in New York's Rockefeller Center, although it is equally effective in style for two-story, relatively compact structures, as contemplated for Napier. Concrete is fire resistant, locally plentiful, quickly applied and at low cost. In the 1930s,

Art Deco was a sign of progress. In all aspects, Art Deco was the ideal choice for rebuilding Napier.

By 1933, a new Napier was ready to receive holiday visitors. Sheila Williams, daughter of architect Ernest Williams, was queen of the Napier Carnival of 1933. A statue of Sheila, commemorating city renewal, sits on Emerson Street in the central business district. She is waving hello to visitors.[85]

Visiting Napier Today

In 1985, Napier's Art Deco Trust was established, to preserve and promote character of the city, as a municipal asset. The visitor center has a video of the earthquake, to tell the story of calamity. The better story is told in the walking guide to city streets. View Art Deco Napier best, from the coffee bar across the street from the visitor center, at Hastings and Emerson streets.

Art Deco Theatre exterior

---

[85] Look again at Sheila. In 2014, a second statue was installed, of a young boy across the street waving back.

Art Deco Theatre interiors

Most of the historic Art Deco buildings of Napier, are clustered along Tennyson and Emerson, to Dickens streets, and at cross streets of Hastings and Marine Parade. Walk from the Soundshell, down Emerson, to the Community Center, in the former Women's Rest home, and cross to Tennyson, as a route back to the ocean. This route runs in front of the Municipal Theater, a premier example of Art Deco. For a treat, tour the inside lobby of the theatre, with its Art Deco ceiling fixtures. More Art Deco buildings are along both sides of Dickens Street.

Along the waterfront, from the central business district, is Soundshell, in the colonnade. The bandshell in a park, is of the perfect scale for intimate Napier, which never grew too large. Further north along the ocean, is *Pania of the Reef*, the goddess of the sea statue. Running to the south, is Marine Parade, with its row of wood houses and mansions of the early twentieth century, parkland, and children's bicycle course, all with a view to the sea of Cape Kidnappers.

Soundshell Colonnade

There is such a wealth of Art Deco buildings in Napier, that the major festival is the summer Art Deco Festival, in February each year. Land visitors find accommodations few and pricey. Cruise visitors find Napier perfect for a stroll, before or after a trip to a local winery, as visitors have been doing for a century.

Mobile Art Deco

Wellington Girl – Katherine Mansfield

St. Paul's Wellington

There is often seen a quest in artists to leave their home city, to free their creative spirit, only to display connection to home in their art. So it was with Katherine Mansfield. Born in Wellington, New Zealand in 1888, when it was an outpost to Sydney, once Mansfield traveled with her family to Europe, she was impatient to leave New Zealand forever. Years later, sitting in rooms in London, or Paris, she wrote some of her best stories, which featured her life in Wellington.

Once Mansfield achieved world fame, Wellington was quick to adopt her, as a daughter of the city. The home at 11 Tinakori Road in Wellington, where she was born, is now open to visitors as a house museum. The home is successful in recreating life, in a prosperous Wellington family, at the turn of the century. Mansfield's father, Harold Beauchamp, came from Australia, to make his fortune in insurance and banking in Wellington. Katherine, the non-conforming daughter, chose to use her grandmother's maiden name for her pen name, Mansfield, rather than Beauchamp.

Mansfield's beautifully written short stories, which give a deep sense of Wellington life, are an ideal introduction to the city. Mansfield, the writer, is a difficult character, about whom to write a story. Regarded by her contemporaries as a gifted writer, her personal life and reckless ways, went well beyond, what her peers could accept. D. H. Lawrence, Virginia Woolf, Bertrand Russell, Bernard Shaw, Aldous Huxley and others of later fame, knew her, loved her and grew impatient with her. Her husband at her death, literary critic and editor, John Middleton Murray, beneficiary of her literary estate, is responsible for marketing Mansfield's stories, so enjoyable today.

Katherine Mansfield died in 1923, at the age of thirty-four, of complications of disease passed to her by her second husband, whom she met in a spa in Germany. She never had an opportunity to see growth in twentieth century Wellington. The small town she fled, became an arts mecca, with iconic architecture, thought daring at the time, an internationally revered museum of Maori culture and New Zealand history, and bookstores and coffee bars, that rival in number and quality the West Bank in Paris, or Mansfield's favorite streets in London.

Green hills and gardens that ring Wellington today, mixed with walkable city streets, of small shops and cafés, and an expanded, inviting waterfront esplanade, would tempt even reticent Katherine Mansfield to come home. Enjoy Mansfield's *The Garden Party* and other stories, on ship, or at a café on the Wellington waterfront, to capture the mind of the city, a century past. Walk streets of Wellington, and linger in Te Papa, the Museum of New Zealand, or the Mansfield House Museum, to put history into visual form. Just wander city streets, to enjoy Wellington.

Turn of the Twentieth Century Wellington – Memories for Stories

Mansfield Home Museum

Maori chief of Hawke's Bay sent warriors south, to explore their island home. Reports of beauty in the southern bay were so favorable, that son of the chief, Watonga, went south to found his own tribe, Ngati Tara, in the name of his son, Tara, sometime after the tenth century. When Captain Cook came through in the eighteenth century, the man of few adjectives in his log, effusively recorded his awe of the beauty of the bay. Given the option, it is to the inner harbor on Cook Strait, which became Port Nicholson, then Wellington, that the great explorer wished to return.

Maori tribal intra-disputed land control, initial attempts to do business with the New Zealand Company by selling land, disputing land boundaries, and resulting deterioration in European and Maori relations, are subjects of other stories. Maori ties to land are ever present in the area of Wellington, regardless of which tribe, descendant of Watonga, is preeminent. Present also, are early business practices of the New Zealand Company, of establishing port settlements, fed cargo from interior settlements. Inland farms and sheep stations began an export economy for the port.

Settlement of the Wellington bay area preceded, and anticipated, the Treaty of Waitangi, by a year, in 1839. New Zealand, as did Australia, began the European era, as a group of provinces, each controlled by private, quasi-military companies, formed to enhance settlement, on behalf of Britain. Eventually, the British parliament wrested control of the territory from the Company, creating a unified New Zealand, in which Auckland was the presumptive capital.

Wellington became capital of New Zealand in 1865, based on advantageous geography, rather than preeminence in population, or economy, which in both instances favored Auckland. In the 1860s, South Island was Maori territory, almost exclusively so, until discovery of gold. Fearful that Britain may establish South Island as a separate territory, the New Zealand Parliament, in Auckland, voted to move the capital to centrally located Wellington, on the Cook Strait.

In 1865, Wellington government house was either the mansion of Colonel William Wakefield, lead agent of the New Zealand Company, or later modest buildings, of absentee provincial governors. Commensurate with its new status, a second Government House was built, in the style of Queen Victoria's favorite retreat, Osborn House, on the site of the Wakefield mansion.

Panorama of Parlimentary Style in Wellington

A fire in 1907, resulted in the appearance of the government complex, as seen in Wellington today. Government House burned and was rebuilt in a city suburb, in the hills, overlooking the bay. Government House is the local residence of the British monarch. Today, it houses the New Zealand Prime Minister. Site of the early Government House, is now an executive office building, known as the Beehive, for its distinctive shape, which opened in 1977. The Beehive is next to Bowen House, the modern steel and glass office tower built in 1991, to house offices of members of Parliament and some government services.

Also lost in the fire of 1907, was the Parliament Building, built of wood, adjacent to the second Government House. Parliament Building was fully rebuilt by 1922, on the same site. This building was initially planned as an ornate neo-classical structure, until World War I and materials shortages intervened. Inability to finish a cohesive executive wing, which were part of initial Parliament Building plans, resulted in the Beehive. To the end of the twentieth century, debates ensued in Wellington, on fate of the Beehive. There were substantial sentiments expressed to demolish the Beehive and complete Parliament Building as originally designed. Costs tempered aesthetic taste. The Beehive endures.

Wellington Parliamentary Library

At the opposite end of the government compound from the Beehive, is the Wellington Parliamentary Library. Opened in 1899, the brick building withstood the fire of 1907, that consumed wooden structures. Considered of Gothic Revival style, think of it as church-like, without a steeple. The building still functions to house books and records of the New Zealand Parliament.

Completing the look of Wellington's governmental core, at the turn of the twentieth century, were Government Buildings, built in 1878, housing government administrative departments, and the Supreme Court of New Zealand, built in 1881. Old Government Buildings, of original wood construction, now house Victoria University of Wellington Law School. Supreme Court capacity was enlarged with a modernist structure, built in 2010, adjacent to the original Gothic building.

Uphill Tinakori Lane

Between the government cluster of buildings, and the harbor below, were the several streets of turn of the century commercial Wellington. From the street along the water, from boat harbor to railroad station, was the snug central business district of Lambton Quay, two streets deep. Two streets further inland from Parliament Buildings, lies Tinakori Road, and a rising hill of homes. In view from the Beauchamp homes, both the birthplace of Katherine Mansfield and the later Beauchamp mansion, looking downhill toward the city, were wooden houses and pubs, some of which still stand. In turn of the century Wellington, these were homes of the less fortunate, featured in Mansfield's short story, *The Garden Party*.

Homes of the well-to-do, sat on streets tiered above the harbor. On Tinakori Lane, is the home in which Katherine was born in 1888. Later, as Henry Beauchamp made a fortune in the insurance business, and became a director on boards of banks and commercial operations, including gas, chemicals and frozen meat, the family moved to a larger Victorian mansion, with a surrounding veranda and tennis court. The larger Beauchamp mansion is now in private ownership.

Between government buildings and homes were churches, one of which is Old St. Paul's. Built in 1866, the simple Gothic Revival structure lacks exterior opulence of the Old Parliament Library. Old St. Paul's, is built of wood, with a high, exposed-beam ceiling, reminiscent of an overturned ship. It has an interior beauty of exposed stained wood, lit by stained glass windows. In this Anglican Church, Katherine Mansfield's parents and the older Beauchamp girls were married.

Interior of Old St. Paul's

Katherine Mansfield – Wellington Girl

By 1900, when Katherine Beauchamp was twelve, Wellington had all the accoutrements of an established national capital. Being a bright girl, she was savvy to the knowledge that businessmen came to Wellington from Sydney, who were unable to achieve success in the metropolitan city of the region. Her father rapidly became a big fish, in what she saw as a small pond. When the Beauchamp family traveled the world on steamer ships, visiting London and Paris, Wellington looked even more provincial. Katherine wanted to see Wellington, only in a rearview mirror.

Katherine Mansfield (public domain)

Biographers portray Katherine Mansfield in several lights. She is either the playful genius, so misunderstood, or the unscrupulous and reckless young woman, who toyed with affections of men and women.[86] Mansfield enjoyed acting roles so often, that she is an enigma to biographers. She invented her name. Initially writing under several pen names, and shedding early her father's name, Katherine chose Mansfield, the maiden name of her beloved maternal grandmother.

---

[86] Antony Alpers, The Life of Katherine Mansfield, Viking Press, London, 1980; Claire Tomalin, Katherine Mansfield: A Secret Life, Viking Press, London, 1987; Gillian Boddy, Katherine Mansfield, A 'Do You Remember' Life, Victoria University Press, Wellington, 2003.

As an actress, Mansfield tried on roles, to test reactions of those around her. Then she wrote with clarity, stories of emotion in her characters. Contemporaries and biographers agree, that Katherine Mansfield brought a fresh voice to literature, and forever altered rules of writing short stories. Virginia Woolf wrote a review for the New York Herald Tribune, of a posthumously published collection of Mansfield stories, in which she described Mansfield as writing with insight to the mind alone.[87]

Mansfield short stories are moments in the life of her characters, in which venue is left ambiguous, and plot is not a factor. She described her own birth in *Aloe*, written in 1915. After a reunion with her brother in London, when he enlisted in the army, Katherine wrote *The Wind Blows*, reminiscent of their days in Wellington, without mentioning a venue for the story.

Homes of Turn of the Century Wellington – Story Material for Mansfield

---

[87] Boddy, at 42.

The Garden Party, set in the Beauchamp home in Wellington, without attribution to place, is a story of a mother, so out of touch with poverty in homes so near, that she sends her daughter, still in her party dress, to deliver cakes left over from the garden party, to the wake for a worker for the family, who was killed in an accident.[88] Thoughts of widow and messenger, contrasted in social class and emotion, are told without sentiment. It is as though the reader is in the moment.

When Virginia Woolf met Mansfield, she thought Katherine was cheap, hard, forcible and unscrupulous. Years later, Woolf said of Mansfield, that she was someone with whom she could endlessly discuss writing, and was the only person of whom she was jealous of her talent.[89] Mansfield was envious of Woolf's talent and of the reliable support Woolf had in her husband.

As a teen in Queen's College London, where her father sent the three oldest Beauchamp girls, Katherine was liked, or hated, depending on which personality she portrayed. There she met Ida Baker, whom Mansfield referred to as her wife. Baker adored Mansfield and traveled to be with her, whenever called upon for support, or a place to stay. For her part, Mansfield treated Baker more as a servant than partner. Baker tended to Mansfield's needs when bedridden, until husband John Middleton Murry arrived from London, to be with Katherine, in her dying moments.

The short life of Katherine Mansfield was punctuated by erratic movement. She returned from school in London, to Wellington, at age eighteen. The next year, Katherine was back in London, and soon pregnant by a young family friend, from Wellington, who she always adored as a musical talent. Realizing the young man could not support her, in 1909 Katherine quickly married a Cambridge music instructor, ten years her senior, George Bowden. Abandoning Bowden immediately after the wedding, Katherine ended up at a German spa, with her mother. After Mrs. Beauchamp left Germany to arrange the wedding of her oldest daughter in Wellington, Katherine had a miscarriage, then ran off for an imagined ideal life, with a Polish man, she met at the spa.

---

[88] Katherine Mansfield, The Garden Party and Other Stories, Constable and Company, London, 1922; Penguin Group, New Zealand, 2010.
[89] Tomalin, at 161, 201 – 204.

Katherine married her Polish lover, Floryan Sobieniowski, with whom she lived only briefly. Quickly disillusioned, when neither could support the other by writing, the pair parted. From Sobieniowski, Katherine contracted gonorrhea.[90] An operation intended to remove infection, spread further infection through her blood, leaving Katherine with pleurisy and arthritis, from which she suffered, often bedridden for weeks, for the remainder of her short life.

In 1911, Katherine published *A Birthday*, in a literary magazine, *New Age*. Among magazine contributors she met John Middleton Murry, who left Oxford to edit the journal. He received Katherine's *The Woman at the Store*, a story set in her past in New Zealand, and they began a relationship. The pair lived together, on and off, from 1912. They married in 1918.

The life of Mansfield and Murry was one of rented homes and borrowed furniture, as they dreamed of a city apartment and homes in the country, on literary income, which consistently left them disappointed. Theirs was a life of young artists, hoping for recognition, in a time of Chekhov and Nietzsche, in the inter-war years in Europe. Their circle of cohorts, became literary greats of the post-World War I era. When Katherine began to receive wide attention, and promise of income, Sobieniowski reappeared, demanding payment for old love letters from Katherine.

After meeting Katherine, D. H. Lawrence amended his about-to-be-published novel *Rainbow*, adding an affair of the woman character with another woman. He was influenced by Katherine and the character she, as an actress trying on parts to test affections of a new friend, played at the time. The novel was banned. Previously enjoying commercial success, Lawrence was financially ruined. His next novel, *Women in Love*, is an unveiled depiction of Katherine. Murry was furious and jealous. As an editor, to whom Lawrence submitted work, Murry refused publication.

In 1923, the year Katherine died, from tuberculosis hemorrhage, her father was knighted in New Zealand. A biography of Henry Beauchamp was compiled, in which a chapter was devoted to the daughter he hardly knew. Estranged

---

[90] Tomalin, at 71-78.

from both parents, in 1921, when ill and writing from bed, Katherine reflected on them fondly, in some of her voluminous letters to Murry and friends.[91]

The battle of Lawrence and Murry, in jealous desire for Mansfield's affection, continued after her death. They each wrote stories of cheating husbands, thinly veiled attacks on each other. After Mansfield's death, Murry published a collection of Katherine Mansfield stories, in his struggling literary magazine. He was accused by Lawrence of profiting on her demise, yet assuring Mansfield a literary legacy.

Wellington Today

Downtown Business District and Cable Car Museum

---

[91] March 1, 1921 letter, reprinted in part in Boddy, at 17.

The central business district of Wellington is not much larger today than it was when Katherine Mansfield departed for London, for the last time in 1908. The two main streets have extended southward around the harbor, to encompass the Museum of New Zealand, Te Papa, on the water. Old harbor warehouses, on the docks, are now shops, which open to eateries along the wharf. The Wellington cable car, and its museum, are popular tourist venues.

South of state government buildings, and the old central business district, is the newer Civic Square of city buildings. Wellington City Hall, built in 1904, in Edwardian style, is now a concert venue. The 1990s planned, Civic Square is between City Hall, and the former central library, now City Gallery Wellington. Nearby is the 1914 Opera House. Wellington presents itself as a city of arts, in a cluster of historic buildings, housing cafés, shops and small hotels, not to be ignored in favor of sites of the national government. For visitors, there are long streets, of many options.

Te Papa Museum of New Zealand

Katherine Mansfield's father, Henry Beauchamp, a director of the Bank of New Zealand, had a part in publication of an early work of his daughter. The Bank of New Zealand has continued that gesture, in an annual literary prize, which until 2010 was the Katherine Mansfield Award. Beginning in 2010, there are five BNZ Literary Awards, of which the top prize is the Katherine Mansfield Award.

Underrecognized in her lifetime, and ever reminiscing of the home she left, Mansfield is continually remembered in New Zealand and in Wellington, where her home is a landmark museum. The home was opened by New Zealand Historic Trust, on the centennial of her birth in 1988. Katherine Mansfield was always a Wellington girl.

Katherine Mansfield - Woman of Letters - Wellington

CHRISTCHURCH RISING

Christchurch began as a perfectly planned town, with a church at its center, located in the midst of god's country in the South Island of New Zealand. The town grew in harmony with its environment, providing places for newly arriving English emigres, joining Maori people, on whose land the town was sited. Christchurch began as a town in 1856, and developed in the post-war quiet of British domination of Maori homeland, in the mid-nineteenth century.

Then on February 22, 2011, the unthinkable occurred. Christchurch sustained a level six earthquake, with the town center squarely at the epicenter. The carefully planned, designed and built city of gardens and old English beauty, was shaken into a pile of rubble.

In the midst of rubble, with the town icon church in ruins, almost two hundred people dead, and half the town homeless, people did not give up their sense of community. Sense of place ran deeper than buildings, which defined a core environment. Sense of community was unshakable.

People of Christchurch were harassed by nature, with an extreme earthquake in 2010, followed by intermittent aftershocks. The February event caused substantial damage, as the culminating blow to months of weakening effects of earlier quakes. After the February quake came several aftershocks, some as substantial as a fresh earthquake. Any distinction between quake and aftershock, is lost on humans, whose lives are torn in mangled homes.

In a battle between humans and nature, nature wins. It is the human response to nature's force, that defines a people and tests their humanity. In Christchurch, there was never a question of whether to rebuild. Questions raised were how and in what way. Signs on public buildings solicited input. Some buildings were targeted for restoration. Others were scraped to be replaced. Outwardly, new buildings will not look like the originals. They will reflect a continuing spirit, which caused people to settle Christchurch, more than one hundred fifty years ago.

Art on the Square - A Christchurch Bouquet

There are cruise guests who enjoyed the cityscape of Christchurch prior to 2010, who, since 2011, refuse to leave the ship, when it docks at the lovely harbor in Akaroa. Akaroa remains charming, as though nothing world-altering has happened. Residents of Christchurch prefer a different attitude. They welcome visitors to vote with their feet, in support of rebuilding efforts. This is the story of Christchurch rising. It is a reflection on the spirit of the people of Christchurch.

The Perfectly Planned Town of Christchurch

Gothic Style City College

The residents of the plains of east-central South Island in New Zealand, chose the name Christchurch for their new home, to tie them to the known in an unknown world. Doing so was common from old world to new. In Christchurch, residents took the further step, of building a town in the same Gothic Revival style of England, with a New Zealand flair. This was home.

History of the acquisition of city land in Christchurch followed the story of many towns in New Zealand. Land of Maori, purchased under various circumstances, by whalers and early farmers, came into question regarding validity and scope of purchase. Land courts stepped in and decided compensation due the Ngai Tahu tribe of Maori, the dominant tribe of the island, at the time. Early Europeans held land, abandoned it, and left farms to stalwart entrepreneurs. Settlers backing development paid court ordered sums, when required, and began city planning.

To build their new city, residents chose Benjamin Woolfield Mountfort, as a single architect, to establish a city design. Born in England in 1825, educated in London, Mountfort was schooled in dark medieval Gothic style, of imposing stone and block. When he came to New Zealand in 1850, Mountfort was a newlywed young man, without a record as an architect. His first projects evidenced a lack of knowledge of local conditions. The aspiring architect became a stationer.

The small town of Waikouaiti, south of Christchurch, gave Mountfort the opportunity to design a church in 1858. The Gothic style building of wood, so pleased town residents, that is in use today. The city council of Christchurch was similarly impressed. Christchurch was granted a city charter in the same year and found in Mountfort a city-defining architect. He was given city commissions.

Mountfort's ability as an architect grew with his new client. His original design for the Canterbury Provincial Council Buildings evolved with needs of the city. Begun as a wood building, it transitioned to stone. Notably, an iron clock tower was added in 1859. Completed in 1860, the buildings still reflect the work of a masterful architect, of which the city was proud.

Architectural historians like to dwell on the nature of Gothic Revival, as a means to display devotion to god in commanding form, typical of early nineteenth century Catholic churches. The effect of choice of architecture, on Church of England members, is not to be understated. Gothic churches were passé in London, by the late nineteenth century. In New Zealand, so far from mother country, nostalgia and god combined to make designs of Mountfort successful.

The position of Provincial Architect was created for Mountfort in 1864. From that point, all of the buildings were touched by his design, even if he was not the primary architect on the project. Christchurch rose as a singular city in New Zealand. Not even England possessed a city, of so many public buildings, of the same design, quality and scale, erected on a grid, carefully mapped with a large central square, satellite squares and well-spaced public parks. The main street ended then, as now, at the Botanical Garden, and buildings designed by Mountfort.

Botanical Garden

In addition to the Provincial Council Building, Mountfort designed and oversaw construction of the Canterbury Museum, between 1869 and 1882, and Canterbury College in 1877, now an art center. The Canterbury Museum looks like a cross between a Gothic Church and a French Chateau, the latter being the muse for Mountfort's design. Out of town, he designed Sunnyside Asylum, looking like a character in a sit-com of aging British actors.[92]

---

[92] Watch BBC Waiting for God, filmed at Oaken Holt Rest Home, Farmoor, Oxfordshire, then see the Sunnyside Asylum, Christchurch, 1891. Mountfort also designed Trinity Church in 1870. By 2010, it was a restaurant.

Canterbury Museum

As Provincial Architect, Mountfort designed several buildings beyond Christchurch. He was a proponent of large wooden Gothic churches, throughout his life. His final, and largest, wooden church, built between 1886 and 1897, is St. Mary's Cathedral, found in Auckland.

For the ChristChurch Cathedral, the Anglican Church chose senior London architect, George Gilbert Scott. Mountfort was relegated to on-site clerk of works, for the off-site architect, when work began in 1864. By 1873, Mountfort was the supervising architect. His imprint can be seen in the tower and west porch. The Cathedral was completed in 1904, six years after Mountfort's death.[93]

---

[93] Mountfort's son Cyril continued as an architect, sometimes using previously unexecuted designs of his father. He was also a devotee of Gothic Revival architecture. The Benjamin Mountforts had seven children.

When New Zealand condensed the number of provinces, Christchurch lost its place as provincial capital of Canterbury province. It remained the second largest city in New Zealand, behind Auckland, with a population nearing four hundred thousand. All that changed in 2011.

February 22, 2011

Christchurch Cathedral February 2011

The iron clock tower, designed by Mountfort, was set on a wooden base. It was reset on stone in 1930, for Queen Victoria's Diamond Jubilee. On February 22, 2011, at 12:51, the clock stopped.

Trouble for Christchurch began on September 4, 2010, when a magnitude 7.1 earthquake struck twenty-five miles west of Christchurch. There was a foreshock of magnitude 5 and aftershocks in the range of magnitude 6. Such distinctions of pre and post-quake are lost, in the midst of the reality of the world shaking around people, in their homes, at five in the morning.

Compounding the visible damage above ground, as a result of the September earthquake, was the effects of liquefaction, occurring in the subsurface, sandy soils. Liquefaction, a term used by engineers of soil mechanics, is now a commonly understood term in Christchurch. Essentially, it is the process by which otherwise stable, sandy soil, containing moisture, is turned into quick sand, by the effects of ground-shaking activity, on a massive scale. When the ground stops shaking, the earth flows, in a torrent of sand. As surface soil moisture evaporates, sand turns to stone.

After the September quake, people of Christchurch attempted to restore normalcy to their lives. They dug cars out of hardening silt. They returned to work in high-rise buildings, of glass and steel, which had not crumpled, as did stone towers of Mountfort's church and public buildings.

On February 22, 2011, a magnitude 6.2 earthquake struck, with an epicenter six miles southeast of Christchurch. The quake lasted ten seconds. The impact was sufficient to turn already weakened infrastructure into rubble. Christchurch was declared a national emergency site.

The Canterbury Television building, a six-story steel and glass structure, was opened for use after the September quake. On February 22, it became an inferno, which claimed the lives of one hundred and fifteen people. Other multiple level buildings, which were reoccupied after September, claimed additional lives, when floors collapsed. Falling masonry struck a passing bus, killing eight people. Forty more people died from falling debris, in and around the central city.

The death toll from the February quake climbed, once recovery efforts ended. Deaths outside of the city became known. Impact-related injury was reported in sizable numbers. Eventually, so many people left Christchurch by choice, or were unable to remain, that it dropped to number three populous city in New Zealand, behind Wellington.

Of structures in the four-street central city, almost half were declared uninhabitable as a result of the February quake. Most impacted were historic structures, built prior to days of earthquake building codes. Notably, the Carlton Hotel, built in 1865, was under repair from the September quake, when it was rendered irreparably damaged in February 2011.

The most dramatic picture of the February quake, is that of ChristChurch Cathedral.[94] The Cathedral sustained minor damage in earthquakes of 1881, 1888, 1901, and 1922. Each time the spire fell, it was repaired with hardwood under-support. The 2010 quake exposed land faults, running through Christchurch, not previously known, bringing the total faults to seven. The February 2011 quake, was followed by over eleven thousand aftershocks, causing compounded damage to the Cathedral.

Totality of damage done to ChristChurch Cathedral, by seismic activity, was destruction of the spire and tower, as well as significant damage to the main building. The rose window, stabilized with an iron support after the February quake, shattered in a quake in June 2011, which brought down the west wall of the main building.[95] The 130-year-old building appeared to be a total loss. The congregation sought temporary space, in the quickly-built Cardboard Cathedral.

Buildings with structural support could not also withstand effects of liquefaction. The twenty-six story Hotel Grand Chancellor, built in 1986, tilted several feet on its foundation, presenting a danger to surrounding buildings. It too, was demolished. In all, more than twelve hundred structures in the central downtown area were demolished, many of which were deemed habitable after the September 2010 quake.

Christchurch Rising

Residents of Christchurch were adamant about rebuilding the core city, even as tremors continued, for almost a year after the catastrophic events of February 2011. Without a central city, there was little reason to rebuild homes in neighborhoods in the surrounding area. At issue was the four-street area of the central downtown, along the Avon River, with ChristChurch Cathedral at the center. The area was mostly devastated beyond repair, yet too lovely a location to abandon. Sentiment of history, loomed large in public discussion.

---

[94] ChristChurch Cathedral in Christchurch, New Zealand, capitalize differently.
[95] The June 13, 2011, Christchurch earthquake was a magnitude 6.3.

What Shall We Do?

The residential area, east of the city, surrounded by the Avon River, was redlined as a ghost town, after the 2011 earthquake. Regenerate Christchurch was created, as a city council and crown planning group, to consider the best use for land. Optimal use as greenspace, competes with practicality and cost in planning decisions. There is an opportunity to woo visitors and advantage residents, if projects have viable funding mechanisms. Projects will be years to completion.

Complicating city council decisions, is attribution of cost to repair public buildings, as well as an inability to control decisions of private property owners. Greek Revival architecture, a creature of nineteenth century materials and tastes, is costly to repair, replicate, or rebuild, even without costs of twenty-first-century building codes. New buildings will never look the same.

The cathedral, although a public icon, is private property. Fate of the cathedral is up to the Anglican Church, despite several legal attempts to force rebuilding. A decision was issued by the Church in September 2017, in favor of rebuilding

Christchurch Museum

ChristChurch Cathedral to the original basic design. The effort is expected to be a ten-year, NZ$100 million program, met by public and private funds. To be determined, is the look of basic design conformance.

In 2012, the restored iron clock tower was unveiled. At a cost of NZ$700,000, it was important to the city council that an icon of Christchurch be visible as soon as possible. The clock no longer advances in time. Time is perpetually 12:51. The iron clock tower is now an icon of resilience.

The former Canterbury Television building space is filled with white pebbles, in memory of those who were lost in the building in February 2011. Other spaces in the central business area, cleared of buildings and debris, are green spaces, waiting new projects. The original city entrance arch on the Avon River, now sits in landscaped space, that leads into open areas, filled with art.

Enduring Stones

As road repair and anchor building projects advance, Christchurch has not forgotten the human impact in the disaster of 2011. Effects of trauma to people are not easily cleared, or repaired, as are home lots, where lives once were lived. Improperly repaired homes, aggravate the healing process. Resident mental health is a primary concern, receiving council attention.

Although issues remain, the message Christchurch transmits is faith, healing and curative spirit. Oversize, artificial grass upholstered, living room furniture sits in an open-air parking lot, inviting people to sit and contemplate what can grow around them. The sculpture of a giant bouquet of flowers is planted next to the ChristChurch Cathedral fence on the city square. Every building that can support a retail shop, attempts to survive. New Regent Street, with its quirky shops, is full of people on any sunny day. The city appreciated the magic of its hometown Wizard.[96]

Linger and Converse

New Regent Street

---

[96] Ian Brackenbury Channell, born 1932, London, has been the official Wizard of New Zealand. Until 2011, he could be found on Cathedral Square. His usual post-earthquake podium was on New Regent Street, the 1930s era pedestrian shopping street, which reopened to shoppers in 2013.

Docking in Akaroa

Akaroa

The volcanic cone, that forms a nodule of fjords, on the central east coast of the South Island of New Zealand, is the site of the little holiday town of Akaroa. Cruise ships dock at Akaroa, from which buses take visitors to Christchurch. The setting in Akaroa is enough to make visitors want to toss their passports in the sea and stay. The volcano is quiet. The town is beaucolic, today.

Maori Chief Te Rauparaha thought the area of Akaroa to be a perfect dwelling site, when in 1830, his tribe captured the land from the Kai Tahu Maori. The Kai Tahu sold their interests to the French in 1838, allowing the French to stand in battle against Te Rauparaha's people. The British, not to be outdone by French, asserted dominion over the area, by deploying a warship to Akaroa.

Rather than fight, the British allowed French farmers of the Akaroa area to retain land, so long as France did not assert sovereignty over the island. Akaroa was known in Maori as Wangaloa, and in French as Port Louis-Philippe. Akaroa is proof, that a beautiful landscape, can bring out the best in everyone.

Dunedin: A Little Bit of Scotland in New Zealand

Distance From Edinburgh

The history of Scotland is that of a people seeking to maintain their identity in the face of invaders from the south; Romans, or Englishmen. Scots seeking religious freedom were willing to travel. In the early eighteenth century, they ventured to Panama, in what became the failed Darien Colony. In 1848, Scots came to New Zealand. On the South Island, they found a paradise that reminded them of home. They named the place Dunedin, which is Gaelic for Edinburgh.

Their new home in the South Pacific had prior occupants, who were not looking for company. The story of the British and Maori is one of treaty, war and lingering difficulty. By 1855, Scots in Britain were so enthusiastic about opportunities in New Zealand, that they emigrated by the thousands. When gold was discovered in the South Island, Dunedin grew to be the largest town in New Zealand. Place names around the newly named River Leith, made it clear to all, Dunedin was a little bit of Scotland, in New Zealand.

Early Dunedin was home to sailors, sealers and farmers. One of the founders was Thomas Burns, a nephew of poet Robert Burns. Inspired by the late poet, who was then enjoying the height of posthumous popularity, the town cast itself as an outpost of the Edinburgh Enlightenment, in the Southern Hemisphere. Dunedin became a town of writers, publishers and book sellers, as well as home to a university, the first in New Zealand. The town self-image is enduring.

Scotland is known for castles. Dunedin has its own castle. Larnach Castle has a short history, although it has prominence, as the only castle in New Zealand. A visit to the castle includes a view of Otago Bay, with soft green hills, interspersed by fjords. The view is classic Scotland.

The story of Dunedin is necessarily short, as the post gold rush years have been quiet. The Dunedin Railway Station, on ANZAC Square, is a signature city timepiece. Erected in 1906, as part of ambitious plans to see Dunedin as an industrial center, it has evolved as venue to a museum and restaurant. Today, many of the railway passengers are tourists on an excursion. The faster paced, twenty-first century city, is on the old town outskirts. When in old town Dunedin, find a book, enjoy a tea shop, and become a student for the day, in this City of Literature.

Of Sailors & Sealers

Captain James Cook arrived in the Otago Bay area in 1770. He and his naturalists spent ten days, in late February to early March, recording local resources, including seals. His reports, widely circulated in various accounts in England, inspired sealers to head south, in search of new waters to plunder.

Lochs of Dunedin

By the late eighteenth century, sailors and sealers arrived at South Island, to trade nails and tools from their ships, for Maori pork and potatoes. As long as the newcomers made no movement to take their land, Maori had amiable relations with Europeans. European seamen knew Maori ate their enemies, so they remained on guard.

One recorded incident, of overflowing tension between sailors and Maori, became known as the Sealers' War. It began, when a sealer became overly agitated over a lost shirt and a knife. He and his fellow sealers attacked the possible thief, sparking reprisals. The sealers left in a hurry, leaving one of their fellows behind. The sealers also left behind the beginnings of European disease, of lasting devastating impact to Maori society.

According to local lore, the sealer who remained behind became absorbed into a Maori community. He is remembered as James Caddell, one of the first known Paakeha Maori, or European/Maori. Among European New Zealanders, there were few people, who were immersed in Maori culture, were accepted by a tribe, and dressed as a Maori, rather than as a European. They covered themselves with Maori-style tattoos. Some were accepted with status in a tribe.

Barnet Burns, no relation to the poet, was a Paakeha Maori, who arrived in New Zealand as a sailor, and went home to England as an expert in Maori culture. He published a book describing his experiences as a Maori chief and went throughout England on the lecture circuit. Burns delighted audiences with his haka performances. Eventually, he was publicly confronted by a man, who had been to New Zealand and exposed as false, Burn's claims of being a Maori chief. The man also confronted Burns, with abandonment of his Maori family.

By the first decades of the nineteenth century, there were secret encampments of whalers and sealers, evading Maori and English officials. By the 1830s, the area between present day Dunedin and Port Chalmers had several active fishing settlements. Dunedin at the head of the bay, was in a prime protected position.

In only a few decades, over-fishing whales significantly reduced their number. Some whalers left the area, while others became traders. Trading in Maori-grown flax, sent north to Auckland, for transport to England, became a lucrative business.

There is a tantalizing tale of the pirate Charlotte Badger. She was an English woman, not a Scot, and not claimed by any descendent in Dunedin, to be certain. She may have been the first European woman to settle in New Zealand, although settle is a relative term. Sent to New South Wales in 1796, at the age of eighteen, for the crime of housebreaking, a general offense for querulous women, she produced a daughter, while serving in the Female Factory near Sydney.

Charlotte was on a ship of inmates, bound for prison in Tasmania, when she and others incited a mutiny, and took the ship to New Zealand. Of the mutineers, Charlotte may have been the only survivor, after an encounter with local Maori. Maori burned the vessel, and ate the men.

Charlotte was resourceful. She became fluent in Maori, and lived as another Paakeha Maori. The last knowledge of Charlotte was in 1826, when she boarded a vessel for the Americas.[97] At age forty-eight, she drifted into local lore, as material for future creative writers of Dunedin.

---

[97] James Caddell left New Zealand the same year as Charlotte. As two of the few Paakeha Maori, perhaps they knew each other. There is a story there.

City of Scots

Robert Burns City Center

The first Scots arrived in 1848, in what would become Dunedin, as part of the congregation of the Free Church of Scotland. Thomas Burns was their spiritual leader. Others of the congregation included builders and a city planner.[98] From inception, Dunedin was a planned community, with a vision of growth. The town concept included a replication of Edinburgh, if not in size, in style.

An octagon formed the city center roadway, bisected across the center by Princess Street, the main thoroughfare. The cross street, Stuart Street, ended at a to-be-built train station. The other cross-street, George Street, runs to the business district. Octagon Park is in the center, where today there are bus bays and weekend markets. High on a pedestal perch, overlooking the Octagon, is the seated figure of Robert Burns. He is *Rabbie Barns* to locals, their favorite son.

---

[98] Charles Kettle (1821 – 1862) designed the street plan of Dunedin. Not a Scot, Kettle is remembered with a statue in a city suburb.

St. Paul's Anglican Cathedral

Around the Octagon, sit major buildings of Dunedin. Most prominent, on the rise of the Octagon, is St. Paul's Anglican Cathedral, home of the Anglican Diocese. Just down the incline, is the Town Hall. Across the Octagon is Regent Theatre. When the city plan was drawn, and sites of the buildings were designated, construction of buildings was only a dream. The 1840s plan of Dunedin was a wish-list. Buildings did not come into being until the 1880s, to the early twentieth century. Dunedin, founded by a religious group, to express their religious freedom, became blessed in a way, they could not predict.

In 1860, gold was discovered in a gully in the Otago Valley. It became known as Gabriel's Gully, for the prospector, who found a quarry yielding gold with each shovel scoop. The Gully is just south of Dunedin. By 1861, Dunedin was flooded by prospectors seeking their fortune.

Between 1861 and 1864, almost twenty thousand prospectors headed to Gabriel's Gully. In the fledgling settlement of Dunedin, workers and shopkeepers abandoned their trades, to become prospectors. The dream of a pretty new-Edinburgh, was exchanged for leaky tents, in the rough.

Over the first decade of the Central Otago Gold Rush, some prospectors transitioned into service providers and tradesmen. Claims were purchased and consolidated by mining companies. By the tenth anniversary of the discovery of gold, the newly rich, including those who struck it rich, or became wealthy by providing services, stepped away from their tents and came back into town. Gold is still mined today in the Otago Valley, as a corporate venture.

Dunedin was a beneficiary of the new wealth. City dreams became a building reality. On the Octagon, first came Dunedin Town Hall, begun in 1878. The Cathedral and theatre, as well as other major buildings on Princess Street, broke ground in the first decades of the twentieth century. On Stuart Street, the Trinity Wesleyan Church was begun in 1870. Otago University was founded in 1869, becoming the first university in New Zealand. All the massive, stone, Gothic style buildings would be at home on streets in Edinburgh.

While Thomas Burns guided the Scottish souls of Dunedin, William Cargill looked to their political and economic future.[99] Born in Edinburgh, Cargill

---

[99] William Cargill, was born in 1784, in Edinburgh, and died 1860 in Dunedin.

began his career in the British army. He and his wife, Mary Ann Yates, were part of the Free Church of Scotland party, that landed in Port Chalmers in 1848. Dunedin became home to their family of seventeen children.

Gothic Dunedin

Cargill became the first Superintendent of Otago Province in 1853, and represented Dunedin County, in the New Zealand Parliament in 1855. It is his definitive Scottish stamp, that pervades Dunedin.[100] From 1855, to the end of the nineteenth century, thousands of Scots emigrated to Dunedin. Their businesses filled streets of the city plan. The monument to Cargill, in the center of Princess Street, built in 1864, is reminiscent of the monument to Sir Walter Scott, on Princess Street in Edinburgh. Climb Mount Cargill today, for a panoramic view of Dunedin.

---

[100] Two other significant immigrant groups in Dunedin were Chinese, who came during the gold rush, and Syriac Christians, who came at the end of the nineteenth century, largely from Lebanon, to escape religious persecution.

William Larnach was a Dunedin notable, who is emblematic of the gold rush age, that built the city.[101] Born in Australia, Larnach was lured to New Zealand by the gold rush. He soon left the gold fields, to become general manager of a bank in Dunedin. As one of the city council members of Dunedin, in the 1870s, he presided during business development, in the post-gold rush era.

Larnach Castle

Larnach made his fortune in real estate, timber and farming investments. At the peak of his wealth, he built Larnach Castle, overlooking Otago Bay. The castle is a visitor destination today. Larnach's investments, and thus his personal trajectory, were impacted by the bust that always follows a boom. He was a member of Parliament, when in 1898, despondent over the state of his personal and public life, he locked himself in a committee room of the chamber, and shot himself.

---

[101] William James Mudie Larnach, was born in 1833, in Australia and died in 1898, in Dunedin.

In a city of writers, Larnach's personal life became the subject of a novel, *The Larnachs*.[102] As a public official, the personal life of Larnach was subject to scrutiny. He protected his estate by putting Larnach Castle in his wife's name. When she died, he married her half-sister. When his second wife died, Larnach married a young woman, about the age of his son. Speculation over a relationship between his third wife and son, as further cause of his despondency and suicide, is a theme now preserved in literature. Visitors to Larnach Castle linger, in the boudoir of the third Ms. Larnach.

Gothic Revival style Larnach Castle was begun in 1871. It is made of local stone, Venetian glass, and carved wooden panels, the work of one family of craftsmen, over a decade. The castle sits among thirty-five acres of gardens, on a working farm. The property is listed as Heritage New Zealand.

Old World Craftsmanship at the Castle

---

[102] Owen Marshall, The Larnachs, Vintage Publication, Auckland, 2011. Marshall, born 1941 in New Zealand, is the award-winning author of more than a dozen works of fiction.

In 1906, the Larnach family sold the castle estate. The current owners have undertaken substantial restoration efforts, which are ongoing.[103] Today, Larnach Castle receives over one hundred and twenty thousand visitors annually.

City of Literature

Publishing Houses and Book Sellers of Dunedin

From inception, Dunedin was a City of Literature. Favorite son, Robert Burns in statue, presides over the center of the city. A plethora of writers blossomed in the Otago bay area, fostered by early establishment of Otago University in Dunedin. Writers need publishing houses and booksellers, both of which were part of the early economy of the city, and are part of its vibrant redevelopment. In 2014, when the United Nations recognized Dunedin as a City of Literature, the organization affirmed what residents knew. Annual book events continue today.

---

[103] The owners are the Barker family; Norcombe Barker is the Larnach Castle executive director.

Robert Burns, the national poet of Scotland, who was raised on a farm, wrote in English, with a Scottish dialect. His sense of local language, made his work universally popular. Most famous of Burns poems are those in songs; *A Red, Red Rose, Auld Lang Syne* and *Tam o' Shanter*.[104] Singing the poetry of Burns, helped the ease homesickness of Scottish emigrants to New Zealand.

Burns loved the ladies, the cause of his early family troubles. He published a few poems, to earn the fare to Jamaica, to escape a domestic situation, then found that acceptance of his work provided opportunities at home. Engaged to one woman, while having an affair with another, he eventually married, but never settled.

Publication of poems never gave financial security to Burns. His views in favor of the abolition of slavery, and in support of the French revolution, added to his difficulties in business associations. He had never had good health. Burns died in 1796, at the age of thirty-seven, shortly after having a tooth extracted. To Scots, he is immortal.

Scots adore stories of young Burns, arriving in Edinburgh in 1786, on a borrowed pony. He was quickly adopted into literary society, where one of the young admirers of his poetry was Walter Scott. In Dunedin, writing in vernacular, in the Burns tradition, influenced generations of young poets. In 1958, Otago University instituted the Robert Burns Fellowship, as a teaching residency, which brought the writing talent of New Zealand to Dunedin. In Dunedin, the spirit of Robert Burns is part of the past, present and future.

Of native New Zealand writers, two of note are tied to Dunedin. Janet Frame[105] and Hone Tuwhare are recognized as representative of writers, whose stories illustrate literary life in Otago Bay. Names of additional writers can be seen in the Writers' Walk of plaques, on the Octagon of Dunedin, emanating from the Robert Burns statue.

Janet Frame's early life was marked by separate drowning deaths of two sisters, and frequent violence between her father and brother. She was in the midst of a teacher-training program in 1945, at the age of twenty-one, when

---

[104] Tam is a drunkard farmer, who shares his stories in a pub.
[105] Nene Janet Paterson Clutha, aka Janet Frame, born and died in Dunedin 1924 to 2004.

she attempted suicide, by ingesting a large quantity of aspirin. Diagnosed with schizophrenia, in 1951, Frame was scheduled for a lobotomy, when a volume of her short stories was published, just prior to surgery. The procedure was cancelled.

Recognition as a writer, gave Frame the ability to travel. While in London and Europe, she was examined by doctors, who believe the schizophrenia diagnosis was in error. Under therapy, with a psychiatrist, who alleviated effects of years of past treatment, Frame wrote several novels. Seven of her novels were dedicated to her psychiatrist.

In 1965, Frame received the Burns Fellowship at the University of Otago. Her most notable work, despite numerous works of fiction and poetry, was her autobiography, written as a trilogy, in the 1980s. The autobiography became a feature film, *An Angel at My Table*. Frame was honored by Queen Elizabeth II, with Commander of the Order of the British Empire in 1983, and was an appointee to the Order of New Zealand. Subsequent to her death in 2004, additional of Frame's works have been published and additional honors received. Posthumous biographies have added to public interest, in the talented writer, with the complex life story, who was designated an Icon of New Zealand, just prior to her death from leukemia.

Hone Tuwhare[106] was born into a Maori tribe and spoke only Maori, until he was nine years old. Informing his future life as a poet, were the teachings of his father, who was a storyteller. Tuwhare initially trained as a boilermaker, working for the New Zealand Railways, while he went to school in the evenings.

When he was seventeen, Tuwhare began writing poetry. In 1964, at age forty-two, a volume of his poetry, *No Ordinary Sun*, was popularly accepted, as a voice of all New Zealanders, whether or not they were Maori. Although Tuwhare's poetry is Maori in tone, filled with cultural perspectives, the themes are drawn from his life, in the aftermath of Communist party membership, through the war years, and decades of social tensions and issues facing New Zealanders.

---

[106] Hone Tuwhare was born in 1922, in north New Zealand, into the Ngapuhi tribe of Maori. He lived his later life, until death in 2008, on South Island near Otago Bay.

Tuwhare held the Robert Burns Fellowship, at the University of Otago, in 1969 and in 1974. In 1999, he became New Zealand's second Poet Laureate. Together with Janet Frame, Tuwhare received the inaugural Prime Minister's Awards for Literary Achievement in 2003. He received an honorary doctorate from the University of Auckland in 2005.

Dunedin by Rail and Road

Dunedin Railway Station

Architect George Troup earned the moniker Gingerbread George, for his design of the 1906 Dunedin Railway Station. The black and white towers of basalt and granite, created a fairy story entrance to Dunedin, when it opened. Even today, surrounding gardens enhance the view.

Railway Building Interior

Dunedin Silver Fern Rail Line

The era of railway transit for local needs died by 1994, when the station ceased to serve regular travelers. The icon building, with interiors of French tile, was too substantial, not to repurpose in a revitalized downtown cityscape. Today, the building houses a restaurant and a museum, The New Zealand Sports Hall of Fame. ANZAC Memorial Gardens in front of the train station are meticulously maintained. The best view of the gingerbread station is across the garden, after a tour of the Cadbury Chocolate Factory, across the street.

Today, cruise visitors dock at Port Chalmers, to board bus tours of Dunedin and Larnach Castle, or stop at the Octagon, to walk the city. They can also board the Silver Fern train, at the Port Chalmers station, for a ride along the scenic Taieri Gorge, ending at the Dunedin station. Either way, a trip to Dunedin is a visit to a little bit of Scotland, in New Zealand.

FRENCH POLYNESIA
Island Gods

Reverence for Island Gods

Three thousand years ago, people left the area of New Guinea and sailed east. Known as the first wave of Polynesians, the people settled uninhabited islands of Fiji, Tonga and Samoa. Less than two thousand years ago, people sailed south into the Pacific, from South East Asian islands, and arrived in Hawaii, Marquesas Islands and Society Islands, among other islands, down to New Zealand, all of which were uninhabited. This became known as the second wave of canoes.

The large triangle of Pacific Ocean, from Hawaii to Easter Island and New Zealand, is regarded as Polynesia. Fiji is grouped with New Guinea and the Solomon Islands, as Melanesia. The Great Migration was accomplished by skilled navigators of stars and tides. Their transit was purposeful and not random. By 1200 CE, Polynesia, that is, the islands of the Pacific, were populated.

Traveling on the long canoes with settlers were plants, to begin new farms, tools, to build huts, make fish hooks and carve wood. Each canoe had a special place for gods. Relationships between people and their origins can be traced today, by similarity of their deities, and the manner of ritual. Some gods kept a watchful eye on the heavens. Special gods had their own traveling cases.

Function in island society was determined by relationship to the gods. Chiefs were close to the gods. They cared for deities in their compound, and were revered through history, as gods. High priests performed rituals and interpreted stars and signs from the gods. Commoners worked for the chief and feared his gods. Among each community were Arioi, depraved, party animals, from all classes of people, who drank heartily, until called upon to serve the gods as warriors.

Archaeologists and historians look for remnants of material culture, to define ritual and social meaning in societies, in the absence of written language. For Polynesians, stories are in their art. Great and prolific carvers of wood, up to the time of European contact, and European written record, wooden remnants of civilization provide a look, at the depth of culture, even when meaning is not discerned. Like the travels of the first navigators, symbolism in Polynesian art is not random. Even body art, the art of tattoo, has meaning in Polynesia, beyond decoration.

This is a little story of peopling Polynesia and the expression of culture in the arts. Items made with care were revered, as embodiment of gods, or effigies of gods. Without written record, island gods have much to tell, about the people in their cosmos and at home.

Arrival of Polynesians

Ancient Canoe

Ancient Transport with Outrigging

In the original dispersal of humans from Africa, so many thousands of years ago, ice across what is now the South China Sea enabled early people to migrate, across the landscape. When the first ice age melted into the sea, islands formed off the coast of South East Asia, and between Australia and New Guinea. People became isolated on islands.

Nine thousand years ago, as water levels rose, people crafted rafts to travel from their island. Over thousands of years, sailors improved their craft and built canoes. Canoes became longer; up to one hundred and fifty feet, or more. Then double hull canoes were launched, connected with outrigging, to stabilize their hulls. Imagine the outer stabilization poles of a canoe, with large twine netting bags of coconuts, secured along the side. Coconuts added buoyancy and a mobile food supply, for months of a voyage.

Reasons for long distance voyages is unknown. New Guinea was a large population area, three thousand years ago. Competition for land, or fighting on the losing side of inter-tribal wars, are most often indicated in historic studies, as impetus to travel.[107] From New Guinea, came the first canoes of Lapita people to reach the Solomon Islands. A thousand years or more later, people sailed further east, to populate islands of Polynesia, Fiji, Samoa and Tonga.

In later voyages, east into Polynesia, not all islands were uninhabited. Some were previously populated, from the Great Migration from Malaysian and South East Asian islands. Archaeologists identify two streams of people: the Lapita people from New Guinea, who populated western Polynesia, and people from Malaysia and islands of South East Asia, who populated eastern Polynesia. There were multiple migrations from the two source areas, and movement between islands. Isolating complete islands, as a single migration group, is rare. Some islands initially populated, were abandoned.[108] Reasons for vacating, and the new destinations, remain a mystery.

The Great Migration, from islands of South East Asia, occurred around the third century of the current era. Although people occupied the Marquesas much earlier, possibly in the first century before the current era. From Marquesas, canoes landed on Hawaiian Islands, in the fourth century of the current era. Easter Island was populated about the same time, by people of the Great Migration. Tahiti and the Society Islands became inhabited from the

---

[107] See generally, Douglas Oliver, Polynesia in Early Historic Times, Bess Press, Honolulu, 2002.
[108] See Peter S. Bellwood, The Polynesians: Prehistory of an Island People, Thames and Hudson Ltd., London, 1978.

third to the ninth century of the current era.[109] Last to see people arrive, was New Zealand, in 1200 CE.

Around 1200 CE, long canoes fell from use. New Zealand became the most southernly habitat for people of the seas. Consider that climate becomes cooler above the Tropic of Cancer and below the Topic of Capricorn. Hawaii sits just within the northern boundary of Polynesia, at the Tropic of Cancer. Easter Island sits just below the line of the Tropic of Capricorn. North Island of New Zealand is about ten degrees further south of Easter Island. By 1200 CE, people looking for new land ran the gamut of the globe, of habitable landscape, for people accustomed to warm weather.

Island Transport

Curious minds of the twentieth century were incredulous of the ability of Polynesian people, to travel great distances, by canoe, without instruments available to eighteenth century navigators. Anthropologist, Ben Finney, built a forty-two-foot Polynesian style canoe, in the 1960s, using the notes of Captain James Cook as a guide. Cook made meticulous notes of the canoes, of native Hawaiians, upon his arrival in 1769.

---

[109] Martial Moutcho, French Polynesia History and Culture, La Provence Print, France, 2017.

In 1975, Finney launched the sixty-foot long Hokule'a from Hawaii, for the three-thousand-mile sail to Tahiti, without modern navigation equipment on board. As his captain, Finney chose Pius Piailug, a master traditional navigator from Micronesia. Guided by stars, winds and ocean currents, Hokule'a arrived in Tahiti, thirty-two days later, proving the ability of ancient navigators to sail among the islands. The Hokule'a returned to Hawaii, amid great celebration by Native Hawaiians.[110]

Cosmos of Oro

In Polynesia, there was a pantheon of gods, prior to arrival of missionaries, in the nineteenth century. At the behest of missionaries, or in some cases by decree of kings, when compliance with missionaries facilitated a king buying guns from European traders, idols were smashed, burned, or surrendered to missionaries. Surrendered gods often ended their journey in European museums.[111]

Polynesians held certain gods in highest regard. Reverence to Oro, a supreme power, was seen across islands of the Pacific, represented in carved effigy. Other gods were local to an island, or island group, and may have begun as reverence for a mortal king of skill and bravery, who led the people well and was deified. As a practical matter, whether always ethereal gods, or mortals elevated to gods, they are all *atua* to Polynesians. Further, a carving of wood, or stone, may embody the god, represent the god, or be godly power in earthly form. All are *atua*.

Cook, and a few of the eighteenth-century explorers, made notes of the physical form of idols, to which natives exhibited reverence; such as, crying at a statue, or leaving offerings, or squatting in quiet. Ethnography as a science came later. Few questions were asked about the name, or place of the god in

---

[110] The sailing was repeated in 1995, with Native Hawaiian Nainoa Thompson as captain. Ben Finney, Voyage of Rediscovery, University of California Press, Berkeley, 1994.
[111] Paul Gauguin wrote of his mistress, in his travelogue of Polynesia, Noa Noa, that she prayed to Taaroa and Jesus.

the lives of Polynesians. Any opportunity for learning was rapidly lost. All that is left, are wonderous artworks of carvers and sculptors, where little inherent meaning is known.[112]

Ahu Sentry

---

[112] This does not mean that the meaning is lost. Polynesians are masters of oral history. Lack of knowledge is in the European, western world of academics, with whom intricate knowledge has not been shared, or the explanation is translated, against a rubric of western cosmology of relating lifeways to western religion.

Gods of life, rain, fertility and harvests, or war have different names across Polynesia, although the root stories of creation of man, day and night, weather and war are constant. In Tahiti, Taaroa is the creator of the universe. Wives of Taaroa gave birth to night. Sons of Taaroa included the god of war. Oro was the god of war and peace in Tahiti, the ultimate arbiter of life forces, even more powerful than Taaroa. The effigy of Oro was kept in the cult of a small, elite group.

Sacred Peaks - Natural Atua

Polynesian island groups are thousands of miles distant from each other, and more remote from the well-font of their origination. Islands developed over time, similar, although different, sacred ritual. High priests gave lessons of *atua* to the king and commoners. Local gods might appear in dreams to anyone. Spirits, not actual *atua*, but life forces in the environment, could occupy a person, and possess their thoughts and deeds.

One of the oldest *atua* of Polynesia is Tane. The name means man. The *atua* image is the god. Placed on canoes of people of Society Islands, Marquesas and Aotearoa, as the north island of New Zealand was known to Maori, Tane led the way to home, on new islands.

SHERRY HUTT | 311

Home for Tane on Huahine Facing the Sea

Huahanie Atua

Papeto'al Marae Platform Huahine

Opunohu Walled Compound, Home for Tane on Huahine

To make *atua* at home on the islands, on Huahine island, for example, the chief brought Tane on his canoe. A compound was built, in which there was a home for Tane. This was the place of ritual practices, known as marae. The high priest house was just outside this low-walled compound. Also, outside the sacred compound, was the place of death. In death, people of importance were disemboweled and placed on a scaffold platform, to disintegrate naturally. When the Missionary War, with traditional believers, ended in 1817, with victory to the missionaries, they burned Tane.

In common to people across Polynesia are marae, the place of ritual and houses of *atua*. New Zealand, the final destination in the migration of the Pacific, has marae that are houses of *atua* and meeting places for tribal ceremony. The wooden, painted structures all have elaborate Maori designs on beams and roof supports, inside and out.

In islands of the Pacific, marae are more likely open places, where gods are placed. On Easter Island, moai statues are often found in a row, on rectangular, gravel and stone raised platforms. On the Society Islands and Marquesas, marae are platforms, long and narrow, faced with flat stones along the raised area, or large level, rectangles, placed one on the next, declining in size, to create a stairstep, pyramid to the open platform of *atua*, at the top.

An exception to the rectangle marae, is Pulemelei, a star-shaped site, on Savai'i Island of Samoa. This marae is one hundred eighty, by one hundred fifty feet and forty feet high. There are sunken ramps around the site, and post holes, suggesting the marae had a protective roof and a promenade to walk up to the top. Samoa has a longer time depth, than eastern Polynesia. With a large, successful population, Pulemelei could serve high priests, with a major ceremonial venue.

The Marquesas are unique as an island group, as there are no surrounding reefs and lagoons, found on other islands in Polynesia. People lived in the interior valleys. Coastlines are not inviting. When eighteenth century explorers arrived, they found the local population not inviting either. In Marquesas, marae were places of human sacrifice. People practiced cannibalism.

On Huahine, in the Society Islands, where resistance to missionaries was most fierce and longest-lasting, marae are well preserved. In places where *atua* figures were burned, or removed to museums, empty places remain. The essence of *atua* still hangs in the trees, on the beachhead.

Beachhead Atua

Life of Arioi – Warrior Elite

On all islands of Polynesia, there were chiefs, priests and commoners. In societies of long-time depth, there were carvers and boat builders, with specialized skills. There also existed a cross-societal strata, fraternal organization, which was voluntary, known as Arioi. Arioi had their own initiation ritual and codes of conduct. They could be found on Society Islands, Marquesas, Cook Islands and the Australs. Of all the islands, Arioi were most visible in Tahiti and Bora Bora.

Arioi proved their worth to the group by: dancing; agility with instruments of war, should they ever be needed; and in a display of good manners. They were in the nature of knights of their era. Arioi spent their time practicing their dancing, swimming and weaving leis, which they wore as crowns, not unlike Roman counterparts of an earlier era, so far away. With their lavish amounts of free time, Arioi organized festivals. They knew how to throw a party.

Warrior Protector of Atua on Marae

Arioi were associated with mysterious To'o, an *atua* of stature with Oro. Privileged to host such an important *atua*, Arioi were the privileged party boys of the Polynesian world. Fed by commoners of the village, in which they existed, served by slaves, Arioi had quick, short liaisons with women. They took no responsibility for any children as a result of their actions. Arioi spent their lives in a party haze, unless and until needed by the chief as warriors. Then they fought.

Tiki and Tattoo

Tiki Boundary Marker

Arioi were distinguished within their group by their tattoo. For Arioi, there were eight grades within the fraternal hierarchy. Status was proudly made visible. All warriors and men of high rank on the islands, as well as women of status, had elaborate tattoo. Tattoo designs reflected social status and achievement, like an indelible medal of honor. Some tattoo was merely ornamental.

The practice of tattoo was known to Polynesians, whether they were descendants of migrants from Melanesia or Malaysia. In Polynesian culture, the art form was at its most elaborate and extensive. Full body tattoo was a mark of affluence. Receiving a tattoo was a mark of manhood, as it took stamina to endure the pain.

Tattoo artists were held in high esteem. Favored artists had a large clientele. In the tattoo process, dye was placed under the skin, by using bone, or tortoise shell needles. Pin prick incisions placed ink, in a laborious process. The dye-tipped needle was tapped into the skin. In some designs, a comb of many needles was tapped in unison, which rendered tattoo a truly painful experience. Tattooing caused bleeding, and in some cases infection, or death.

Notable were people of high rank, with face and full body tattoos. Slaves were marked with tattooed buttocks. It was impossible to go to another village, or island, and not be identified. Tattoo artistry was often localized. It gave distinction to place. Some artisans repeated traditional designs, with additional original designs in their work, as a special signature.

Designs in tattoo are seen across Polynesia, repeated on bark cloth, wood carvings and carving on shell. Pottery with designs, so prevalent in western Polynesia, in early cultures in the migratory era, fell out of practice in Eastern Polynesia. Much of the material culture of Eastern Polynesia is represented in wood carving, cloth and woven mats. Ceremonial bowls, paddles and war clubs have intricate carving of tattoo style designs, as well as anthropomorphic designs, known as Tiki.

Although little is known of Polynesian *atua*, there is no doubt, that the carved, human-like statues, ubiquitous in the islands, have mana. These are Tiki, carved *atua*, whether representations of gods, actual gods, or spirits captured in the figure. Tiki may be small, like an amulet worn on twine, or carved onto a club or bowl. They were often carved on canoes.

Aura of Island Gods Today

Large Tiki, of several feet high, to about ten feet, carved of wood, or stone, marked boundary areas of chiefdoms. Tiki inhabit marae. A Tiki in a museum exhibit, lacks the aura of a Tiki *in situ*, on a marae platform. Most potent, are Tiki in the position of original placement.

Cultural History Preserved Today

At the Paul Gauguin Museum in Tahiti, Tiki found in the area have been relocated to museum grounds. Out of context of place, they still project mana. On Huahine, or Nuku Hiva, of the Marquesas, there are Tiki around the island, in open air marae sites, at, or close to, their original habitat. There is a sense of power of place, even felt by those uninitiated in Polynesian cosmos.

Walking marae grounds today, on any of the Polynesian islands, the feeling of invading the aura of an unseen force is inescapable. *Atua* have power. Seen and unseen, physically diminished in time, depleted by removal, or destruction during the missionary era, *atua* have endured.

Island Gods at Home Today

Papeete Tahiti

The French in French Polynesia

The French portrayed Polynesia to the world, as a garden of bliss, though they knew life on the islands to be a difficult existence. Painters, poets and politicians repeated descriptions of lovely islands, a thousand miles from land. The eighteenth century was an era of sea exploration. In the nineteenth century, powerful nations claimed colonies. France asserted its place among the powerful commercial nations of the world, by staking claim to Polynesia and making it French.

French corsairs of the eighteenth century were among the first to sail by Tahiti. Able sailors though they were, their interest was in quick capture of loot, not discovery of land-based opportunity. That was the domain of governments. Later, English, French and Dutch sailors sailed to the islands, on official missions, to create maps, on behalf of government and commercial sponsors. They found meager real estate, no obvious export items, and few people.

Brief visitors, whether pirates, explorers, or refugee mutineers of the HMS *Bounty*, left an indelible mark on development of the islands. They forever changed native lives by bequests of guns and disease. Guns enabled a lesser tribe to become dominant. King Pomare I began a short-lived dynasty of rulers of Polynesia, begun with English weapons, and ended with the lack of English support, when French asserted control. Disease greatly reduced the native population.

Less obvious in the first decades, was the critical, indelible, change to native culture that arrived with European missionaries in 1700. Oral history of centuries was replaced in missionary teaching, by Christian Bible stories. High priests of tribes, next to a chief or the king in power, were replaced by missionaries, from foreign lands. The code of island ethics, became European and Christian. Missionaries made the step to European law and government, a natural transition.

Three French Ladies in Tahiti

Though United States and British captains, who visited Tahiti and saw value in the islands, pressed their governments to annex some, or all of the islands, it was the French who asserted control. French conquest was not quickly, nor easily achieved. By 1885, the French Colony of Oceania, as Polynesia was called, was administered and defended by France, from a base of operation at Papeete, on Tahiti. American, British and German entrepreneurs garnered much of the successful commercial business on the islands. For France, the islands were an expense.

This is a short political history of Polynesia, from native kings and queens to French governors. Though French in government, most locals found little relevance of government in their lives. Polynesian islands are popular tourist destinations today, for what the French were unable to achieve, in mastery of the landscape. Where nature is oblivious to government, beauty survives.

Arrival of Europeans

French Polynesia is a combination of five island archipelagos, including: Society Islands, in which Tahiti and Moorea lie; Gambier Islands; Tuamotu Archipelago; Marquesas, which includes Atuona Oa island of Hiva Oa, where

Gauguin died; and Tubuai Islands. Society Islands is the name given by Captain James Cook, to honor his sponsor the Royal Society, when he visited in 1769.

Fishing Traditional Style

As a group of islands, French Polynesia covers an area, if overlaid on Europe, that runs west to east from southern Spain to Gdansk, northern Poland, and south into the Mediterranean, to Croatia on the Adriatic. The administrative center is Papeete, on Tahiti. Of a total of one hundred and fifty thousand residents today, two-thirds live on Tahiti and Moorea. It is not surprising that numerous sailors, whether adventurous pirates, or purposeful explorers, stopped on one or more of the islands, as they transited the South Pacific.

It is difficult to assess the population of the islands, prior to arrival of Europeans. By 1800, after effects of disease and confrontation reduced the population, it is estimated that sixty thousand natives occupied the island groups in total. By 1900, the number was reduced to three thousand.[113]

The litany of explorers arriving in Polynesia includes Antoine Bougainville, sailing for France, who came by in 1768 and 1771. He called the islands New Cythera. Bougainville was preceded by Englishmen Cook and Samuel Wallis in 1767, and Dutchman Jacob Roggeveen in 1722, reputed to be the

---

[113] Jean-Louis Saquet, The Tahiti Handbook, Avant et Après, Singapore, 1999, p. 94.

first European on Bora Bora. These men created maps and wrote reports of gardens and lagoons, made to seem glorious, in comparison to long days at sea. Missionary groups relied on information of Bougainville, Wallis and Cook to assess, whether natives could be saved by conversion to Christianity.

Seasoned explorers were observant of effects on native people, from prior contact with the outside world. Cook noticed declining health in women, no doubt the effects of prior visits of buccaneers and corsairs, pirates by other names, from England, France and Spain. Spanish explorers reached Marquesas as early as 1595, bringing guns and disease. By the time missionaries from England and France arrived, in 1797, potential subjects for conversion were reduced in substantial numbers.[114]

Bougainville Marker 1768 Papeete

---

[114] See generally, Martial Moutcha, French Polynesia History and Culture, La Provence Print, France, 2017.

Bougainville Landing Point Memorial

Cook Memorial Papeete

In 1789, mutineers, led by Fletcher Christian, arrived in Tahiti on the HMS *Bounty*. They landed during a critical period, in the inter-tribal wars of the future Society Islands. Mutineers stayed on Tahiti five months, during which time they gave guns to a minor chief, who parlayed the advantageous firepower to overcome rivals and take control of the islands.

Christian had twenty-four sailors with him, when he reached Tahiti. Sixteen chose to remain on the islands, when Christian decided he must sail to lesser known turf. His concerns were justified. Not long after Fletcher Christian departed Tahiti, a British captain arrived, who made Captain Bligh seem like a permissive saint. The captain corralled all sixteen mutineers, including those who ran into the volcanic hills of the island and those who hastily built and launched a schooner. Few of those captured survived to stand trial in Portsmouth.[115]

Unified Tahitian Dynasty

Symbol of Tahitian Monarchy

---

[115] See: The Real Captain Bligh, this itinerary.

Chieftain Tu Tina Mate, who controlled Tahiti, utilized guns received from Fletcher Christian to dominate other contenders for king of the islands, that is, the Society Islands. When he conquered Moorea, he dubbed himself King Pomare I.[116] His son, Tu, became Pomare II in 1815.[117]

Despite the action of Pomare II, to become Christian in 1812, prior to becoming king, English missionaries preferred to see his infant son be established as king, upon birth. The action of the missionaries is curious. Though they were anxious to break native traditions, they employed the ancient Polynesian tradition of consecrating the heir to the kingship shortly after birth. In custom, the act established succession without turmoil. For the missionaries, the custom was an opportunity to control education of a proper Christian Tahitian monarch, in ways of the Church of England.

Church Pomare III

---

[116] Pomare I lived from 1745 to 1803.
[117] Pomare II lived from 1774 to 1821.

Whatever hopes the missionaries had for Pomare III, died with him six years later. Pomare III had an older sister, Aimata, who was overlooked by the British missionaries. In 1827, Aimata, as Queen Pomare Vahine IV, began her fifty-year reign.[118] She was revered by her people, befriended by British counsel George Pritchard, who became her close counsel, and detested by the French, for her strong, independent spirit.

Queen Pomare Vahine IV

---

[118] Pomare IV was born in 1813 and died 1877. Her husband was King Tapoa II of Bora Bora. That is another story.

Pomare IV had a son, who succeeded the Queen, as Pomare V in 1877.[119] The wife of Pomare V was a native of Tahiti, of half Tahitian and half Jewish heritage. She lived to 1934, as the last royal of the islands, although she never ruled. Pomare V was an active king, for only three years. In 1880, he gave his royal islands to the French, and abdicated the title. In 1891, the last king died.

Witness to the outpouring of grief of island natives, upon death of their king, was Paul Gauguin. He wrote in his journal, *Noa Noa*, that the people showed much emotion for the dead king. They held funeral rites in native tradition, despite Christian services. Then, people went back to their daily business, as though nothing in life was changed. In fact, much had changed at that moment. Tahiti went from monarchy to French annexed territory.

Pomare Monument next to Breadfruit Tree in Papeete Parking Lot

---

[119] Pomare V was born in 1839 and died 1891.

Missionary Era

Missionary Church, Papeete

Missionaries, of the London Missionary School, arrived in French Polynesia in 1795.[120] Believing that life would be blissful in Tahiti, they were surprised at simplicity of native life. People lived in grass huts, wove mats and simple cloth, and grew vegetables. Fishing and gardening were not difficult, nor time consuming, so natives felt their life was ideal. Missionaries came to tell them differently. Once people felt deprived, they found Christian god. Although for many it was facial conversion.

Pomare II was impressed to become a Christian in 1812, when he realized that as a Christian the missionaries did not denigrate him to his people, when he purchased guns from European traders. With guns, he could maintain power on earth, regardless of who held power in the next life. To show his sincerity, Pomare II issued what is known as the Code of Pomare.

---

[120] Moutcha, p. 126.

Natives knew what was taboo, known in island cosmos as *tapu*, without written rules. The Code of Pomare was an English code of ethics, in the model of early nineteenth century England. In the Code, young girls were to remain chaste, until marriage in the church. They could have one union. The Code ended ritual sacrifice of humans, or animals.

In the world of island missionaries, mana, the strength of the person, was protected by god. It was no longer a death sentence to injure the mana of the king. Animals and objects lost their mana. Animist priests and kings lost prestige.

Christian Cemetery Marker in Atua Style on a Pyramid Marae

In customary native life, ceremony, death rites and important events, such as induction of a new king, were conducted by priests on marae. The existence of marae is seen throughout the greater Polynesian ocean triangle, from Hawaii, to Easter Island and Aotearoa. The marae consists of a raised platform, although styles of platforms vary across islands and time. Gods are on marae. Missionaries caused maraes to lose relevance for the people. They were left to deteriorate.

Within mission schools, there was no room for oral history of cultural traditions of the people. Canoe building, reading stars and winds, practical and not religious, were lost concepts. By the time the people of the islands lost their freedom to the French, they had already lost their culture.

French Protectorate from Whom?

Sainte Famile Moorea

In 1838, French Commodore Dupetit Thouars arrived in Papeete, and threatened Queen Pomare IV with removal by force, if she did not abdicate in favor of the French government. The Queen turned to her trusted advisor, Englishman, George Pritchard. Pritchard sailed to England, to convince the British Parliament to offer the Tahitian Queen a British protectorate. In his absence, Thouars annexed Marquesas, in the name of France, and returned to press Queen Pomare to abdicate. She sailed across the bay to Moorea, to hide from the French.

Working among chiefs of the islands, adverse to the interests of the Queen, was Hitoti a Manua, descendant of a powerful chief, overcome by Pomare I with his guns.[121] The Pomare rival urged chiefs in the islands to support a French annexation of Tahiti. In response, the Queen told her people, that Britain would not abandon them. In fact, by that time, Parliament had done so.

By the time Pritchard informed the Queen of her precarious situation, French governor of Tahiti, Armand Bruat arrived in Tahiti. In 1843, Bruat announced that he possessed orders of the French king, to annex Tahiti, regardless of the position of Queen Pomare. The Queen, in defiance, flew the Tahitian flag over her Papeete palace. The French governor sent soldiers to tear down the flag.

Bruat built a French fort in Tahiti, then arrested Pritchard, and expelled him from the islands. By 1844, the French held the island. That did not mean all of the islands acquiesced to the French. For the next three years, a bloody, island by island, battle ensued.

French Fortress Lighthouse

---

[121] Hitoti a Manua was born 1770, and died in 1846, shortly after the French takeover of Tahiti.

France annexed Gambier islands in 1881, then fought against stiff resistance in Huahine. People of Huahine, impervious to missionary attempts to Christianize them, gave the French Catholics no better welcome. So bloody were battles on Huahine, that when the French finally overcame their native adversaries in 1897, French citizenship was withheld from the island until 1946. In 1958, when France offered a referendum on the issue of independence, and sixty-five percent of islanders voted to remain a French Overseas protectorate, voters on Huahine said no.

Victory over Polynesia was declared by France in 1885, when they named the administrative unit French Colony Oceania. The Austral Islands were made a French colony in 1900, completing the span of French control in the Pacific. During World War II, when Germany invaded and quickly controlled France, French Colony Oceania fought with the Free French, under Charles de Gaulle.

Papeete Lagoons Constructed and Real

In 1957, the name of Polynesia was changed to simply French Polynesia. Polynesia became autonomous in 1984, and an Overseas Collectivity in 2003. All the verbiage aside, France does not want to lose contact with its islands, and the reality is, that the islands want French financial support, along with independent governance.

English, US and German businessmen came to Tahiti, once France established a stable government. Members of multinational families married locals, one of whom married Pomare V, and reigned as Queen Marau, although she did not rule, into the twentieth century. These families sought wealth on the islands. Several of them succeeded. Their efforts were little bothered by the French, who were their benefactors.

French resources were used to build docks and an airport. French military kept the peace and French bureaucrats managed the infrastructure of government. The French gained their colony. It served to give prestige to a nineteenth century colonizing power. That was all.

Today in French Polynesia

Tahiti a Cruise Favorite Destination

Today, cultural traditions of native people are taught in French schools, as local history. Students learn about native culture in trips to museums. Native Tahitians are a small minority population. Foreign-owned hotels and business dominate the landscape. The largest source of island income is tourism, little of which is realized by natives. A monument to Pomare V stands outside

Papeete. Next to the shrine is a breadfruit tree; the tree that brought Captain Bligh to the islands. His sojourn ended in a mutiny, that brought mutineers back to Tahiti, where English guns aided Pomare I, to begin his dynasty. The cycle of history is ever present in Tahiti.

Over-Water Bungalows in an Idyllic Lagoon

Papeete is still the administrative capital of the French Autonomous region. An autonomous region is of higher independent standing than a department, protectorate, or colony. Society Islands has a representative in the French parliament. Since 1987, France has supported the French University of the Pacific, in Papeete.

The islands are known for their history in French nuclear testing, which began in 1963. There were anti-testing demonstrations on the islands, and in France. In 1985, the French government blew up a yacht owned by environmental group, Greenpeace. Testing ended in 1996, with the South Pacific Nuclear Free Zone Treaty. The French military left the islands, and the economy collapsed. In 2009, the French government offered compensation for the effects of nuclear testing on locals.

The economy of the islands has recovered with income from tourism and vanilla exports. Pearl farms are a large part of the economy on some islands of Polynesia, such as Bora Bora. Bora Bora has its own story.

Docking in Moorea Today

In 1856, cotton plantation owner in Tahiti, William Stuart, brought Chinese laborers to the islands, to compensate for the dearth of local labor. During the US Civil War, known in Tahiti and England as the War of Succession, cotton prices were high. Supply of cotton to British mills was disrupted, by the war raging in the American south. Tahitian cotton was a profitable substitute product. After the war, American cotton, joined by cotton from Asia and Arabia, entered the market. Cotton prices for Tahitian island exports dropped precipitously.

When cotton plantation production was reduced in Tahiti, many Chinese workers returned to China. Some stayed and joined entrepreneurs on the islands. The Stuart cotton plantation on Tahiti became a golf course in 1970.

Today, China vies with Australia and France, in support of the Society Islands, in French Oceania. In exchange, China seeks fishing licenses, in the vast ocean surrounding the islands. In this regard, the People's Republic of China is in competition with Taiwan for access to fishing areas of the South Pacific. Future struggles of China, in its effort to merge Taiwan into China, may play out in the fishing waters of the South Pacific around Tahiti.

Native Tahitians, never the beneficiaries of foreign politics, are likely to turn inward to their island home, for cultural survival. Although the tourism economy has not made locals wealthy, appreciation of visitors for Tahitian culture, is an incentive to keep culture ongoing. Never lush, always sparse, Polynesia was Polynesian prior to being French. So, it will continue without France.

Recyled Housing Tahitian Style

Still Natural in Tahiti

Gauguin Idyll

Paul Gauguin in Tahiti

Paul Gauguin was prompted to change his career to art in Paris. He found his artistic soul in Tahiti. Gauguin was a responsible family man, dabbling in art as his secret passion, when Camille Pissarro challenged him to paint full-time, if he wanted to consider himself a painter. Absent an income, Gauguin spent winters in Pont Aven, on the Brittany coast. To truly come to the essence of art, Gauguin fled France to Tahiti. It was his desire to experience primitive culture in native habitat. Tahiti was warmer than France. The cost of living was almost nil. He could afford Tahiti.

Gauguin was bold as a painter, yet underestimated himself as a writer. The subject of many volumes of art analysis and critique, he is best described in his own words. In his travel diary of his first years in Tahiti, *Noa Noa*, Gauguin wrote to his wife Mette, that critics are literary men. They try to describe art, as it relates to writing and literature.

Painting is not literature wrote Gauguin. Literature unfolds slowly and explains itself. Painting is viewed in an instant. Critics write what they know. They do not know art. They do not understand my painting.[122]

This complaint of Gauguin of art critics, was expressed after a positive critique of *Study of a Nude*, also titled, *Woman Sewing*, Gauguin's breakthrough painting. The simple painting of Mette's house maid, naturally repairing her shirt, gave him a place among Impressionist artists of Paris, and space in galleries. If this was what the public wanted and expected, and if this painting defined his place among a group, then Gauguin wanted to turn elsewhere. To join a Paris cadre was not the reason Gauguin gave up a comfortable life as a stockbroker, his family and security.

---

[122] Paul Gauguin, Noa Noa, The Tahitian Journal, Dover Publications, New York, 1985 translation and printing of the 1919 journal. The thoughts related above are not a direct quote.

Paul Gauguin escaped from Paris to Pont Aven, on the north Brittany coast. He came impoverished and alone. In Pont Aven, Gauguin found his passion and unique style of art. He also found a bevy of companions, who wished to emulate his style. Founding a school of art, averted hunger, it did not satisfy his need to explore the core of his artistic being.

Though Gauguin went between Paris and Pont Aven several seasons, with an eventful side trip to Avignon, he wanted to paint Tahiti. It was a place he heard of, yet had never been. To reach the primitive core of his art, he sought primitive people. In Tahiti, a French possession, he found pretensions of France on the distant islands. He also found the beauty of people caught between native and French life, as was he. In Tahiti, Gauguin created works for which he is best known. This is the story of the painter in his ideal habitat, which made him famous, and ended his life.

Success at the Bourse

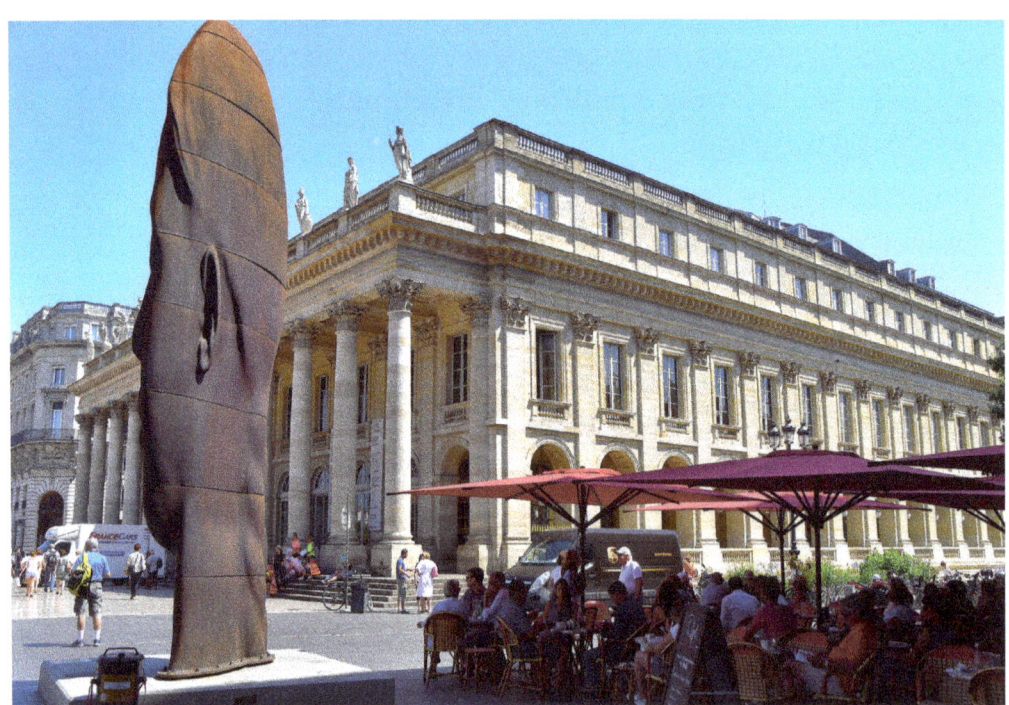

French Bourse Bordeaux

The personal life of Paul Gauguin was as nuanced, as his later development as a painter. Eugène Henri Paul Gauguin was born in France in 1848, to French political journalist, Clovis Gauguin, and his French-Peruvian wife, Aline Maria. To avoid a hostile political climate in France, in 1851, the family sailed to Peru. Clovis died on the voyage, leaving the widow, and two children under the age of four, to seek residence with her family.

For Gauguin, life under patronage of his wealthy great uncle gave him every advantage. For four years, the little French contingent lived well in Lima, in a household of servants and indulgences. When in 1855, Gauguin's paternal grandfather died, and his mother decided to return to France, to administer the estate, it was a financially disastrous decision. The elder Gauguin's estate was small. It offered a meager existence to the three Gauguins. They lived not in Paris, but in humble style in rural Orleans. Meanwhile, back in Peru, the patriarch of the wealthy family also died. In her absence, Gauguin's mother missed out on her ability to share in lucrative bequests.

Paul Gauguin was accustomed to wealth and to speaking Spanish. He did not fit well, in the modest French country life. He bragged about descending from the Borgia family, on his father's side, and from a Spanish proponent of worker's rights on his mother's side.[123] At seventeen, he left school, without completing his studies, to join the merchant navy.

While Gauguin shoveled coal below deck, the job of an engineer's assistant, he heard stories of a Polynesian paradise, which he never saw. When he switched from the merchant to the military navy, it was not as an officer. Returning home, six years later, Gauguin learned his mother died, his sister married

---

[123] Gauguin's maternal grandmother, Flora, was born in Spain. She married a French painter, Antoine. Their daughter, Gauguin's mother, was born in France. Flora left home to campaign for women's and worker's rights. It was the 1820s, and Flora believed that women should receive equal pay to men. Antoine thought Flora should stay home. Antoine sought sole custody of their daughter. They fought. Antoine shot Flora. She died of her wounds. Their marital squabbles, the shooting, and the fight for custody of their child, were headline news. Gauguin may have inherited his swarthy complexion from the Spanish side of the family, and his artistic ability through his maternal grandfather. Lawrence and Elisabeth Hanson, Noble Savage: The Life of Paul Gauguin, Random House, New York, 1955, p. 9.

a Chilean merchant, his mother's home had burned, and remaining family possessions were pillaged.[124] Gauguin was impoverished, aged twenty-three, and alone.

Gauguin's Grandmother Flora Tristan 1838 – Women's Rights Activist (public domain)

Gauguin was given an opportunity for a respectable life, when a friend of Gauguin's mother found him a job at the French Bourse. He did well as a stockbroker. Gauguin proved to be intelligent, hardworking, and capable. He

---

[124] Hanson, p. 19.

used his tall, strong stature, his dark features, and his abundant self-assurance as business assets. Within a few years, Gauguin achieved affluence.

Gauguin was a self-described rascal with women, although he desired a family. At a boarding house, where he often went for dinner, he met a Danish visitor to Paris, Mett-Sophie Gad. She was his opposite. Mette was raised in a household of civil servants. She wanted no excitement from life. In 1873, when Mette was twenty-three and Gauguin twenty-five, they married. Over the next ten years, they had five children. They lived a quiet, advantaged life, as Gauguin went to work every day at the Bourse. Secretly, he began painting.

Paul Gauguin & Mette Sophie Gad by Julie Laurberg, 1885 (Royal Danish Library)

Art as a Passion

Paul Gauguin 1891 (Louis-Maurice Boulet de Monvel public domain)

For nine years, Gauguin lived a double life. Although historians rarely record Gauguin as enjoying his wife's company, he did enjoy his children. He applied himself as a stockbroker and enjoyed the ability to provide luxuries for his family. By all outward appearances, Gauguin was successful.

Gauguin's spare moments were spent painting. If he could be a success as a stockbroker, he felt he could be a success at anything, with enough effort. He never lacked self-confidence in his ability.

In 1876, Gauguin met Camille Pissarro. Pissarro was a family man, so dedicated to his art, that he was willing to live an improvised life, living on the faith that his belief in his art would vindicate him. Pissarro displayed his work with a group of painters, who shared his unconventional style of painting unromantic subjects, caught in a point in time. Their paints were applied softly, as though to catch the light. One of the painters, Claude Monet, created *Impression Sunrise*, which was emblematic of the group's philosophy of art. Thereafter, the group of painters was known as *Impressionists*.

Impressionist painters did not enjoy the label. They thought of it as a means to corral their art and deride it. The mainstream press and respectable art galleries refused to give recognition to impressionistic works. Meanwhile, many of dealers hedged their bets, by purchasing canvasses while they were cheap.

In Gauguin, Pissarro saw a man with some talent, but he had a more important feature. Gauguin had an income, and thus could be taught to appreciate the artists of Pissarro's flock. He could purchase their work, sustain their lives, and give greater acceptability to their efforts.

Pissarro introduced Gauguin to Monet, Cézanne, and Renoir, who all avoided Gauguin as an amateur. Works of these artists were selling without his help. Wisely, Gauguin purchased a Cézanne. He purchased the works of other Impressionists, including Pissarro, Monet, Manet, Renoir, Sisley and Daumier, as if to buy his way into their group, by owning their art.

In 1881, Gauguin discovered that his children's nurse, Justine, had been a nude model for Delacroix. Gauguin convinced Justine to pose for him. The result was *Study of a Nude*.

The painting was an instant sensation. It was regarded as a masterpiece. Gauguin had innocently shattered notions of portrait painting. Not only had he painted an ordinary person, in the act of an ordinary event, mending her blouse, Gauguin captured Justine as she was. He painted with compassion. She was made immortal with every crease and bulge of a forty-year old woman, including the hunched shoulders of a hard life. The model was captured in an act, not posed.

Paul Gauguin Study of a Nude 1880 (NyCarlsberg Glyptotek)

As a result of *Study of a Nude*, Gauguin was accepted into ranks of the Impressionists. Mette fired Justine. Mette also curbed Gauguin the artist, telling him to apply himself more at the Bourse.

With four children and Mette expecting a fifth, there was little time to paint. In an exhibition in 1882, Gauguin showed his canvasses next to those of Renoir. Unfortunately, he had not created any new works, to carry through on brilliance seen the prior year. Gauguin was dismissed as a one-time event.

His fellow painters levied the harshest sentiment. Monet challenged Gauguin, by saying no one is a painter unless he loves painting more than everything else. Being a great painter was not a part time endeavor. A true painter must have passion for art. It was a pivotal moment in Gauguin's life.

At age thirty-four, with five young children, and a wife feeling abandoned, Gauguin needed to make a choice between a comfortable life and painting. In 1883, he quit his job at the Bourse, to paint full time. He moved his family from Paris to Rouen, to follow Pissarro. Two years later, with savings depleted, the Gauguin clan moved to Copenhagen, to live with Mette's family.

Living with in-laws left Gauguin miserable. He was unable to paint, between complaints from his wife and his in-laws. In May 1885, Gauguin left Mette and four of the children in Copenhagen. He took his six-year old son, Clovis, and went back to Paris.

Life in Paris was difficult. Except for Cézanne and Renoir, Impressionists were unable to sell their work. In order to support Clovis in a boarding home, Gauguin accepted work as a sculptor. He could barely afford to purchase canvass.

There was a small bright light, when at an annual showing of Impressionists, some of Gauguin's works sold. In addition, Gauguin's sculpture received acclaim and a patron. Gauguin had sufficient funds to pay his debts and reestablish himself. He wrote a letter to Mette, inviting her to bring the family to a seaside resort, where he would paint. Mette was unmoved by the offer.

Gauguin spent the summer of 1886 in Pont Aven, in search of his passion as an artist. In the winter, artists left the seaside for home. Gauguin had no home without Mette, so he returned to Paris. It was then, that he met Vincent Van Gogh.

Gauguin and the Van Gogh Incident

Van Gogh Yellow Cafe Arles featured in painting

Van Gogh, with his red hair and ever-present pipe, was easily welcomed into the group of Impressionist painters. He had a terrible temper, which isolated him. That his brother Theo was an art dealer, made him attractive to the Impressionists.

Van Gogh's art was clearly impressionistic, although unique. Gauguin recognized that Van Gogh found his passion. The two became close. It would be a mistake to consider them friends.

While in Paris, Gauguin and Van Gogh argued. They parted, when Gauguin returned for another summer at Pont Aven. Gauguin eventually left Pont Aven for Arles, to join Van Gogh. After yet another argument, Gauguin returned to Pont Aven. Between trips to Paris and Pont Aven, Gauguin garnered sufficient funds to make his first sojourn to Tahiti, in search of his passion.

The infamous argument of Paul Gauguin and Vincent Van Gogh, took place in Arles. In the story of Paul Gauguin, it was a brief chapter, definitive of nothing. In popular culture, the incident remains one of the best-known moments in the art world. Paul Gauguin came to Arles on a whim and left in a hurry. He was in Arles nine weeks.

Van Gogh's yellow house is a local landmark in Arles. Supported by his brother, Theo, Van Gogh spent days and nights at the local pub, immortalized in the painting *The Cafe, Arles*.[125] Although Van Gogh is a celebrated resident of Arles today, during his lifetime, locals kept their distance. They did not appreciate Van Gogh's art, his frequent violent outbursts, or the company he kept.

During Gauguin's second summer in Pont Aven, Van Gogh sent several letters to him, requesting that Gauguin come to Arles. Van Gogh sent a self-portrait to Gauguin and requested one in return. Eventually persuaded, Gauguin left Pont Aven for Arles. He could hardly afford the trip.

Art historians have long debated why Gauguin went to Arles. In Pont Aven, a patron funded his life. Arles was no better place to paint. Some historians speculate that Gauguin was keenly aware of how Van Gogh's brother could assist struggling Impressionist artists to sell their works. Without explanation, Gauguin made the trip.

---

[125] Local guides are pleased to point out the pub, although they admit that Van Gogh was never popular with locals, due to his intake of absinthes and his carousing with local ladies of the night.

The two painters lived in Van Gogh's house in Arles, for no more than nine weeks in 1888, before they argued again. An angry Gauguin grabbed his belongings and went running from the house. An angry Van Gogh ran after him, screaming. What happened next, has been debated ever since.

In the historic account of the day, a depressed Van Gogh returned to his home, severed his ear, wrapped it, and gave it to one of his ladies. A recent version of the story has emerged, due to sleuthing historians. In the new version, Gauguin, the expert at fencing, drew his sword, turned on the pursuing Van Gogh, and swung at him. The severed ear was retrieved by one of them, wrapped and delivered at a brothel. Gauguin tossed his sword into the river, as he left the city.

The two artists made a pact of silence, to protect Gauguin from arrest. Van Gogh made up the story of having severed his own ear.[126] In all versions, the two artists never spoke again.

By 1889, Van Gogh was dead. He lived his last years on the verge of mental and physical collapse. Financial support and artistic appreciation from his brother were not enough to sustain him. Theo died shortly thereafter.

Pont Aven: Bold Lines and Color

In Pont Aven, Gauguin defined his art. He first left Paris, because he was destitute. A benefactor paid for his keep at an inn in the country. It became a repeat refuge. The Brittany village provided quiet surroundings at a modest price. The seaside and village were excellent subjects for art. It was warm in summer and the light was perfect for painting.

Gauguin did not see himself as a landscape painter, though he tried. His subjects were people of Pont Aven; the women in starched white hats characteristic of Bretons, and their children. Painting townspeople in daily chores was the Impressionist style. Gauguin painted in stark reality and simplicity, that took

---

[126] Henry Samuel, "Van Gogh's ear was cut off by Friend Gauguin with a sword," Telegraph, Paris, May 4, 2009. http://www.telegraph.co.uk/culture/art/art-news /5274073/Van-Goghs Last visited 9/27/2020.

him beyond Impressionism. It was in Pont Aven, that Gauguin developed as a master post-Impressionist. He perfected his signature style of bold lines and simple shapes.

A Vison After the Sermon Paul Gauguin 1888 of Breton Women in Pont Aven (National Gallery of Scotland)

Gauguin was impressed by Van Gogh's use of bold color. He was also interested in cloisonné work of a new member of the Pont Aven group of artists, Emile Bernard. Bernard used broad strokes of black in his work, to separate bold color, which was something new to Gauguin.

Impressed by cloisonné, Gauguin painted women of Pont Aven, in their tall, starched, white hats. He outlined white hats in broad, black, brush strokes. In his second stay in the town, when he remained through a change of seasons, Gauguin painted houses capped in snow. The results were paintings of almost all black and white.

In his next evolution of art, Gauguin added color between heavy black lines. The results were paintings such as *Yellow Christ*[127], a bright masterpiece, initially thought too daring for display, even in Paris. Art historians, looking back at this time in the life of Gauguin, remark that in Pont Aven, he created his greatest paintings, prior to relocating to Tahiti.

Image of Gauguin & Yellow Christ in Pont Aven

---

[127] The Yellow Christ, 1889, Albright-Knox Art Gallery, Buffalo, N.Y.

Although Gauguin went to Pont Aven in 1886, as an impoverished refugee from Paris, other painters saw his work as refreshing and new. They strove to emulate his art. When Gauguin next returned to Pont Aven in 1887, he found other artists drawn there, to be near him. The growing band of Impressionists in Pont Aven, was a cult of Gauguin aficionados. Gauguin was no longer the outsider, attempting to buy his way into the clan of Impressionists. He was the master painter of Pont Aven. His style was widely regarded as the Pont Aven School of Art.

Gauguin needed more than appreciation of disciples to sustain him. To survive, he sold works of Impressionists, purchased in his days at the Bourse. He could not part with the Cézanne.

Mette and Gauguin kept up their correspondence, but Gauguin never accepted her invitations to rejoin the family. During one of Gauguin's absences from Paris, Mette arrived to retrieve Clovis, who had been left in Paris with a caretaker. She returned to Copenhagen, with several canvases by Gauguin and his friends.

Gauguin in Pont Aven

Gauguin continued to paint in Pont Aven. Finally, in 1891, Gauguin sold thirty canvasses at a show in Paris, at the Drouot Hotel. This was the largest single success during his lifetime. The Impressionist artist Degas purchased the Gauguin painting entitled, *Beautiful Angela*. With proceeds from the sale at the Drouot, Gauguin headed to Polynesia, to realize his dreams.

Gauguin in Tahiti

Idyllic Visions of Moorea

In 1889, Gauguin visited the Paris *Exposition Universelle*, where exhibits of exotic places rekindled thoughts of Polynesia. He imagined a place of pure light and primitive people, unaffected with pretense and commercialism of Paris. Always the able writer, Gauguin submitted a grant application to the French Minister of Public Education and the Fine Arts. Grant funds for travel were awarded in 1891. He was free of civilization. His adventure in primitivism began.

At the time, France had colonial holdings in Tahiti, Madagascar, Viet Nam, Mauritius and Java. All were possible destinations for Gauguin. He sought a primitive culture to paint. When Gauguin arrived in Papeete, he found French bureaucracy and pretense, far from home. Initially disappointed, Gauguin was determined to live like a historic local, away from town.

It was more difficult for Gauguin to adjust to life in the tropics, than he imagined. In his diary, *Noa Noa*, Gauguin repeatedly expressed his appreciation for the local man, who rented him a hut and fed him. Gauguin quickly realized, natives were superior to Europeans, who were incapable of self-support. Primitive life was complex, not crude, or uncivilized. Idyllic paradise was an illusion.

Gauguin's first painting of a local girl, is a study in respect for her noble stature, her pride in wearing a western dress for the portrait, and her obviously non-European features. Gauguin could smell perfume in flowers she wore. In his painting, flowers shower down upon the subject. *Tahitian Woman with a Flower* is art evoking a sensory experience.[128]

Though Gauguin felt sympathy for natives, living part in their old ways and part as French protectorates, he too was a hybrid. He was a European going native, always a creature of his former life. He was lonely in his hut in paradise. He drank absinthe, a holdover from days in Arles. Tahitian words appeared on his canvasses. They became as iconic of Gauguin, as his signature.[129]

Gauguin's teenage mistress assuaged the loneliness, yet she did not interfere with his continuous painting. From her, Gauguin sought an education in the cosmology of islanders, of Atua, sons and grandsons of Taaroa. Of his companion, Gauguin wrote that she venerated Taaroa and Jesus. In his paintings, Gauguin melded Christian and native cosmology. He and Tahiti were fused.[130]

From 1891 to 1893, Gauguin created some of his best-known works, while in Tahiti. He sent canvasses home to Mette to sell. None sold. Gauguin was now aged forty-six. He was an artistic success, who could not sell his art. He returned to Pont Aven.

---

[128] Catalogue MUDEC, Museo Delle Culture Milan, 2015, exhibit Gauguin – Tales from Paradise. *Tahitian Woman with a Flower* 1891, is in the collection of Ny Carlsberg Glyptotek, Copenhagen.
[129] MUDEC, at 25.
[130] Noa Noa, at 41. Recent social commentary of Gauguin, condemns his acceptance of a fourteen-year-old mistress, while in Tahiti.

Paul Gauguin Woman with a Flower 1891 (Ny Carlsberg Glyptotek)

Tahitian Floral Inspiration

Inspiration in Tahiti

When Gauguin returned to Brittany, he was accompanied by his muse from Tahiti, Anna. Anna thought highly of her painter and by association, she thought highly of herself. She did not blend with locals in Pont Aven. When a child smirked at Anna, she struck him. The child's father confronted Gauguin. The two men locked in a physical struggle. Gauguin's ankle was broken.

The father of the child was a fisherman, whose friends never developed a regard for Parisian painters of Pont Aven. They had less regard for Gauguin and his muse. A group of townsmen sought out Gauguin and beat him unconscious.

Once Gauguin sufficiently recovered from the attack, and could travel, he left Pont Aven, for the last time. One of the final Pont Aven paintings was *Watermill in Pont-Aven*, in 1894. Gauguin went to Paris. His objective was to raise money from art sales, to fund a return to Tahiti. Gauguin was despondent. He wished to remain in Tahiti, for the remainder of his life.

Gauguin remained in Tahiti from 1895, until his death in 1903, at the age of fifty-four. Unfortunately, it was a long, slow, painful death. Just prior to leaving Paris in 1895, Gauguin spent time with a prostitute, from whom he contracted syphilis. The last eight years were spent creating some of his finest work, interspersed with bouts of debilitating pain, or in an absinthe fog.

Tahiti as Muse for Gauguin

Among works created on the second trip to Tahiti, is the 1897 masterpiece, *Where Do We Come From? What Are We? Where Are We Going?*[131] The painting is a unified expression of primitive soul, through color, brush strokes and subject. As Gauguin wrote of painting, that it is more than depicted on canvass, this work is rightfully dubbed a masterpiece, for its complex inclusion of levels of meaning. There is no doubt of the title. In the upper left corner, of the twelve-foot-wide canvas, Gauguin wrote the title, in French.

Gauguin 1897 Where Do We Come From? What Are We? Where Are We Going?
(Boston Museum of Fine Arts)

The large painting was not critically well received in Paris. Not understanding the achievement, the leading critic wrote that *Where Do We Come From?* was not true art. Another artist wrote of Gauguin, that he found it amazing, that one man put so much mystery, into a single canvass.

For six more years, Gauguin painted and sculpted, believing in his art, yet despondent over lack of acceptance in Paris. *Woman with Mangoes*, in 1899, is a painting on carved wood, which if not identified, would leave most viewers incredulous, that it was created by a European, on the cusp of the twentieth century. The work is a study in ancient technique and mysticism.

For the last decade of his life, carving symbolism of ancient gods on wood, and formed in clay, were more numerous than Gauguin paintings on canvas. Painting on wood, or burlap, was less costly than canvas. The medium was also closer to primitive life in artistic context.

---

[131] In the collection of the Boston Museum of Fine Arts, Boston, MA.

In 1903, Gauguin became embroiled in an argument, with the French government in Tahiti. He was accused of libel, a criminal offense, and sentenced to three months in jail. Before the jail term could begin, Gauguin died. The cause was heart attack, brought on by an overdose of morphine, to dull pain. He died May 8, 1903, and he is buried in Calvary Cemetery, Atuona, Hiva 'Oa, in the Marquesas Islands of French Polynesia.

Legacy of the Artist in Tahiti

Paul Gauguin Museum Tahiti

Gauguin's legacy to the art world can be seen in modern art masters of the twentieth century. In the 1890s, a Gauguin painting was hung upside down at an auction house, by mistake, and laughed at by bidders, before it sold for a pittance. Today, a Gauguin can sell for tens of millions of dollars. His works are in major art collections of the world.

The place of Gauguin's modest dwelling in Tahiti, is now The Paul Gauguin Museum, an art school and pilgrimage site, to the place where he painted. Primitive stone art is displayed on the grounds. Gauguin would not appreciate formal placement of the stones. He thought the works primitive, not crude, and best arrayed in a natural setting.

Gauguin Painting Among Island Gods

In Tahiti, Gauguin found an honest natural setting in which to paint, not one contrived to be so. The islands were his muse. He painted what his mind envisioned. Tahiti cleared his mind for thoughts, pure and sensational. Gauguin painted Tahiti of Tahitians, not a European impression of a Tahitian. In his art, Gauguin moved Impressionism beyond Paris. Tahiti holds Gauguin's body, as it should be. It was in Tahiti, that he found his passion, expressed in art.

William Bligh by Alexander Huey 1814 (National Library of Australia)

The Real Captain Bligh

The popular image of Captain Bligh of the British Admiralty is of a tyrant, flogging sailors trapped in the infamous ship the HMS *Bounty*, on a perilous journey. The words mutiny and *Bounty* have been locked together for two centuries, through scandalous news accounts and five movies. Hollywood movies are great cinema. They are not to be relied upon to pass a history exam.

William Bligh was no saint. He was also a lieutenant, not a captain, hoping to prove his merit for a captaincy, independent of work performed, without attribution, for the world-famous Captain James Cook. Bligh, long on technical ability and short on patience with officers, wanted the *Bounty* mission to Tahiti to be a perfect voyage. His trusted friend and mate thwarted his desires.

The mutiny of Christian Fletcher is a small part of this story. Life of mutineers hidden on Pitcairn island has its own story. Survival of Bligh and men cast off with him, and the fate of some men who sailed with Christian, their apprehension and trial, supply the drama in this tale. The true story, although different from Hollywood versions, is an amazing adventure.

Bligh's public, personality profile took a journey from loving husband and father, who was a diligent commander and talented navigator, to become synonymous with bad behavior in the British admiralty. The transition has been attributed to Bligh's vengeful actions at the trial of mutineers, his rise through the ranks from commoner "before the mast," and changing public attitudes away from tolerance of absolute power in maritime authority. Most effective in shaping the lasting image of Bligh, was Charles Laughton's portrayal of him in the 1935 Hollywood movie, *Mutiny on the Bounty*, in which Clark Gable played the maltreated Fletcher Christian.

In an effort to put the *Bounty* back on keel, this story floats through the life of William Bligh before, during, and after the mutiny. Dissention followed Bligh from England, in its slavery era, to New South Wales, Australia, and the transportation era. For these few pages, walk the decks of his ships and decide for yourself how history should regard William Bligh.

The Era of Bligh

Breadfruit Tree

William Bligh was born in 1754, in England. The date and place are important to his story. His was an age of England's desire to utilize its colonies to provide trade goods, transported around the world by a naval fleet, superior to any in the world. Maintaining good discipline on ships was critical, to protecting cargo and returning ships safely home. Officers had broad powers to punish unruly sailors. The captain of the ship had unquestioned, absolute power.

Eighteenth century English society drew hard lines on rank by birth. An English sailor of common birth could rise to the level of an officer, only upon demonstration of exceptional ability. James Cook, who mapped the southern extent of world, while maintaining a strictly moral character, was such a man. Horatio Nelson, whose deft military strategy at sea, resulted in numerous victories, for which credit was given to high-born gentlemen officers for decades, was such a man. William Bligh served as an officer, under the command of both of these men. Cook gave no credit to Bligh for contribution of Bligh's navigational skills to Cook's successful voyages.

Bligh was the son of a customs officer. It was a respectable position for a man of the working class. Bligh first went to sea at age seven, as a captain's personal servant. His rank was third class. His life was spent on lower decks; a world unknown to seamen of upper-class society.

At sixteen, Bligh was an able seaman, who was promoted, on ship, to midshipman within months. Upon returning to England, Bligh was given no credit for the earned advancement. Intensely ambitious, Bligh was made to repeatedly prove his worth, each time he was hired for a crew. Owners of ships filled their better-paid crew positions on a patronage system. Bligh had no family connections. He had not attended schools, from which gentlemen matriculated to officers.

In an effort to achieve officer status on merit, Bligh overwhelmed naval officials with his technical navigation ability, until he was given command of a small vessel patrolling the Irish Sea for contraband. He was twenty-one, with greater visions of his career. Within a year, Bligh was appointed as Sailing Master to James Cook, for the third and final of the Cook voyages to map uncharted islands of the Pacific. After the demise of Cook in 1779, in an altercation with Hawaiians, it was Bligh, who completed the survey of the islands, for which he received no credit.

On the voyage with Cook, there was ample opportunity for Bligh to display his navigational ability and his stamina. He also displayed his irritability, when lower seamen underperformed. Bligh was easily disappointed, and quick to lash out with foul language.

In the English naval service of the eighteenth century, flogging and other physical punishment, frequently and harshly imposed on sailors, was routine. Scholars comparing treatment of sailors by Bligh, to other English captains of the era, have found Bligh to be less heavy-handed than most, when it came to punishment.[132] Bligh was singular in his ample use of derogatory language.

Gentlemen of the time, in judgement of Bligh, attributed his swearing to the fact that he was not a gentleman. A gentleman could flog sailors at whim, as sailors were an uncouth group. Bligh was, however, a man "before the mast," that is, a man who rose from the lower decks of common sailors.[133] He would never be accepted as a gentleman. His verbal abuse was unacceptable.

Demanding and unforgiving of crew, while at sea, at home, Bligh was deeply devoted to his wife Elizabeth and their four daughters. Elizabeth Betham was born in Glasgow and raised in Edinburgh, among family associates, who were key thinkers of the Scottish Enlightenment.[134] To eighteenth century Scots, ability ranked above noble birth. They married in 1780, at age twenty-six. Until her death in 1812, Elizabeth was supportive of her husband, through each career crisis.

Elizabeth's uncle, Sir Joseph Banks, needed an able ship's captain, willing to accept unglamorous assignments. Bligh was so willing to demonstrate his ability as a captain, that he accepted the position of Master of the HMS *Bounty*, with double duty as purser, while remaining in the official status of lieutenant. Bligh planned to earn a captaincy, by a flawless voyage.

The mission of the *Bounty* was mundane at best and a foolish errand. Banks was a principle with investors in Caribbean plantations, profiting on slave labor. The investors, acting on information from botanists, gained from Cook's voyages of discovery, decided that Polynesian breadfruit could be an

---

[132] Greg Dening, Mr. Bligh's Bad Language, Cambridge University Press, 1992.
[133] Accommodation for common sailors "before the mast," was cramped in comparison to larger quarters for fewer officers behind the mast. Before the mast was synonym for low class, commoner crew.
[134] See Cruise through History, Itinerary X Port of Edinburgh, Edinburgh in the Age of Enlightenment.

inexpensive means of feeding slaves in the Caribbean.[135] Bligh was assigned to transport botanists, who would collect plants, to transplant in Caribbean islands, as a new food staple.

The HMS *Bounty* was a small merchant sailing vessel, purchased by the Royal Navy in 1787, for the purpose of the breadfruit mission to Tahiti. The ship measured ninety by twenty-four feet, with a depth of hold of just over eleven feet. In the best of circumstances, the *Bounty* had a capacity of forty-four crew. In seven months, the ship was modified to transport the maximum possible breadfruit plants. The crew area was condensed, to about a third of the original living space. The number of crew was not reduced. Bligh sailed with forty-six men, including two botanists.

When the *Bounty* sailed, just days before Christmas, it was a cramped, unhappy ship. The captain held lives of the crew and responsibility for the ship, yet, as a lieutenant, he had no imperative of authority from his employers. The crew gave Bligh no loyalty.

Aggravating circumstances, was the dual position of Bligh as purser. Pursers held the pay of seamen and inventory of stores. Pursers had a reputation for being corrupt, often personally claiming pay of deceased seamen and selling provisions on the side. Bligh was honest, never self-dealing. Regardless, the prevailing assumption as to pursers was attributed to him. His response to insolence was profuse verbal abuse.

The trip to Tahiti entailed ten months at sea. Bligh was frustrated in attempts at a direct route around South America, due to storms at Cape Horn. He turned east, to reach the South Pacific by sailing around Africa. Once in Tahiti, Bligh allowed five months on one island, for the sailors to recoup, while the botanists collected breadfruit plants, loaded with care on the *Bounty*. During that time, idle sailors developed close relationships with families on the island. Men, long at sea, enjoyed the women, climate, and relaxed life on land.

---

[135] Authoritative information on the voyage of the *Bounty* is gained from Sir John Barrow, The Mutiny and Practical Seizure of HMS *Bounty*, the Folio Society, London, 1831, reprinted 1976. A contemporary of characters in this story, Barrow, born in 1764, was a founder of the Royal Geographic Society, for which he served as president in 1820. Although not unbiased, the account is gathered from primary source documents.

Mutiny and Survival

Bounty First Landing Monument Papeete, Tahiti

The great irony of the mutiny, which occurred on the *Bounty*, was that it was led by the man to whom Bligh had shown favoritism, while at sea. At sea, Bligh maintained three shifts on deck. He placed his long-time friend, Fletcher Christian, in charge of the third watch, over more senior men, and despite Christian's lesser experience at sea, than other possible appointees.

To call what happened on the Bounty a mutiny, suggests there was a cadre of angry sailors, organized to depose their captain. This was not the case on the *Bounty*. Fletcher Christian acted solely, to push the revolt at the end of his watch, to incredulous sailors.

The mutiny occurred three weeks into the homeward sailing. After months of an idyllic life, of no responsibility, a routine under strict naval discipline was hardest on those least accustomed to life at sea. Christian was such a man.

When he succeeded in gaining the support of a small group of men, Christian ordered that Bligh be awakened and bound. Christian yelled at Bligh, "That is the thing, I am in hell." What he meant, has been the subject of argument ever since. Supporters of Christian suggest, that Bligh nagged Christian to the point of desperation. Supporters of Bligh suggest, that Christian was longing for a return to life in Tahiti. Christian provided no answers.

On the morning of April 28, 1789, Bligh wrote in his log, that plants were thriving and all men and officers were in good health. He was still in bed, when three men burst in and bound his hands. Three more men, one with a gun, pushed Bligh and eighteen officers and crew into the twenty-three-foot-long launch. Christian threatened Bligh's life at gun point. Other men tried to give additional provisions to Bligh and those in the launch, but were restrained. One man was able to grab Bligh's papers and throw them after him, into the small boat. Christian would not allow Bligh any navigational charts.

Mutiny HMS Bounty by Robert Dodd (British National Maritime Museum public domain)

Under British law of the sea, all those who aid, or acquiesce to, a mutiny are guilty as primary parties to the act. Many more men attempted to join the party, about to be set adrift, and take their chances with Bligh, but were restrained from doing so. Still others, were confused, or fearful of drowning in a launch, which promised certain death. All remaining on board *Bounty* were eventually judged as mutineers, unless proven innocent. Less than ten, were actual mutineers.[136]

The dangerously crowded, and critically under provisioned, boat was set adrift. Exposed to the equatorial sun, and lashed by waves in storms, Bligh kept moving westward, drawing on memory of experiences as a navigator with Cook. Much of the sea around him was uncharted. Using only a sextant and his pocket watch, Bligh navigated toward a known port. He added islands to Cook's maps, where the starving sailors caught birds barehanded and found fresh water.

In the forty-one days at sea, in the small boat, Bligh's navigational skills and stamina were assets. He navigated through the Great Barrier Reef, and on to Timor. Bligh kept a diary, as if keeping a ship's log. He wrote of his concern for the men, and of their experiences on shore. He distracted the men from their dire fate, by educating them on navigation, should he be lost at sea.

All but one of the men, under Bligh's care, survived the ordeal of a 3,600-mile sailing, although some were so ill, that they perished on the return voyage to England. The one sailor lost, was stoned by natives, when a small party from the boat ventured on shore, looking for fresh water. When the boat reached the Dutch-controlled harbor of Kupang, on the island of Timor in Indonesia, those on the pier were aghast, at the emaciated men, arriving in the small boat.

By March 1790, Bligh was back in England, arriving on the Isle of Wight. He was prolific in his diary of events at sea, intent on negating impact of the mutiny on his career. Bligh was lauded for his handling of the mission, and valor when set adrift. He was promoted to commander.

---

[136] At the time of the mutiny, there were 46 men on board the *Bounty*. Only the doctor died in the voyage. According to Bligh's log, the man was a heavy drinker and had no regard for his own health.

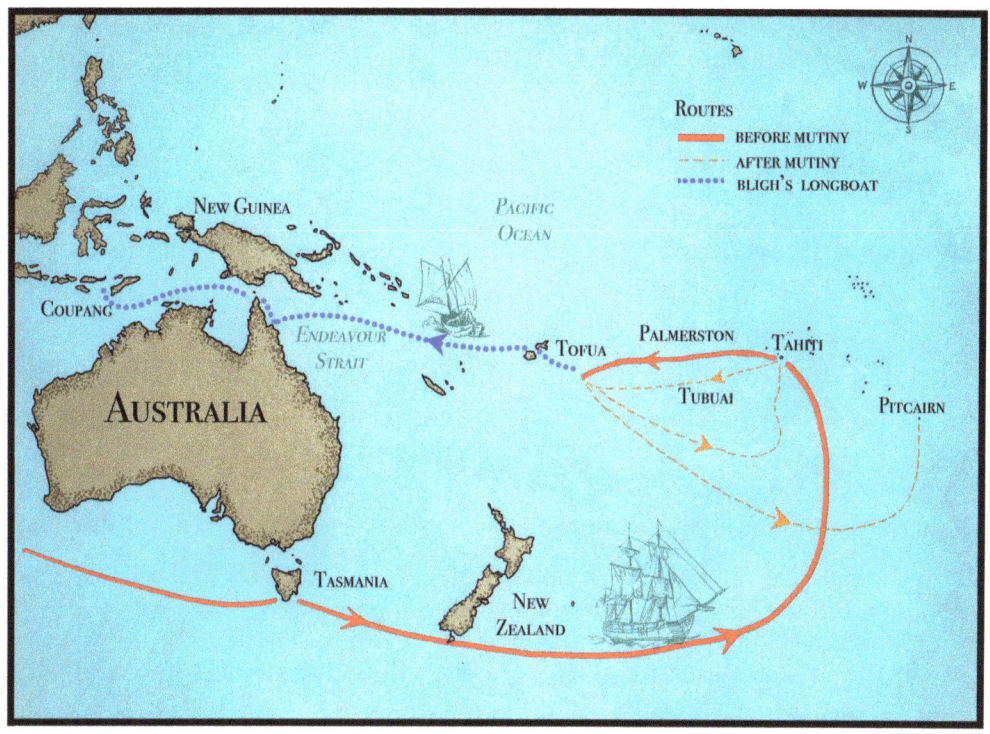

Digby Art - Travels of Captain Bligh and the Bounty

The name of Bligh might have been little remembered in history, but for later events of the trial of mutineers, upon returning to England, and Bligh's behavior at the trial. He sought vengeance, when a cooler disposition would have worked in his favor. Once again, lack of social status acted to the detriment of Bligh, despite his career standing and personal accomplishment.

The Royal Navy sent Captain Edward Edwards on the HMS *Pandora* to Tahiti, in 1791, to locate the mutineers. In Tahiti, they found fourteen of the sailors, who had remained on the *Bounty*, and who parted company with Christian, when he sailed with remaining mutineers to an unknown place, to evade capture and punishment.[137] Despite having declared to Captain Edwards their

---

[137] Of the 27 men remaining on the HMS *Bounty* after the boat with Bligh and 18 others was set adrift, an altercation on the return of the *Bounty* to Tahiti, post mutiny, left two dead. Fourteen men remained on Tahiti and were apprehended by Captain Edwards. Eleven men, including Christian, sailed on to places unknown. The fate of these eleven men is the story of Pitcairn Island.

innocence in the mutiny, all were treated as prisoners. They were chained and transported to England for trial, housed in a locked box on the open deck, as though they were cargo.

Captain Edwards was a fitting character for the personality of a captain portrayed in Hollywood as the Bligh of the *Mutiny on the Bounty* film. He ordered frequent punishment of men on his ship. When the *Pandora* shipwrecked on the same Barrier Reef, through which Bligh had safely sailed, Edwards ordered the ship abandoned, with no regard for the prisoners chained in their cell. Only the valor of a sailor, who risked his life to unlock the chains as the box slipped below the water, allowed all but four of the prisoners to survive.

Enough of the *Pandora* was salvaged to enable construction of a suitable craft, to sail the survivors to safety. In September 1792, the ten surviving prisoners arrived in Portsmouth. There they received a much-publicized trial.

One of the prisoner-survivors, sixteen-year-old Peter Heywood, wrote to his mother, stating his innocence of the mutiny and of his near-death experience under Captain Edwards. Heywood was not critical of Bligh. Bligh had an abundance of wrath to unleash on the youth, since his was the face Bligh last saw, before he was dragged onto the deck of the *Bounty* and pushed into the boat.

During the trial in Portsmouth, Bligh was most critical of Heywood. He wanted to see Heywood hanged. Heywood was from a family of gentlemen. His sister published his letter to their mother and an attorney was hired to represent Heywood. In contrast to Heywood, Bligh appeared the uncouth commoner. Heywood's defense put Bligh's pre and post mutiny character on trial.

At the trial, six of the ten returned sailors were found guilty of mutiny. Bligh's condemnation was the deciding factor, although Heywood had a strong defense. Heywood and another of those found guilty, James Morrison, were given a reprieve. Four men were executed. Heywood went on to a career of distinguished service in the Royal Navy. Bligh returned to sea as a ship's captain.

At Sea with Captain Bligh After the *Bounty*

Captain Bligh Welcome to Sydney

At the end of the eighteenth and beginning of the nineteenth century, England was continually at war with France for domination of commerce at sea. Although Bligh damaged his ascendancy to the status of gentleman, by his conduct at the mutiny trial, his record as a competent captain was unblemished. At the Battle of Camperdown in 1797, Bligh displayed valor and sound leadership.

Bligh twice had the opportunity to serve as a captain under Admiral Horatio Nelson. At the Battle of Copenhagen in 1801 and the Battle of Trafalgar in 1805, Bligh proved his ability and bravery. The Battle of Trafalgar was fatal to Nelson. The great admiral was given the news of his victory, just as he breathed his last breath. The battle rendered Napoleon's navy no longer a threat in the Mediterranean. Bligh was given a terrestrial assignment in New South Wales, Australia.

New South Wales and the Rum Rebellion

Once again, Sir Joseph Banks came forward to direct the career of William Bligh. Britain needed a strong leader, with a no-nonsense personality, who would accept a position, which required sailing to the South Pacific. The position of governor of New South Wales carried a title of which a gentleman could be proud. In truth, it was an assignment to clear an intransigent mess, which had ended the career of two prior reform-minded governors of the Australian province. Bligh took the risk. For him, sailing into controversy was not new terrain.

At the time Bligh arrived in Sydney in 1805, the Transportation Era was in high gear. Transported convicts were conscript slaves of local landowners. The landowners included, and were in business deals with, men of the military, that is, the all-powerful New South Wales Company.

Freed convicts and voluntary settlers were at the mercy of the NSW Company, which set prices high and kept availability of imported commodities scarce. Soldiers of little talent in England were becoming wealthy landowners in Australia. Two governors sent to Sydney to corral the Company were recalled at the behest of the Company, citing a creative list of misdeeds.

Bligh immediately jumped into controversy. He found the captain of his transport ship to be involved in questionable deals with the NSW Company. Bligh denied the captain his commission and sent him back to England to face a court martial. Banks deflected a demand for Bligh's recall.

Next, Bligh distributed food staple items from government stores to settlers, who needed aid after a flood. The Company had hoped to profit from the misfortune of settlers and were livid at the loss of sales at high prices. Bligh found the Company was paying settlers for the crops, using rum as currency. The rum was produced in illegal stills, depriving Britain of taxes. Bligh decreed that rum could no longer be used as barter currency. He ended imports of illegal rum.

Bligh termed revolt of the military in New South Wales, the *Rum Rebellion*. The overthrow of the civilian government by the Company had little to do with rum. Bligh issued arrest warrants for soldiers involved in illegal commerce. In return, the New South Wales Company issued its own warrant for the arrest of Bligh in 1808, and held him prisoner in the Government House.

Soldiers subject to charges were released, due to an inability to locate judges and jurors to hear the case. The Company portrayed Bligh as a coward, who was not a gentleman. Bligh was relieved as governor by a new man sent from London. Bligh was given command of his return ship.

Eventually, Britain resolved the military coup in New South Wales, by recalling the entire Company to service in England. To remain in Australia would have been a mutiny. Bligh was elevated to Rear-Admiral in 1810 and given an administrative job in the admiralty offices.

Bligh was able to enjoy two years of a peaceful home life, before his adored Elizabeth died in 1812. Bligh remained devoted to their daughters. He died of cancer in 1817.

Popular Media and Memory

The saga of the mutiny on the HMS *Bounty* was popular material for London theater almost immediately upon the return of Bligh. Scripts were made even more spectacular by the trial. Early productions featured Bligh as heroic and mutineers as dangerous pirates.

In 1814, the last surviving mutineer from the *Bounty* was located on Pitcairn Island. Twenty-five years post mutiny, John Adams, not his real name, gave a remorseful account of the events to his would-be rescuers. He had become the patriarch of a colony of the progeny of *Bounty* sailors.

The English sailors became enamored of Adams. They saw in him a repentant sinner, who used the Bible from the *Bounty* to teach the young of Pitcairn to read and speak English. In excusing his part in the mutiny, the sailors returning from the island cast Adams in glowing terms and in so doing, recast Bligh as the villain in the episode of the mutiny. In the nineteenth century Royal Navy, floggings were passé. Captains were expected to be gentlemen. Sailors were professionals.

Bounty Memorial Tahiti

There have been five films made of the *Mutiny on the Bounty*. In each, Bligh is portrayed as the vicious captain and Christian is either noble, or his actions are forgiven as the reaction of a man pushed to the breaking point. The first two *Bounty* films were Australian; a silent film in 1916, and the 1933, *In the Wake of the Bounty*, starring Australian born Errol Flynn as Christian.

In 1935, Charles Laughton portrayed the punishment prone captain and Clark Gable was the idyllic Christian. Women loved this film. In 1962, Marlin Brando was almost a saint, giving water to an ill seaman, only to have the ladle kicked from his hand by the cruel Bligh. Finally, in 1984, Anthony Hopkins added intelligence and scheming to the depth of character in Bligh, as he and Christian, played by Mel Gibson, battled to mental exhaustion in a contest of inner strength.[138]

Mutiny on the Bounty films are telling of evolving attitudes to limits of authority, even at sea. Today, the name Bligh has become a cliché for abuse of power. Perhaps it is now time for a twenty-first century version of *Mutiny on the Bounty*. Might the new version portray Bligh as a victim of assumptions of a class-oriented society, and Fletcher as a man whose weakness caused the death of dozens of sailors? Not likely. The cliché is so much fun.

---

[138] Each of the films had a replica HMS *Bounty*. See also, Caroline Alexander, The Bounty, Viking Press, New York, 2003.

Bora Bora, Beautiful Isle

Bora Bora: Operation Bobcat and the Beautiful Isle

Bora Bora is the Polynesian island known for divine beauty. Such was the opinion of the island people who arrived in the fourth century of the current era. Quite literally, they called it Pora Pora, creation of the gods. When the Dutch arrived in 1722, they agreed with the locals and mapped the island to be forever known as Bora Bora. Captain James Cook arrived decades later and had the same opinion. Bora Bora is a gem among so many beautiful islands.

Contributing to the beauty of Bora Bora is the coral reef that surrounds the island, creating a welcoming, peaceful lagoon. The first inhabitants waded into the lagoon to easily snare dinner. Visitors today snorkel into a clear-water bay of rays, small sharks and assorted marine life.

Like the other islands of Polynesia, Bora Bora is the defunct tip of a volcano. This volcano has two peaks that frame the landscape. The lagoon is the creation of mountain mass below the water, with coral reefs that peek above the waterline, sufficient to create atolls. Atolls, the beginning of land mass, is substantial in a few spots on the coral ring of the island to support development.

In the aftermath of the bombing of Pearl Harbor in 1941, the United States established a supply base on Motu Mute atoll, the northernmost tip of the Bora Bora reef and the largest atoll in the string. Instantly, Operation Bobcat, as it was called, doubled the population of the island, with up to six thousand service men and women. The airstrip built for the war effort remains today as the commercial airport servicing Bora Bora, bringing resort guests from Papeete, from one hundred and fifty miles across the sea.

From ancient long-distance travelers, looking for a new home, to military operations seeking peaceful harbor, to resort guests and cruise visitors headed to clear warm water, or a cocktail, all have found a peaceful, garden existence on Bora Bora. The tiny island deserves its moniker. This is the short story, of the little, beautiful Polynesian island.

Coconuts and Copra – A Royal Life on Bora Bora

Iconic Bora Bora View

For more than a thousand years, people lived on Bora Bora, although little is known of their daily life. People brought coconut and other plants on canoes, enough to sustain crops for a small population on the small island. Bora Bora, though beautiful, is not a plentiful garden. Between the beach and volcanic mountain, there is little farmland. From first landing, population grew slowly.

There are two major maraes on the island, evidence of two strong clans. In inter-clan warfare, chiefs vied for total control of the island, or at least, control of scant farm land. The cycle of search for land, to sustain a population, that brought people east and south to Polynesia, continued on larger populated islands.

Warfare and the desire to control turf by the two clans of Bora Bora, engulfed the nearby island of Raiatea. At times, one or the other clan was dominant, and at times Bora Bora came under the control of the clan on Raiatea. When Captain James Cook came by in 1777, his native guide Tupaia explained that

Bora Bora was in recent history relegated to a place of pirates and thieves. Among the motley bands of Bora Bora, a warrior chief rose, Teihotu Matarua, known simply as Puni.

Bora Bora was known to have a vibrant band of Arioi, the warrior brotherhood of party boys of the islands, always ready for a luau, or a battle. As leader of Arioi, Puni had control of all of Bora Bora, an island of warriors, when he took control of Raiatea, a place of families. At this time, Raiatea was a place of a large and significant marae.

Cook recorded as Tupaia explained, that at the time of their arrival, Puni was dead and his nephew, Tapoa I, was chief of Bora Bora, Raiatea and the island of Tahaa. The islands had local subservient chiefs on Bora Bora and Tahaa, while Tapoa I lived on Raiatea. It was a time of peace.

The royal line of Bora Bora continued for the next century, occasionally intermarrying with the Pomare dynasty of Tahiti. The last monarch of Bora Bora was Queen Teriimaevarua III. Her father was a king of Raiatea and Tahaa. His sister was of higher rank, a descendant of Pomare. She was Queen Teriimaevarua II at the time of her death in 1873.

In descent from her aunt, Queen Teriimaevarua III reigned from 1873, until she abdicated to the French in 1895. She lived to be sixty-two and died in 1932, in Papeete. She married a member of the Pomare clan, a direct descendant from Pomare I. The couple had no children together. In the tradition of providing successor royalty, they adopted two daughters of the queen's husband. Neither would reign.

France annexed Bora Bora by fiat in 1888. In exchange for her cooperation, the French allowed Queen Teriimaevarua III designation as monarch until 1895, when they demanded her abdication. From 1895, to her death in 1932, Ari'i Otare Teriimaevarua III Pomare, deposed and divorced from her Pomare husband, lived in Papeete as simply Ari'i Otare, the last of the royal era.

Copra is the dried meat of the coconut. Coconuts are worthy of a story of their own. As a source of food and water, coconuts are good travelers on long-distance voyages. From Malaysia, coconuts made sea transits west to the coasts of Madagascar and Mozambique. Coconuts came south to the islands of Polynesia on canoes of the first arrivals.

Bora Bora Island Church

In addition to supplying water and food to rowers on long voyages, the fibrous outer bark of the coconut was rolled and braided into twine. Hollow shells were manufactured into domestic items.

Copra is produced by grating the meat of the coconut, then grinding it with a hard stick, against a firm bowl of wood or rock, then boiling the pulp. In the boiling water, coconut oil is extracted. The remainder pulp makes good animal feed. So useful was the coconut, that it sustained villages and became a basic crop. On the islands, people found breadfruit, which also sustained them. Still, it was coconut, through the ages, that provided oil, food for animals in the absence of grass, and eventually, in the era of French control and an export economy, a reliable export commodity.

Operation Bobcat

Bora Bora Location for Operation Bobcat (US Naval History Archive)

The South Pacific Area Command, under Admiral Chester Nimitz, established a supply depot on the Bora Bora atoll in 1942. In four years of operation, the task force dubbed Operation Bobcat, saw no direct action. Small enough to be strategically insignificant, it was in the middle of the large ocean, near nothing, therefore able to supply forces from all directions. Defense of New Zealand, if necessary, was tasked to come from the little island of Bora Bora.

Nine supply ships were stationed on Motu Mute, always ready for action. Six to seven thousand service people entertained themselves in the lovely lagoon and in Vaitape, as they waited out the war. For the islanders, working for service people, it was the highest level of activity and economy seen on the island up to then and since.

Supply Depot for Pacific Command (US Naval Archive)

The 13th Coast Artillery Regiment set up eight, seven inch-forty-four caliber guns around the Bora Bora atoll, in the event of incoming enemy fire. There was none. The unused guns remain in place today, as an open-air museum piece, of a time when the Pacific was ablaze with big guns and war planes.

The most famous memento of a military presence on Bora Bora, is the Rogers and Hammerstein musical *South Pacific*. The play premiered in 1949. Buoyed by success of the play, the 1958 movie of the same name featured top Hollywood stars, some of whom had singing voices dubbed in by other artists. The movie music was produced into a top-selling album. Both productions were based upon the 1947 book by James Michener, *Tales of the South Pacific*. Bloody Mary became the most loved character in the book, the play and the musical.

In the book, play libretto and movie script, a sailor fathered mixed-race children. The story vehicle was Michener's comment on racism of the era. Mary Martin and Ezio Pinza brought the play to garner ten Tony Awards. Controversial subject matter, encased in a love story and brilliant musical score, made the play the second longest running on Broadway.¹³⁹ In 2008, when the revival of *South Pacific* opened on Broadway, it snagged another Tony for best revival. Themes of the play are relevant today.

Fourty-four Caliber Guns (US Navy Military Archive)

Bora Bora Today

On Bora Bora today, a lady stands next to a pile of coconuts, holding a large sharp knife, just waiting to cut a nut and sell a coconut water healthy drink to visitors. Many visitors head to Blood Mary's, an island institution since 1979, where tomato juice is spiked and the atmosphere is a party any Arioi would be pleased to attend.

---

[139] Longest running play at the time was the Rogers and Hammerstein musical Oklahoma, which revolutionized musical theater.

Bloody Mary's on Bora Bora

When travelers succumb to tourist pursuits on Bora Bora, they are keeping alive island history. The large thatched roof and coconut tree stump stools of Bloody Mary's, are similar to native festival huts. Each July, Bora Bora hosts a Heiva Festival, like an Arioi event. A party atmosphere, with open-air huts and relaxation, drinking and eating, with music and merriment, was just their style.

When the military left Bora Bora in 1946, tourism became the economic driver of the island. The first hotel, Hotel Bora Bora, opened in 1961, takes credit for instigating over-the-water bungalows, seen now throughout Polynesia.[140] There are now seven resorts operating on atolls, or motus of Bora Bora, the ring of coral reefs that form the lagoon. Hotel main services are located on the atoll. Rows of tiny thatched roofs, on strings of bungalows, appear from the air as little fern pods bursting from the shore. Restricted access to resorts over the lagoon give them exclusivity. The perennially calm water and climate make Bora Bora a year around choice for vacationers.

---

[140] In 2008, in the aftermath of a world financial downturn, Hotel Bora Bora and other small hotels closed. At last visit it had not reopened.

Bloody Mary's Celebrity Register

Lagoon and Atolls of Bora Bora

As if natural atolls were not enough, St. Regis Resort created a man-made island along the reef. Motu Marfo is a private island, within the island reef. When Bloody Mary's is teeming with visitors, ogling the list of celebrities who have enjoyed themselves at the bar, the celebs are likely sunning on private islands within Bora Bora lagoon.

Air Tahiti provides service between Papeete, Tahiti and Bora Bora. The Bora Bora airport does not accommodate larger commercial aircraft. Expect Air Tahiti to weigh your carry-on luggage, as well as your checked baggage. Private aircraft and seaplanes are most prevalent on the small atoll airstrip, that was so state-of the-art in 1942.

Today, half of the population of Bora Bora of ten thousand, live in Vaitape, the largest city on the island. This is the ferry and cruise ship port. It is also home to the proliferation of shops and art galleries, dependent upon tourism for their existence.

Come to Bora Bora to swim with the rays and enjoy perfect weather in a beautiful setting. Always beautiful and minimally populated, Bora Bora is likely to remain so in the future.

Bora Bora Business Conference

Bora Bora Commercial District Vaitape

Moai of Rapa Nui Perpetual Watchman

EASTER ISLAND

Katherine Routledge
Legacy of Easter Island

Katherine Routledge, blessed and cursed with intelligence, affluence and curiosity, shocked her Quaker family by going to a land less traveled, far into the Pacific, on a purpose-built ship, she commissioned, to examine a people few in the academic community considered worthy of study. Routledge embarked on an adventure in 1913, in an age of curiosity about the natural world, when women were not welcomed as scientists. She employed ethnography, a new scientific method, in which Routledge preserved knowledge of the lifeways of a people, who were slowly disappearing.

Routledge's revelations of Rapa Nui culture, their origination, development of technology enabling massive monolithic sculpture, and decline, pushed the body of knowledge forward in contributions, the conclusions of which were confirmed over time. Prohibited from presentation of her research paper at the Royal Geographic Society in London, due to her gender, the paper was read to the large audience by her husband. His separate archaeological work on Easter Island of the Rapa Nui, was dwarfed by Katherine's use of ethnography, to gather credible facts, illuminating life on the distant island.

The story of Katherine Routledge and her time on Easter Island, land of Rapa Nui, is a story of determination surpassing limitations on gender. Her effort to study the culture in its meaningful context, occurred in an era when objects of culture were most often plundered for display as curiosities. Her efforts preserved a body of knowledge, that would otherwise have been lost, greatly diminishing understanding the meaning of mysterious giant stone sculptures of the island.

Katherine's story is also a story of ethnography as a science. In the early twentieth century, archaeology was advancing, as organized examination of ancient sites, to determine knowledge through context of remnant artifacts on the landscape. In archaeology, present day people, and their oral history, have little relevance to examination of excavated habitation sites. While archaeologists seek to reconstruct what happened in a place, and often focus upon burials, battlegrounds and palaces, ethnographers ask why events occurred in the lifeways of a people. Katherine spent years on Easter Island, probing distant memories of the oldest residents, to connect lifeways to the ancient past, in order to determine origination of the population and give meaning to the effort absorbed in creation and placement of Moai on Easter Island.

Easter Island is a fascinating place, with a fragile ecosystem and a small historic population. The people of Easter Island and their Moai have their own story. This is a story of pursuit of knowledge under extreme circumstances, by an unlikely heroine. Heightened visitor enjoyment of Rapa Nui, the native name of Easter Island, is the legacy of Katherine Routledge. Preservation of knowledge, upon which to build the story of Rapa Nui, is Routledge's gift to all who marvel in mysteries of the past.[141]

Moai Anakena Beach

---

[141] Papers of Katherine Routledge were discovered and curated by anthropologist and author Jo Anne Van Tilburg in, Among Stone Giants, Scribner, New York, 2003; see Katherine Routledge, The Mystery of Easter Island, 1919, reprinted by Adventures Unlimited Press, Kempton, Ill., 1998.

Becoming Katherine Routledge

Katherine Pease was born in England in 1866, to a Quaker family of intergenerational wealth.[142] Her father, always depressed, died at age fifty-two, leaving Katherine, aged six, with independence and social mobility. From her Quaker values, Katherine gained a distain for dogma and a respect for opinions and cultures of others. In her summers spent in Cornwall, Katherine developed curiosity about stone monoliths and ancient people.[143] In her extended family there were educators and scientists. Though she was tutored at home in the Victorian style, entire libraries of diverse knowledge were available to her.

Katherine Maria Routledge in 1919 (public domain)

In 1882, Katherine was a debutant, presented to Queen Victoria by her uncle, a baron. Rather than marry, in 1891, Katherine announced she was headed to Oxford's Somerville Hall. Oxford began admitting women in 1879.[144] Katherine had no desire to marry a cousin, as had her siblings.

At college, Katherine lived alone. She studied anthropology, a course of study for which there was no degree. Degrees were not awarded to women at Oxford, even if earned, until 1920.

---

[142] The estate of Katherine's father at death was valued at $21Million in 1872. Tilburg, at 16.

[143] There are several standing stone circles in England beyond Stonehenge, some in Cornwall.

[144] Sommerville Hall, now Sommerville College, was one of the first two Oxford women's colleges. Margaret Thatcher and Indira Gandhi are Sommerville alumni. Sommerville was non-denominational. The other women's college was Anglican Lady Margaret Hall.

In 1904, while on a study trip to South Africa, Katherine met forty-six-year-old William Scoresby Routledge. Six feet tall, tan and handsome, he was a would-be adventurer, living well above his income, on a homestead in Kenya, supported by an annuity from his father. Never a lady's man, Scoresby enjoyed dressing well and living in comfort. Throughout his life he never had an income, other than from family or Katherine. She adored him. Scoresby, admitted to the Royal Geographic Society by age twenty-six, held the academic allure denied to Katherine as a single woman. They shared an interest in archaeology. That interest was enough for Katherine to base a marriage.[145]

The courtship and marriage were not romantic. Scoresby accepted a prenuptial contract of twenty thousand pounds and signed a release to the Pease estate. The couple honeymooned in Nairobi. In Nairobi, Scoresby collected specimen for the British Museum of Natural History and Katherine secured the release of two young village girls, who had been taken captive by the British commissioner. When the commissioner was removed from service, the British social circle excluded the Routledges. Katherine took the matter to Parliament, which cheered her courage to advance human rights.

While the couple lived in Southampton, they craved adventure. Scoresby learned of Easter Island. They studied notes of Captain James Cook, who described great statues, on a barren island, occupied by a starving population. He named the island for the Christian holiday on which he landed in 1774. In 1910, Katherine and Scoresby developed a research plan to determine: whether the remaining population on Easter Island was Polynesian, Melanesian, or Peruvian. Scoresby planned to archaeologically investigate the island, while Katherine interviewed the people.

The couple held no romantic assumptions about an island of a lost continent. They approached their self-assignment as scientists on an adventure. For both, the project made their marriage and their lives meaningful. Fortunately, they required no outside funding for their research.

---

[145] Katherine learned enough about genetics in college to understand that her father's depression, the early death of her two depressed aunts, and the psychosis of her brother were hereditary. After a bout of scarlet fever, as a child, Katherine sometimes heard voices. She did not want to bequeath her heredity to a child.

Two Years with the Rapa Nui

Mana at Easter Island 1914 (collection British Museum, public domain)

There are carved stone monoliths on the Marquesas Islands and Austral Islands of French Polynesia, as well as evidence of pre-eighteenth century occupation of Pitcairn Island. None of the statues are as large and well-defined as those on Easter Island. Katherine Routledge is credited with relating Moai of Easter Island in time depth and development of technology, to a population of Rapa Nui people, with Polynesian ancestry. Her inquiry occurred from 1914 to 1915.

Katherine commissioned construction of a yacht, on which she, Scoresby and six crew could sail to Easter Island. She christened the boat, *Mana*. Joining the couple on the expedition were an Oxford trained geographer, a geologist, and a naval navigator, on loan from the Royal Navy. The Navy man, Lieutenant Richie, knew what the civilians did not, and that was the potential for outbreak of a war. The loan of Richie was not gratuitous. He was gathering military intelligence.

Between Katherine's exacting standards on ship, and the pompous attitude of Scoresby, crew left the ship at each port and were replaced by fresh locals. While still in the Atlantic, the geographer left the expedition, went to the Sudan, and later distinguished himself as an archaeologist. A greater loss was felt at Punta Arenas, where the cook left the ship with Pease family cookbooks.

The Routledges left Southampton on *Mana* on March 25, 1913. They crossed the Atlantic, traversed the Magellan Strait and stopped at Robinson Crusoe Island of Chile. On their travels, an inlet in the Patagonia Fjords was named *Mana Canal*. *Mana* arrived at Easter Island on March 29, 1914.

Upon arrival, the couple found that most of the indigenous population lived in the one town of Hanga Roa. The island was under control of the Chilean government, which installed a company agent as local despot. People were herded into a compound, and excluded from access to Moai and traditional sites, while company agents roamed with cattle and sheep across the island. Katherine and Scoresby were expected to lodge in the government house.

Rapa Nui Settlement in Hanga Roa

One fact was immediately apparent to the couple. Diminished circumstances of Rapa Nui culture were the result of external impacts. The emaciated people before them could not build giant stone statues. Locals stood among evidence of their past like distant ghosts. Scoresby was enthused to excavate, to find the past civilization, while Katherine had the desire to discover what people knew of their past, as a means to determine links to their heritage.

At the time the couple arrived, they were indeed viewing a people on the brink of extinction. Once a robust population, in a closed and fragile environment, their landscape was irrevocable altered once Spanish and French sailors arrived in the seventeenth and eighteenth centuries. Rats from ships feasted on palm nuts, eventually denuding the island of trees. European disease decimated the people. Pirates captured people as slaves, who were taken to Chile. In the nineteenth century, when some survivors were repatriated, they returned, bringing more disease.

Easter Island Ranchland

Scoresby went off to explore caves created as the result of cooled lava tubes of three volcanoes, from which the island was formed. Katherine sought the eldest of the island, to search their memories. In her research notes, Katherine credits her introduction to Juan Tepano as critical to her access to information.

Tepano spoke Rapa Nui and Spanish. He also knew a little English. Among his people, Tepano was regarded as being apart. He served in the Chilean army. He was a man bridging indigenous and European cultures. Katherine knew a little Spanish. Working together, Katherine gained insight to the island. Tepano gained a protégé and patron. Together they achieved documentation and preservation of a culture, the survival of which neither could accomplish working alone.

Katherine's First Base Camp on Rapa Nui

Tepano introduced Katherine to the elders of the island, some of whom could remember life prior to arrival of the missionaries in the late nineteenth century. Traditional ceremonies, held at *ahu* sites around the island, ceased upon introduction of Christianity, at insistence of the missionaries. Prominent of *ahu* sites was Orongo, place of the birdman ceremony, at the east end of the island. Although the area was off limits to islanders, and to the displeasure of her Chilean hosts, Katherine made it her base camp for the year, while she attempted to learn the local language.

In the origination stories of Easter Islanders, were tales of birdmen. In piecing together mythology surrounding birdmen, with traditional ceremony, Katherine pondered whether ancient sailors arrived at the island by following birds. Ancient sailors populated the Pacific islands, in the great Malaysian migration, one thousand years ago, following stars, currents and birds. In the depths of memory, Rapa Nui elders recalled bird migrations to the island, in numbers of such staggering quantity, that birds were harvested to supplement islander diets.

From its inception, so far back no one could remember when, and up until discontinued upon arrival of Christian missionaries in the 1860s, the birdman ceremony was among the most important of annual events. Until decimation of the population, Rapa Nui were living among several clans, each with dominance over a portion of the island. A young, male contender as a future clan chief, proved his ability by representing his clan in the annual birdman ceremony.

Each year, birds arrived on the islands, building nests and depositing eggs in those nests on the island and its several, surrounding rocks, above sea level. The birdman ceremony was held each year, during nesting season, when eggs were most likely in the nests. It was during this season that sharks, following prey, were densely clustered around the island. Presence of sharks made the birdman competition all the more challenging.

Orongo Site of Birdman Ceremony

The Rapa Nui version of shaman lived in small stone, clustered, cubicle dwellings along cliffs of the *ahu* site of Orongo. At this place, the birdman ceremony was held. Symbols of birdmen, carved into rocks at the site, illustrate the importance of place in cosmology of islanders. From the cliffs, young men dove into the sea, swam to the nearby tiny island of rocks, retrieved an egg from the nest, and swam back to adoring crowds. The first young man to return was the birdman of the year. Shark mortality among contestants was high. The gods delivered the winner.

The winner of the bird-man competition, gave his speckled tern egg to his chief. For a year, his shaved head grew uncut hair. He had special food prepared. He gave a name to the year and lived as a god, until the next competition. Then the birdman slipped back into the general population.

Katherine examined Moai to consider how they were created and positioned. Most important to her work on cultural derivation, was why the Moai were created. Even after leaving the island, Katherine continued to examine likeness of Rapa Nui Moai to other stone monuments of Polynesia and Melanesia. From Polynesia, across the Pacific, technology was replicated and size increased. As she learned the cosmology of island people, Katherine tied Rapa Nui to Polynesia. Her conclusions, based upon documented research, are the accepted origination theory today.

By placing Moai in relation to technology and style of Moai of Pacific islands, Katherine dated Rapa Nui culture, at its height, from 1100 to 1500, when Moai were created. Only a sizable, successful population, with sufficient food for workers, could devote so much time and energy to giant Moai. During times of strife on the island, there was hiatus in construction. As the population diminished, Moai were no longer produced. Smaller carvings, around dwellings of chiefs, were created in wood, a scarce resource. Dwellings were of stone, with turf roofs.

While Katherine lived among the Rapa Nui, she grasped nuances of meaning lost on those whose prior research was based upon brief visits and logs of sailors. Scoresby several times sailed to Valparaiso for supplies. On one visit he was hospitalized with dysentery for several months. Freed from European lifeways, Katherine became close to Tepano and islanders, such that she went beyond folk-fictions created for visitors, to gain the trust of elders. Her detailed notes became a record of a people, whose personal knowledge of cultural history was

Birdman with Egg (Orongo Visitor's Center)

Hanga Roa Moai in Rapa Nui National Park

Example Rapa Nui Dwelling this one at Orongo Ceremonial Area

waning with each death. Katherine connected two hundred people to their genealogies, documenting one hundred years of memory.[146]

In 1914, German ships arrived at Easter Island. These ships sailed only at night. They used the island as a rendezvous point and asked only to obtain fresh water. French and English prisoners were left behind. From Germans, Katherine learned of the assassination of the Archduke Ferdinand of Austria and of the war in Europe. Her greatest concern was for Scoresby, due to arrive on the island, at any moment on *Mana*. Fortunately, there were no incidents on the island. Stranded prisoners spent time helping Katherine in her research. When months later a Swedish ship arrived, the captain offered transit back to Europe for all who wished to leave.

Science and Skepticism

Katherine and Scoresby left Rapa Nui at the end of August 1915. They sailed to Tahiti, where Katherine met the widow of Pomare V. Then they sailed to Hawaii and San Francisco. Scoresby sailed the *Mana* through the Panama Canal, while Katherine toured the US by train. She went to Los Angeles, the Grand Canyon and Chicago. In Washington, DC, she saw the lonely Moai in the Smithsonian Museum. The couple reached home in Southampton, at the end of June 1916.

In November, Scoresby presented Katherine's paper at the Royal Geographic Society, where she was excluded. Scoresby received the Royal Cruising Club Challenge Cup for his voyage to the Pacific. Spurned by scientific societies for asserting that the Rapa Nui were Polynesian, Katherine was adored by the press. That the Royal Society debated research of a woman was intriguing.[147]

In the early 1920s, Katherine went to Tahiti and the Austral Islands. She observed similarities in sculpture, that was small and unimpressive compared to that of Rapa Nui. When she listened to native women describe gods and ceremony, using some of the same names used by Rapa Nui, Katherine drew further connections of Polynesian ancestry to Rapa Nui.

---

[146] Van Tilburg, at 132.
[147] Today, the conclusions of Katherine Routledge are supported by DNA evidence.

In 1925, Katherine was elected as a fellow of the Royal Geographic Society. In a will written that year, she left the home to Scoresby and her papers to the Society and the British Museum. By 1929, the family history of darkness fell upon Katherine. She was hospitalized until her death in 1935, at age sixty-nine. Scoresby moved to Cyprus, where he died in 1939.

Legacy of Katherine Routledge

Silent Road Warriors Today on Easter Island

Visitors to the National Natural History Museum of the Smithsonian Institution today, walk through the north entrance and quickly past the lone Moai, removed from Easter Island in 1886, for display as an object of curiosity. Absent context, the stone statue has little meaning. A dozen of its fellow Moai sit in such a state in museums around the world, while thousands of travelers each year, expend considerable funds, to visit four hundred remaining Moai *in situ*. Travelers understand the value of context. The legacy of Katherine Routledge is preservation of meaning that heightens enjoyment of travel, such as views of Moai at sunrise, on their home turf.

Importance of visible indicia of culture to a people, heighten international efforts at preservation of Moai, which continue to remain in place. Part of the legacy of Routledge, is the field of Rapa Nui study, leading to in situ site management. After the paper of Routledge was presented in London, Moai were no longer curiosities to simply take home and display at random.

Fifty years after the Routledge theory of Rapa Nui population was presented to the London Royal Geographic Society, Norwegian geography student Thor Heyerdahl sought to disprove the woman's view, by testing his theory that Easter Island was populated by white men from Chile, who sailed west on a raft. His tale of *Kon Tiki* is a wonderful adventure story. By sailing to Easter Island on a raft, Heyerdahl proved that contact between islanders and mainland South America was possible. However, the prevailing scientific view today, adopts the wisdom of Routledge, that people came to Easter Island from Micronesia, in the prior millennium.

Other legacies of Katherine Routledge reverberate through academia. Acceptance of ethnography, sometimes known as cultural anthropology, as valued science, and of women scientists, seeped slowly through the halls of institutions, encased in tradition. Open access of women in the Royal Geographic Society began in 1913, nudged, no doubt, by Routledge and others.

Women in the male dominated field of archaeology, such as famed Petra archaeologist, Agnes Conway, worked in the shadows for years, until their work was discovered.[148] Scottish archaeologist Christian Maclagan, born in 1811 and died in 1901, financed her own study of Pictish stones, just before Kathrine completed her college studies in 1906. Cultural anthropology was often relegated to regard as a women's science, until men realized they failed to grasp meaning in stone alone.[149]

---

[148] Agnes Ethel Conway was born in 1885 and died in 1950.

[149] Even today, oral history is often discredited by archaeologists as lacking factual credence, or historical merit. Key to grasping meaning in stone was Alice Kober, who pioneered the decipher of Linear B. Inspiration to Routledge were few known scientists, such as British ethnographer Anne Walbank Buckland (1832-1899); Lady Hester Stanhope (1776-1839); or Routledge's American contemporary, Annie Marion Maclean (1869-1934); and British contemporary, Dame Bertha Phillpotts (1877-1932). A beneficiary of Routledge was Barbara Freire-Marreco (1879-1967), who completed Oxford studies in anthropology in 1908. Another contemporary at Oxford, Gertrude Bell (1868 – 1926), has her own story in Egypt, CTH Itinerary V.

Travelers to Easter Island aim for the destination, with excited anticipation. The island is not easily on the route to somewhere else. Go armed with the story of Moai and of the people of the island, given by Routledge, in vindication of her effort. She would prefer that you simply wander and enjoy.

Rapa Nui Hotel

Walking Moai of Easter Island

Waiting to Walk from Rana Raraku Quarry

Easter Island, more than a thousand miles away from anywhere else, fascinates visitors with its population of almost nine hundred stone giants. Standing like sentries, with backs to the sea, some with hats, all with expressions of long past island chiefs, statues mystify viewers with their creation and installation. Amazing, but true, most stone giants were created in a single quarry, then walked into position. The story of these mute sentries is an intriguing prelude to a visit.

This is also a story of island people, who arrived on Rapa Nui, the island Europeans call Easter Island, in the eleventh century, as part of the larger, ongoing, migration of peoples of the Pacific. Early Dutch, Spanish, French and English explorers documented conditions of people on the island from the seventeenth century. When the population went into decline, statue building ended, likely in the sixteenth century. The story of people and their monuments is intertwined.

Based upon reports of sailors, various theories developed to explain the statues. Katherine Routledge spent over a year on the island, adding to the body of knowledge of the people and their lifeways. Her literally ground-breaking scientific assessments are relied upon in this story. Routledge also has a separate story of accomplishment. Research continued through the twentieth century, as Easter Island statues, the Moai, evolved from objects of curiosity, to subjects of scientific investigation. This story is indebted to scientists, who recorded detailed measurements and made conclusions adding great insight to mysteries of Easter Island.

The few people of the descendant population of Rapa Nui will be seen by visitors, who spend three days or fewer on the island. This story begins with the story of the people, to give context of place as a prelude to a visit. Part of the story is evolution to a high functioning people and decimation, to the point of marginal existence, the result of environmental and human factors.

The focus of this story turns to Rano Raraku, the island quarry of volcanic stone, where almost all of the stone giants began their existence, before the giants walked the earth to their final ahu, the ceremonial site. Some island mysteries have plausible answers, told here. Other mysteries remain. This is the story of the walking Moai of Easter Island, the island its people call Rapa Nui.

People of Rapa Nui

Easter Island began as the creation of three volcanos. Lava tubes permeate the island. The first inhabitants were birds. Albatross, terns, boobies, herons, parrots, pigeons, doves and owls came to the island, where seeds of palms, shrubs, grass and ferns were deposited. Volcanos left fresh water pools on the land, where birds congregated. The little dot in the vast Pacific was a haven.

Volcanic Landscape–No Vegetation to Support Community

Hotu Matua, the first human, came to Easter Island, the ultimate Polynesian frontier, in the eleventh century. Rafts, or double-hulled canoes, were the most likely transportation. People brought yams, sugar cane, banana, chickens and small Polynesian rats. Nets of coconuts supplied water and food on the journey. Their new home was a sparse sixty-three square miles of island.

Hotu Matua

Relationships between people, as they continued to migrate across Polynesia, can be seen in *ahu*, the ceremonial practices and names given to gods. People of the sea from Melanesia, north of Papua New Guinea, came in waves, with other migrating Pacific peoples. Most islands are a mix of peoples, from Melanesia and New Guinea, over several migration flows.

People of Easter Island are Polynesian, likely of northern Melanesian origin, as people came south and east. Their DNA evidences less of a mixture of Pacific peoples, than much of Polynesia. When Marquesans, for example, invaded Polynesia in the 1200s, they did not venture as far as Easter Island.[150] Distance provided inherent protections.

Ahu Anakena - Place of Hotu Matua Landing - Moai of Chiefs

Sons of Hotu Matua became chiefs, each with their own section of Rapa Nui island. Inter-generational leadership was hereditary. Intra-tribal tensions were not unusual. Organized battles between tribes were rare. By the time of European contact in the eighteenth century, there were ten Mata, that is tribes, on Rapa Nui. Chiefs were subordinate to Makemake, supreme, ethereal god of men.[151]

---

[150] See, Steven Roger Fischer, Island at the End of the World, Reaktion Books, London, 2005, p. 39.
[151] See generally, Catherine and Michael Orliac, Easter Island: Mystery of the Stone Giants, Abrams, Inc., 1995.

People fished near the shore, using nets. In winter, when tuna was scarce, only chiefs could eat tuna. Chickens, brought on the first rafts, roamed the island. People enclosed their rock dwellings with simple wood screens to keep out chickens. They planted yams, banana and breadfruit.

As the population became successful, and thus larger, more land was cleared for farming. Giant palms, of the species that covered the island upon arrival of people, were slow growing. These hundred-foot palms were long living, yet slow to regenerate. In contrast, rats brought to the island proliferated from a few dozen to millions in just a few years.[152] Rats ate palm nut seeds. Fewer palms meant fewer coconuts to feed the population. The poor soil did not support vigorous cultivation of food plants. There were food shortages and theft of food between tribes.

In examining a cave on the island, twentieth century researchers found evidence of cannibalism. Cannibalism, as a form of ceremony, was performed by chiefs. There is no evidence of general community cannibalism. Although specifics of ceremonies on Easter Island are unknown, it is not unusual among Pacific islanders of pre-Christian history, to practice ritual cannibalism, in which war chiefs ingested the power of an adversary, through consumption of the deceased's body.

Kings, or chiefs, had a paternal role in their community. They slept in new houses, to bless them. Their role as king was marked by ear ornaments and tattoos. Initially, only chiefs bore tattoo.

People built low, stone houses, in an oblong shape, with a turf roof. Remains of a few houses can still be seen, now random on the landscape. Lives on the island evolved from lava-tube caves to houses. Along the east coast, now the site of Orongo, the birdman ceremony, shaman lived in a cluster of stone buildings, arranged like cells, along a path above the cliffs. The housing cluster, off limits to Rapa Nui since Chilean government control, are now protected as an historic area.

---

[152] Terry Hunt and Carl Lipo, The Statues that Walked, Counterpoint, Berkeley, 2012, pp. 15-29.

Flanking entrances to homes were palates of wood, carved with a form of writing, now indecipherable. Wood was scarce, so decoration was precious. Carvings protected the home and its occupants from evil, with blessings. Depth of meaning of designs, or written blessings, was lost over time. As the population declined, survival not ceremony was the priority. By the end of the nineteenth century, when missionaries brought Christianity, few elders retained knowledge of the cosmology of the ancestors. Carvings were destroyed or hidden. By the time Katherine Routledge arrived in 1914, none of the elders could read messages on the few existing carvings.

Europeans and Rapa Nui

Moai In Situ on Ahu Tongariki

The first European known to land on Rapa Nui was Dutch seaman Jacob Roggeveen, in 1722. He landed on Paasch, that is Easter, so he named the island Paasch Eyland, Easter Island. His island stay was brief. Islanders, curious about the white gods from the sea, pulled at clothing and weapons. The Dutch pushed the people back, with obvious revulsion. Islanders pelted the Dutch with rocks. The encounter ended when Dutch sailors shot and killed about a dozen islanders, refreshed their supply of water, and sailed away.

It is not known how many European ships came to Easter Island over the next fifty years. Rogue captains did not keep logs for publication. Nothing reported by the Dutch encouraged trade, or search for wealth. Still, as location of the tiny island appeared on maps, it was a known source of fresh water and safe harbor when in need. Any mistreatment of natives, was not reported. Unintentional harmful impacts left to diminish island people were European disease and rats from infested ships. Rats ate crops and palm nuts. They had no natural predators on the island.

By the time English Captain James Cook arrived at Easter Island, in 1774, the population was showing debilitating effects of European contact. Cook knew Spanish ships reached the island in 1769. He observed people wearing feathered hats and possessing *muskets*, as evidence of Spanish visitation.[153] Though Cook was ill and did not personally explore the island, he sent men to canvass the island, to report on resources and assess the population.

Cook's shore party observed no animals, a few birds, and a small population of about seven hundred people, lacking vigor. Men and women had tattoos and little clothing. They ate sugarcane and plantains, which were roasted on small fires, fueled with grass. Three canoes of wood were spotted, although the source of wood was unknown. Cook surmised the boats were made of drift wood, or materials left by visiting ships. A system of chiefs was evident, each with distinct land domain.

Cook was impressed by the size and workmanship of giant idols, on platforms, he reasoned were of religious distinction, though he was unable to discern their meaning. He did observe that the people gave no reverence to the statues. If they were of importance, at one time, that time had passed. Island people referred to the statues as *Moi*, and *Areeke*, meaning chief (spelling provided by Cook). Through the language barrier, Cook determined that the Moai had names of chiefs, who were now sleeping. He reasoned that Moai were monuments to burials of deceased chiefs.

---

[153] Logs of Captain James Cook, entry March 1774, published initially by Cook in, A Voyage Toward the South Pole and Round the World, Volume I, 1777, at EasterIslandTravel.com, last accessed September 9, 2020.

Moai Ahu Akivi

The next European of record to visit Rapa Nui was Frenchman Jean-François de Galaup, Comte de la Pércouse, in 1788. Pércouse was a French naval captain in aid of the Americans, in the American Revolution. He sailed in search of a Northwest Passage from the Atlantic, around Australia and the Pacific. His ship and life were lost in an altercation with natives in the Solomon Islands. His posthumously published *A Voyage Around the World in the Years 1785 – 1788*, gave a glowing report of his interaction with Easter Islanders. Pércouse reported that, unlike Cook, he and his crew arrived healthy. He found the natives in no need of a chief, as the small population was peaceful. Upon departing, the French left seeds, sheep and goats on the island.

Over the first half of the nineteenth century, Easter Islanders learned from visitors to cultivate crops and herd animals, rather than slaughter all existing stock. The male population became more robust, although women of the island had few children and were frequently ill. Occasionally, Spanish or pirate ships came to the island to take young men as slaves. It is estimated that by 1860, the population was ninety percent reduced of its high culture numbers.

By 1867, the last of the royal line of Easter Island chiefs was defunct. The last chief died of tuberculosis at age thirteen.[154] Remaining islanders adopted Rapa Nui as the name of their island. Long abandoned traditions were reinvented, with modifications. In the birdman ceremony, young men no longer swam to the little pile of rocks to retrieve a bird egg. Instead, young people recounted history in a pageant. People of the island were dependent upon trade with whalers and occasional government supply ships from Chile. Skills of ancient islanders were long forgotten.

Recreated Moai – front & back

---

[154] Fischer, p. 101.

Missionaries arrived in the mid-nineteenth century, to bring Christianity to Rapa Nui. People equated Jehovah with Makemake. Names of gods changed. To people, it was all the same *mana*.

Ahu Tongariki Prior to Restoration (collection British Museum public domain)

The population of Rapa Nui rebounded to about nine hundred, when in 1869, a sheep rancher contracted with the Chilean government to manage Easter Island. He removed a third of the population to his plantations in Tahiti and turned the island into a sheep ranch. A diminished number of islanders were restricted to a small area of land, near the port in Hanga Roa.

Lost Friends & Empty Spaces on Ahu

The next owner of the sheep concession made a pretense of buying island land from illiterate islanders. He exiled the missionaries, to facilitate his sheep raising enterprise. When islanders revolted against enslavement, the landowner retaliated by tearing out their yam crops, resulting in massive famine. To escape death, islanders voluntarily left the island, when supply ships came to port. The native population of Hanga Roa was reduced to almost zero.

In 1868, a British ship arrived and removed a Moai. In 1886, Smithsonian excavators came to Easter Island and took a Moai. Islanders referred to removals as lost friends. In 1888, Chile annexed Easter Island as domain of Chile. Moai were placed under government protection.

By 1914, and the arrival of Katherine Routledge at Hanga Roa, Easter Island was a single purpose, Chilean outpost, sheep ranch. Islanders and their well-being were not a consideration for the government of Chile, beyond survival. The little population was fully dependent upon the government. Routledge stepped beyond the government, and in defiance of the local agent, to find the stories of the people and their cultural roots and practices. Her published research raised awareness of Rapa Nui culture world-wide. The Chilean government took a heightened interest in the people, their well-being and their survival. Rapa Nui was developed as a tourist destination.

Walking Moai

Sources differ on the age of Moai, the stone giants of Easter Island. Most Moai came into being within a range of from 1100 to 1500 CE. Ninety-five percent of all Moai were quarried and crafted in Rano Raraku. Moai were lifted from the quarry and transported to their sleeping place on an *ahu*, ceremonial platform. Fronts and backs were carved at the quarry. Eyes were cut when the giant was installed. Each Moai is a likeness of a chief of Rapa Nui, upon death. All Moai are male.

Researchers have documented eight hundred and eighty-seven Moai on Easter Island, although the actual number may be closer to one thousand.[155] A little fewer than half of all Moai are still in the quarry, in stages of development.

---

[155] Jo Anne Van Tilburg, Among Stone Giants, Scribner, New York, 2003, p. 2.

Visitors Walk Rano Raraku Quarry where Moai Walked

There are three hundred *ahu* platform sites identified on the island, of which a third had, or still have, statues. Other sites still await their Moai.

Moai irreparably cracked in transit to *ahu*, were left in the roadside. Most Moai range in height from ten to twenty-six feet of solid stone. There is one Moai, still in the quarry, that if raised, would be sixty-nine feet tall. Carving Moai and transporting the giants to an *ahu* was a massive undertaking. Over time, size of Moai increased. Their design and elongated facial features became somewhat standardized. A few Moai wear hats, or crowns, of round, red stone.

From Moai found in various stages of creation at Rano Raraku, the process of carving has been determined. About ten men were needed to carve a single Moai. They carved the front and back, while the Moai was prone. As the stone cutters went around the girth, a trench lowered workers around the stone. Next, the statue was raised, in its place on the incline of Rano Raraku, a steep hillside, by digging into the hill supporting the statue. Once upright, with the lower body buried, the face was carved, beginning with the nose. The nose set the special relationship for other facial features. Today on Rano Raraku, there are Moai facing out from the hill, their lower bodies not visible below the soil level. Half buried Moai give a dramatic appearance to the quarry.

Walking Moai (photo credit Alexa Nicolaides)

Moai Awaiting Friends

Moai in Process – Largest Potential Moai

Meaning and reasons for creating Moai was unknown, until Katherine Routledge came to Rapa Nui and talked to elders. Moai were imposing reminders of chiefs, whose spirits continued to keep watch over Rapa Nui. Size and number of statues were indicia of strength of a tribe and its chief. Moai walked to their sleeping place, perched on *ahu*, the ceremonial platform, commanded by Makemake.

Running from the Rano Raraku quarry was a road, where Moai left their beginnings to reach their *ahu*. Choice of quarry site makes abundant sense. It is easier to move large objects going downhill. The technology of walking giants was mythology, until years of investigation illuminated clues.

Various theorists offered versions of walking Moai. In 1972, Erich Von Daniken applied his extraterrestrial explanation for the Nazca Lines in Peru, to Moai of Easter Island.[156] Thor Heyerdahl came to Easter Island, on his *Kon Tiki*, to support his theory that the island was populated from Chile. He demonstrated his solution to the walking Moai, by placing statues on sledges, slipping into place, facilitated by transit over squashed sweet potatoes, or banana skins. According to Heyerdahl, one hundred eighty islanders were necessary for the placement of Moai. According to engineers reviewing Heyerdahl's theory, the entire population of fifteen hundred islanders was necessary to move Moai, using such a process.[157]

In 1998, a public television show staged a Moai transport.[158] An assumption was made that the Moai were transported prone, and rolled on logs, with workers constantly bringing logs forward. The television show reported that fifty to seventy workers could move a statue nine miles in five to seven days. At the site, twenty workers were needed to raise the statue with ropes. Television writers made assumptions that statues were built in a stable society with

---

[156] For more on Daniken's theory of Nazca Lines see Cruise through History Itinerary 9 Ports of South America, Port Arica, Peru, Mystery of Ancient Marvels, 2018.

[157] Liesi Clark, Past Attempts, for NOVA, pbs.org. Last accessed September 10, 2020. For more on Thor Heyerdahl and Galapagos, see Cruise through History Itinerary 9 Ports of South America, Port Ecuador.

[158] 1998 Nova, for Public Broadcasting Station, informed by work of Jo Anne Van Tilburg.

surplus food. They also assumed that Rapa Nui once had abundant trees, cut for logs to roll the Moai into place.[159]

A Czech engineer offered another answer to the mystery of walking Moai. In the early 1980s, Pavel Pavel used a fifteen-foot, twelve-ton piece of concrete, to demonstrate that Moai could walk, with adequate assistance. Pavel used seventeen workers, holding ropes tied to the center of the Moai, to wiggle it, that is, walk the statue, side to side, as it progressed forward.[160] As the statue walked, there was damage to the base. An experienced cadre, using this method, could move the necessary distance and go up a ramp. At *ahu* sites, there is evidence of ramps, formerly in place.

A stunning site on Easter Island is Ahu Tongariki, a long platform, with fifteen Moai, now all standing in a row. In the late twentieth century, when Moai were lifted from where they fell and resituated on *ahu*, only one was still standing at Ahu Tongariki. At Anakena beach, place of the first landing of Hotu Matua and his six sons, a single Moai stands on a bluff overlooking the beach. Inland on the beach is an *ahu* with six Moai, some which have red stone cylinders on their heads. At this place, Katherine Routledge began to unravel some of the mysteries of the Moai.

Last of the Moai was created for a chief at Ahu Akivi, at around 1500. There are seven Moai at this site. All Moai are on a long *ahu*, positioned to face out to sea. In the sunset of the Spring Equinox, the Moai are aligned in the light.

By the sixteenth century, the human population on Rapa Nui was in decline. Absent surplus food for workers, and there existing fewer strong men to form and move Moai, construction ceased. In uncertain times, the birdman ceremony developed on Hoa Hakanana'a, at the east end of the island.[161] For two centuries, the birdman ceremony was a tribute to order in life and a prayer for birds arriving on the island to feed the people.

---

[159] The assumptions and depiction of moving Moai are similar to the concept of building Pyramids of Egypt.
[160] Hunt and Lipo, p. 79.
[161] Hoa Hakanana'a is also the name of the Moai removed in 1868 from Orongo, the site of the birdman ceremony and taken to the British Museum in London, where the Moai remains today.

Rapa Nui Ahu Akivi

In the eighteenth and nineteenth centuries, fallen Moai were left on the ground. Coincidently, in the eighteenth century, Europeans arrived in Rapa Nui. European ships brought more rats and disease. The population further declined. Food was scarce. Competition and food theft between tribes escalated to war. In anger, one tribe toppled Moai of chiefs of another tribe. Near the beach, Moai were susceptible to large tidal wave action. Moai lost their *Mana*; their reverence. The icons of Rapa Nui culture, built large and placed as a conspicuous show of strength, lost their force.

Visiting Easter Island Today

Today on Easter Island, of the population of four thousand, a little more than half are Rapa Nui. The Chilean government occupies a management station, examining everything from environmental impacts of sheep and tourism, to health of the native population. Those islanders with pre-European connection to the island, pursue land claims. Meritorious land claims are resolved through transfer of national park land, not private land. Addition of Rapa Nui National Park to the list of World Heritage Sites in 1995, provides the park some protection.

Curtain Call - Final Memorable Shot of Ahu Tongariki

Owing to the great size of Moai, difficulty in transporting in ships of the nineteenth century, and preservation action of Chile since 1888, most Moai are *in situ* on Easter Island. Some Moai in private or museum collections have been repatriated to Rapa Nui. Most appreciated by visitors are the Moai, raised to original standing position, *in situ*. No virtual experience replaces being there.

Today, when cruise ship tenders dock in Hanga Roa harbor, the crescent-shaped tourist hotel on the bluff above the wharf is in view. Accommodations for air/land travelers is limited. Cruise ship travelers, afforded a two-night overnight at Easter Island, have the same opportunity to visit all the Moai sites as air/land travelers, without the logistics of check in/out, and without impacting the environment. More flights will result in more hotels, until Hanga Roa takes on the appearance of many developed tourist havens. Fortunately, most *ahu* sites are beyond Hanga Roa.

Regardless of transit mode, comfortable walking shoes are an important travel item. There is so much to see, and most Moai viewing requires walking. The hill of volcanic tuff stone, that constitutes the quarry of Rano Raraku, requires walking many steps and a bit of energy. Dramatic views of Moai, with buried bodies and exposed heads, can be viewed from the site entrance, without missing out on the drama of place that is Easter Island. Take a bus to Anakena beach, where Hotu Matua first came ashore with his sons. Then take the iconic Easter Island photo of Ahu Tongariki, fully restored in 2004, where fifteen Moai look inward, with the sunset at their back. This is the Rapa Nui experience to enjoy.

Pitcairn Island

PITCAIRN ISLAND

Bounty Mutineers Escape to Pitcairn Island

The story of the Real Captain Bligh continues on, in the necessary sequel of the adventure of the escape of the mutineers. To complete the story of the HMS *Bounty*, is to follow factual travails under the mutinous captain, Fletcher Christian. Questions remain, of what happened on the *Bounty* after Bligh was set afloat to die, and what is the real story of Pitcairn Island. To his death, Captain Bligh asked about the fate and location of Christian, with good reason.

When Captain Bligh and eighteen sailors were set adrift in a longboat, twenty-seven men remained on the HMS *Bounty*. Not all were mutineers. In fact, the mutiny was an almost spontaneous act of just a handful of unsavory characters. There is no question that Christian was the leader of the mutiny. Though Hollywood drama has created an image of Christian as a sad hero, this story will adhere to facts. As this story shows, reality is fascinating and mysterious.

From part one of this story, the story of Bligh, it is known that the British Navy sent out ships to locate HMS *Bounty*. The first stop of the *Bounty*, after setting Bligh adrift, was back to Tahiti. Christian was savvy in his prediction that British ships would make Tahiti their first stop in a search for mutineers. Of the twenty-seven men, two died in a post-mutiny altercation and fourteen remained on Tahiti, when Christian and the remaining ten mutineers sailed to places unknown. In 1791, Captain Edwards apprehended surviving sailors on Tahiti and treated all men as mutineers, to be held for trial. Fate of the fourteen, and eventual trial, are part of Bligh's story.

This is the story of the eleven men, who sailed away from certain capture on Tahiti. The final port of the HMS *Bounty* was Pitcairn Island, where remains of the ship rest today. Ten men made a life on Pitcairn Island, with the women they brought from Tahiti. Theirs is a continuing story of descendants on the previously uninhabited island. The fate of Fletcher Christian is a separate chapter, in what began with the mutiny on the *Bounty*.

After the Mutiny

Landing Site HMS Bounty & Place of Burnt Remains

After the mutiny, Fletcher Christian proved to be even less of a leader than a sailor. Sailing back to Tahiti was the best initial option. Aided by a compliment of knowledgeable sailors, the ship handled well. Once back in Tahiti, the shock of the event abated and reality pounced on the remaining sailors. Most of the men wanted to distance themselves from Christian. When the HMS *Bounty* sailed from Tahiti, with a crew of ten, they had no direction, or plan, and little sailing skill.

At the eventual trial of mutineers, in Portsmouth, years later, when exoneration of survivors seemed the better part of British naval discretion, the whole affair was boiled down to Fletcher's distain for Bligh, or at least Fletcher's dismay over a life at sea, without the comforts of his Tahitian mistress.[162] The two men who assisted Fletcher in mutiny were dead. Remaining for trial were men caught in the crossfire of an action that surprised them, and in which they took no part, other than failing to resist. In British naval law, neutrality in the face of mutiny was not an option. Since Fletcher was not present at trial, he became a convenient receptacle for remaining blame.

---

[162] Sir John Barrow, The Mutiny and Piratical Seizure of HMS Bounty, London, 1831, Folio Society edition 1976, at 80.

Fletcher earned a lack of regard, immediately upon reaching Tahiti. When questioned by the daughter of the island chief, as to the whereabouts of Bligh, Fletcher told her that Bligh sailed off to take the breadfruit plants to Captain Cook. The men remaining on Tahiti evidently feared reprisal upon arrest by British officers less than a fate directed by Christian. Christian loaded the HMS *Bounty*, and with his remaining crew and twelve island women, set off for places unknown.

From the end of May to the end of June 1789, the motley band tried to make a home on the Austral Island of Tubuai. Once again, Christian had an opportunity to display his lack of leadership, or knowledge of rudimentary skills for survival. He decreed that a fort be built. He had no idea how such a fort would be built, what it should look like, nor how to direct construction. After a month of failed attempts, Christian abandoned his plan and the whole group sailed away.

Just where the HMS *Bounty* sailed after leaving Tubuai is unknown. Christian did not keep a log book. If he had attempted to do so, he would not know what to record. Knowledge of sailing, wind speed, or direction of the winds, were never matters he desired to learn from Bligh. Bligh, love him, or hate him, was a master geographer, upon whom the great Captain John Cook relied. When Pitcairn Island was spotted, by chance or luck, the crew were happy for land, any land. Years earlier, Cook searched for the island, twice, never spotting the little dot in the big ocean.[163]

Life on Pitcairn Island

In some accounts, there were eight men remaining on the HMS *Bounty*, when it landed on uninhabited Pitcairn Island. In other accounts, there were six men and nine to twelve women. Violent fights among the men were common. Some fights were deadly.

---

[163] Pitcairn Island is one thousand, one hundred and twenty acres, of which there are only ninety acres of level land.

Inhospitable Docking and Little Flat Land

Christian ordered that the HMS *Bounty* be burned, to avoid detection of the mutineers, should British patrols float within view of the island. Even burning the ship was a failure. Rather than harvest the wood for other uses, the *Bounty* was burned to its hull. Even today, remnants of the ship's stem stick above the waterline, signposting the haven of mutineer descendants.

Christian's next order was to divide the island into sections, assigned to each man. It was his last order as an incompetent leader. Island women had no status, as they had enjoyed at home. So little level land was available, that men consolidated holdings as the few remaining mutineers died of illness, or in fights. The north side of the island was rocky terrain, deemed uninhabitable. When Christian caused a fight with another man, by trying to steal the man's island wife, Christian disappeared to the north island, to live as a hermit. He was not spoken of again.

In 1809, an American private clipper ship, the *Topaz*, arrived at Pitcairn Island, where they found a malnourished, but otherwise thriving colony of natives, led by one Englishman, who called himself John Adams. His actual name was likely Alexander Smith. They were impressed by the fluent English spoken by the young natives. Adams told the Americans an amazing tale.

John Adams House Pitcairn Island by Sir John Barrow 1831

The American sailors learned of the mutiny on the HMS *Bounty*, and of the men who landed on Pitcairn Island, with women kidnapped from Tahiti. The men fought among themselves until there were four men left. Two of the men created hostility by mistreatment of the natives. Adams and a man by the name of Ned Young, hid until the tension was over and the two men were dead.

Young died in 1800. Adams claimed to be father of most of the children, who identified as either children of Adams, or Young. Adams was proud of teaching the youth to be literate in English, using the ship's Bible as his only teaching tool. Adams had no desire to leave his island.

In 1814, a British frigate located the last surviving mutineer from the *Bounty* on Pitcairn Island, with his colony of forty souls. Twenty-five years post mutiny, John Adams, gave a remorseful account of the events to his would-be rescuers. He had become the patriarch of a colony of the progeny of *Bounty* sailors.

Adams taught his girls to make clothing and restrain from promiscuity, which had been the native tradition that so enthralled sailors on the *Bounty*. When couples married, their patriarch performed the service. Adams died in 1829, on Pitcairn Island.

In 1831, the British government sent a ship to remove all who wanted to relocate to New South Wales. There is some irony in the choice of location. Captain William Bligh was a former governor of New South Wales.

Instead of Australia, those who wished to leave the island were returned to Tahiti. The new arrivals felt out of place among pure Polynesian locals, whose customs differed from their English-infused morality. They wanted to return to their home. British officials were concerned that given supplies, the Pitcairn people would overpopulate their environment and starve.

English sailors arriving in 1814, became enamored of Adams. They saw in him a repentant sinner, who used the Bible from the *Bounty* to teach the young of Pitcairn to read and speak English. In excusing his part in the mutiny, the sailors returning from the island cast Adams in glowing terms. In so doing, they recast Bligh as the villain in the episode of the mutiny. In the nineteenth century Royal Navy, floggings were passé. Captains were expected to be gentlemen. Sailors were professionals.

Fletcher Christian Mystery

When Fletcher Christian disappeared over the back side of the rock that is Pitcairn Island, islanders never spoke with him again. Never popular, the more the men and their island wives sailed with Christian, the more they were glad to be rid of him. Attempted wife-stealing exhausted their patience with the man, who led them to their dire circumstances. He was of no use in their miserable lives. No one sought him out.

Portsmouth of Fletcher Christian

Years later, when someone ventured near the cave, where it was thought Christian was living, there was no one home. Appearances were of a long empty abode. People assumed that Christian fell to his death from a rocky cliff into the sea. He was not mourned. There were no monuments erected to mark his time on Pitcairn Island. When British ships arrived at Pitcairn, decades after arrival of mutineers, the sole surviving mutineer, and island historian, John Adams, reported that Christian died in a fall to the sea. No one questioned his explanation.

In their first years on the island, people noticed sails of vessels in proximity to Pitcairn Island on two or three occasions. They had no reason to hail the vessels for aid. Arrival of British vessels meant certain arrest. To the knowledge of islanders, the vessels sailed around the island and sailed away. High within a rocky home, viewed from the sea, the island appeared uninhabited.

Although location of Pitcairn Island eluded Captain Cook, it appeared on seventeenth century Spanish maps. French sailors were aware of the island, although they had little reason to land. It is problematic for sailing ships to dock on Pitcairn Island, even today. On the chance that a French ship landed on the north side Pitcairn Island, and found its sole occupant, Fletcher Christian, a shipwreck survivor, it was plausible for the French to believe that he was a sole survivor. Imagine the irony, with an absence of remorse, as Christian sailed away to Europe, leaving behind the mess he created.

It is not far-fetched to believe that Christian reached England, where he was reunited with his family, who shielded him from discovery. The mutiny trial was an ugly affair. The blame for mutiny was placed on Christian. Only the sour temperament of Bligh left him without champions.

Bligh, who knew Fletcher Christian well, and mentored the man to his own peril, recorded in his writing that one day he thought he saw Christian in Portsmouth. He saw the man from the rear and recognized him by his gait and stature. He called out to him. The man quickly disappeared among a throng of people.

In 1808 and 1809, there were rumors of Christian arriving home and living in the Lakes District of Cumberland, in northwest England. Another sailor on the HMS *Bounty*, who had the opportunity to know Christian on a daily basis, was Peter Heywood, a young midshipman. Heywood was standing behind Christian, when Bligh was bound and taken prisoner. So close to Christian was Heywood, that Bligh maintained at the mutiny trial that Heywood was a conspirator. In his days in jail, prior to release and exoneration, Heywood had time to reflect deeply on the appearance of Christian.

One day, as Heywood was walking near the dock in Plymouth, he saw a man from behind, that reminded him of Christian. Heywood called out to the man. The man walked away. Heywood walked faster, as did the man. Finally, Heywood ran to confront the man, face-to-face. As they looked at each other, Heywood was certain that he was gazing into the eyes of Fletcher Christian.

The man turned around and sped away, saying nothing. For Heywood, the incident brought back all the pain of the mutiny, arrest, near death experience on the British rescue ship, and the trial. Heywood never pursued the incident, nor made further inquiry. He never forgot seeing Fletcher Christian back in England.[164]

---

[164] Sir John Barrow, 1976 edition at 233.

Portsmouth Queens Hotel – Did Fletcher Christian Stay Here?

Pitcairn Island Today

Few Houses, Small Population, No Easy Visitor Access

Once the Pitcairn Island community was discovered, and its patriarch deceased, three Englishmen decided to take his place. One man married a daughter of Adams. Another of the new arrivals decided that as a preacher, he should be exempt from work. He was not appreciated by the locals. The British government decided that to keep the peace, he should be removed. In an effort to take responsibility for the lightly inhabited island of British and Tahitian descendants, in 1838 Britain claimed Pitcairn and three closely situated islands, as part of a British protectorate.

Over the next century, Britain supported Pitcairn residents and urged them to relocate. Some left, although most of those who relocated soon wished to return. The population of Pitcairn Island has been just under one hundred into the twentieth century. Many Pitcairn natives have the surname of Young, or Christian.

Today, farming and fishing on Pitcairn Island supplement supplies brought to residents by British ships. Crafts created on the island are sold to guests of passing cruise ships. Bee keeping has become popular in Adamstown, on disease-free Pitcairn.

Cruise ships seldom make landings on Pitcairn Island, despite listing the location as a port on the itinerary. There is no dock to support a large ship and mooring with small ships is dangerous. Steep steps lead from the water to the settlement. There is no island infrastructure to support tourism on location. At-home stays for the very adventurous are possible, from expedition ships.

Mutineers of the HMS *Bounty* brought attention to Pitcairn Island. Today, Britain seeks to protect the fragile environment for the few locals and the ecosystem, in which fish and birds thrive. Locals celebrate Bounty Day as a public holiday every January 23, to recall the day in 1790, when fate brought a permanent population to the island.[165]

For cruise guests, it is fascinating to anchor close to the island, where remnants of the HMS *Bounty* are still visible, and consider the story of Fletcher Christian and the impact of his actions. Consider also, the likelihood of locating this small rock in the great nothing of the north Pacific. No tale spun by John Adams, or anyone else, is too large to fill that space.

---

[165] There is evidence of prior habitation of Pitcairn, although long prior to 1790.

INDEX

A

Aboriginal People Australia
   Eora, 23
   Gagadju, 128
   Gurindji, 27
   Jagera, 165
   Noongar, 109
   Turrbal, 165
   Wurundjeri, 63, 147
Antipodeans, 71
ANZAC (Day, Remembrance), 172-174, 288, 302
Archibald Prize, 55
Architectural Style
   Art Deco, 13, 33, 42-47, 56, 60, 239, 245-258, 304
   Art Nouveau, 42, 43, 237, 254
   Baroque, 168, 255
   French Chateau, 239, 277
   Gothic (Revival), 13, 41, 112, 174, 237, 264, 265, 275-278, 293-296
   Icon, 32-33, 45-46, 49-50, 68, 103, 260
   Italian Renaissance, 237
   Mission (Prairie), 253-254
   Moderne, 43, 254
   Neoclassical, 173
   Palladian, 112
   Queenslander Classic, 169
   Steel & Glass, 33, 43-45, 163, 174-175, 239, 263
   Territorial, 14, 37-38, 112, 178, 228
   Victorian, 36, 40-42, 48, 66, 71, 111-112, 265, 395
Arkley, Howard, 72

B

Badger, Charlotte, 290
Banks, Sir Joseph, 197-198, 201, 368, 376
Batman, John, 62-64
Battles
   Camperdown (1797), 375
   Copenhagen (1801), 375
   Gallipoli (1915), 158, 172-173
   Kellett Street (1929), 53
   Trafalgar (1805), 376
Bentham, Jeremy, 81
Bligh, Captain William, 11, 13, 15, 31, 37-38, 47, 79, 326, 336, 364-379, 429-436
Boomerang, 129
Bougainville, Antoine, 247, 323-325
Bourke, Governor Sir Richard, 41
Boyd, Arthur, 72
Broome, Sir Frederick Napier, 147
Brown, William, 224, 234-236
Bruat, Armand, 333
Burns, Robert, 13, 288, 297-298, 300
Burns, Thomas, 288, 291
Busby, James, 211-212

C

Campbell, John Logan, 234-236
Cargill, William, 293-294
Carlotta, Les Girls, 51
Code of Pomare, 321, 330, 331
Conder, Charles Edward, 72

Cook, Captain James, 11, 17-18, 22, 28, 33, 41, 73-78, 80, 123-125, 187-208, 211-216, 223-233, 247-249, 262, 288, 307-308, 314, 323-325, 365-368, 372, 381-383, 396, 415-416, 431
Copra (coconut), 382-384

D

D'Urville, Jules Dumont, 200
Dampier, William, 20-21
   A New Voyage Round the World, 20-21
   A Voyage to New Holland, 20-21
Darling, Governor Ralph (Australia), 32, 41
Davidson, Roby, 135, 145
Devine, Tilly, 51-60
Dobell, Sir William, 51, 54-57
Dutch East India Company DEIC, 17, 19, 151

E

Earhart, Amelia, 157-158

F

Fenians, 82-83, 118-119
FitzRoy, Captain Robert, 67, 163, 168, 219-226, 235
Flinders, Mathew, 19, 38
Frame, Janet (Janet Paterson Clutha), 298-300
   An Angel at My Table, 299
Fremantle, Sir Charles, 108
French, Leonard, 72

G

Gabriel's Gully (Gold Rush), 293
Garland, Cannon David John, 173

Gawler, Governor George, 102
Gilmore, Dame Mary, 51, 56-57
Goyder, George Woodroffe, 151-154, 160
Great Migration, 11, 177, 184, 304-306, 400, 410
Green Ban, 58
Greenway, Francis Howard, 39

H

Hahn, Captain Dirk, 92-99
Heysen, Hans, 93, 99-101
Hill, Ernestine, 135, 145
Hinkler, Herbert John Louis, 158

I

Idriess, Ian, 135, 143-145
   Forty Fathoms Deep, 135, 143
Impressionists
   Bernard, Emile, 353
   Cézanne, Paul, 347, 349, 355
   Gauguin, Paul, 12, 308, 318-329, 340-363
      Beautiful Angela, 356
      Pont Aven School, 352-356
      Noa Noa, 308, 329, 341, 357
      Study of a Nude, 348
      Tahitian Woman with a Flower, 358
      Where Do We Come From? What Are We? Where Are We Going?, 361
      Woman with Mangoes, 361
      Yellow Christ, 354
   Monet, Claude, 347-349
      Impression Sunrise, 347
   Pissarro, Camille, 241, 347-349
   Renoir, Pierre-Auguste, 347-349
   Van Gogh, Vincent, 349-353
      Yellow Café, 350

J

Jansz, Willem, 18
Johnson, Amy, 156

K

Kemp, Francis Roderick, 71-72
Keneally, Thomas, 135, 146
   The Chant of Jimmie Blacksmith, 146
King, Inge, 71-72
Kings, Queens and Other Royals
   Elizabeth I (England), 78
   Elizabeth II (Britain), 229, 299
   George III (Britain), 75
   George IV (Britain), 108, 211
   Marau (Queen Tahiti), 334
   Pomare I (Tahiti), 321, 327, 333
   Pomare II (Tahiti), 327
   Pomare III (Tahiti), 328
   Pomare Vahine IV (Tahiti), 329
   Pomare V (Tahiti), 329-334
   Tapoa I (Raiatea), 383
   Tapoa II (Bora Bora), 328
   Teriimaevarua III (Bora Bora), 383
   Victoria (Britain), 41, 147, 207, 212, 214, 221, 262, 279, 395

L

La Trobe, Governor Charles, 65, 67
Larnach Castle (Dunedin), 288, 302
Larnach, William, 296-297
Lawrence, David Herbert (D.H.), 135, 145, 156, 260, 269-270, 343
Leigh, Kate, 51-53
London Missionary School, 330

M

Mabo, Eddie, 28
MacRobertson Trophy Air Race, 158-159
Macassans People, 19
Macquarie, Governor Lachian (Australia), 25, 30, 32, 37-42, 46-48
Marae, 187, 313, 315, 318-319, 331, 382-383
Michener, James, 386
   Tales of the South Pacific, 386
Mikimoto, Kochichi, 386
Moai, 12, 313, 392-427
Moondyne Joe (Joseph Bolitho Johns), 107, 115-117, 121
Mountfort, Benjamin Woolfield, 276
Mungo Lake, Australia, 124, 128
Murry, John Middleton, 260, 268-270
Museums
   Auckland Art Gallery, 238-240
   Auckland War Memorial, 182, 241
   British Museum (London), 197, 371, 396, 406, 424
   Broome Pearl Museum, 139
   Cadbury Chocolate (Dunedin), 302
   Canterbury Museum (Christchurch), 277
   City Gallery (Wellington), 271
   City Hall (Brisbane), 168
   Contemporary Art (Sydney), 43
   Darwin Aviation Heritage Center, 154
   Gallery of Modern Art (Brisbane), 175
   Ian Potter Museum (Melbourne), 73
   John Cadman Cottage (Sydney), 35-36
   Mansfield House (Wellington), 260
   Mint (Sydney), 40
   National Gallery Victoria & NGV International (Melbourne), 73
   National Natural History of the Smithsonian Institution (Washington, DC), 406
   New South Wales Gallery of Art, 55
   Newstead House (Brisbane), 167
   Paul Gauguin Museum (Papeete), 362
   Queensland Art Gallery (Brisbane), 168, 175
   State Library Victoria (Melbourne), 166

Te Papa Tongarewa National Museum (Wellington), 206, 229, 260, 271

N

Namatjira, Albert, 131-132
Native Lands Act (New Zealand), 220
    Native Land Court, 218
    Waitangi Tribunal, 218
Native Title (Australia), 28-29, 218,
    Indigenous Land Fund, 29
    Native Title Amendment Act, 29, 228
    Wik Peoples v. Queensland (1996), 28
New South Wales Company, 23, 38, 79, 81-82, 219, 222, 235, 376-377
New Zealand Company, 23, 219-228, 261-262
Nielson, Juanita, 51, 57-58
Nimitz, Admiral Chester, 385
Noland, Sydney, 72

P

Pascoe, Bruce, 135, 145-146
    Dark Emu: Black Seeds: Agriculture or Accident?, 145
Pércouse, Jean-François, 416
Pinctada Maxima, 133
Pitjantjatjara Land Rights Act, 27
Pritchard, George, 328, 332-333
Pritzker Architecture Prize, 47

R

Roseate Pearl, 143-144
Roggeveen, Jacob, 323
Rudd, Prime Minister Kevin, 29
Rum Rebellion, 37, 376

S

Ships
    Astrolabe, 248
    HMS Beagle, 153, 166, 219, 235
    HMS Bounty, 11, 13, 321, 326, 365-379
    Catalpa, 118-119
    HMS Endeavor, 197-204
    SS Fortitude, 167
    Kon Tiki, 407, 423
    SS Koomba, 144
    Mana3, 12, 397-398, 405
    HMS Pandora, 373
    Topaz, 433
Simpson, Edwin Colin, 135, 145
    Adam in Ochre, 145
Slap sticks, 129
Smith, Sir Charles Edward Kingsford, 158
    Southern Cross (airplane), 158
Smith, Sir Ross Macpherson, 156
Social Darwinism, 26
Songlines, 11, 129-132
Sopwith Camel, 158
Southern Cross Pearl, 142-143

T

Tarpeian Way, 48
Tattoo, 127, 185-188, 201, 289, 304, 316-318, 413, 415
Tasman, Abel, 11, 19-20, 190, 193-194, 197
Terra Nullius, 17-18, 22-24, 28-29, 123
Tiki, 316-318
Torres, Luis Vaes de, 18
Transportation Era, 12-13, 19, 32-44, 62, 64, 67, 75-89, 92, 107, 110, 113-114, 120, 126, 135, 163-165, 193, 219, 366, 376

Treaty
South Pacific Nuclear Free Zone (1996), 336
Waitangi (1840), 11, 191, 206-250, 262
Tuwhare, Hone, 298-299
　　No Ordinary Sun, 299

U

Utzon, Jørn Oberg, 46

W

War
　Boer War, 173
　First Maori War (1860), 191, 219-224
　Maori War (1863), 224- 227
　Missionary War (1817), 313
　Sealers' War (1810), 289

World War I, 12, 42, 92, 99, 102, 156, 158, 164, 172, 263, 269
World War II, 12, 43, 50, 54, 69, 92, 103, 145, 149, 154, 157, 161, 334
Woolf, Virginia, 260, 267-268
World Heritage Sites
　Australian Convict Sites (Hobart), Fremantle Prison, 13, 114, 120
　Kakadu National Park, 160
　Rapa Nui National Park, 426
　Royal Exhibition Building (Melbourne), 66
　Sydney Opera House, 47

www.ingramcontent.com/pod-product-compliance
Lightning Source LLC
Chambersburg PA
CBHW040419130526
44592CB00052B/2848